Fit for Purpose

How Modern Businesses
Find, Satisfy, & Keep Customers

David J Anderson
Alexei Zheglov

Blue Hole Press
Seattle, WA

Fit For Purpose
How Modern Businesses Find, Satisfy, & Keep Customers
Copyright © 2017 Blue Hole Press

ISBN: 978-0-9853051-1-6

First Print Edition , 29 November, 2017.

Contact info@leankanban.com for rights requests, customized editions, and bulk orders. Additional print copies of this and other Kanban publications can be purchased via leankanban.com / shop.

Library of Congress Cataloging-in-Publication Data
applied for; available at www.loc.gov.

Printed in the United States.

Cartoon in chapter 11 used with permission, Peter Steiner /
The New Yorker Collection; © Condé Nast

Taxi image on cover and page 1 courtesy of Google Images

Cover and interior design by Vicki Rowland.

Contents

For Nastya — DJA

. . . .

For Lilia, Sasha, and Dasha — AZ

SECTION I

Introducing
Fitness-for-Purpose

Introduction

MOST PEOPLE ARE FAMILIAR with the concept of evolution of species to best fit their environment. This book is about how to evolve your products and services to be the best so that you satisfy your customers, earn their loyalty, and keep them coming back for more. If you can do this successfully, your business will be resilient, robust, and positioned for long-term success. Fit-for-purpose products and services produce a win-win-win of enthusiastic customers, happy employees, and superior economic results. We hope you'll find this book fit-for-purpose, and that you'll keep coming back for more!

Who Should Read This Book?

This book is intended for product managers, service designers, service delivery managers, and those who work in product strategy, strategic planning, market research or marketing, or those who oversee these functions in senior executive roles.

What Can You Expect?

The book lays out the thesis of the Fit-for-Purpose Framework and the concept that you should segment your market by customer purpose and then design, implement, and deliver your products and services such that each customer segment perceives what you offer to be fit-for-purpose. To do this, you must understand the customer's goals and objectives and the criteria they use to make selections in the market. You must understand why they choose you and what they hope to gain from selecting your product or service. We will introduce Fit-for-Purpose surveys and a Fitness Box Score as means to understand your market and how well you are serving it.

Along the way we will visit techniques with which you may already be familiar, such as Net Promoter Score (NPS), Balanced Scorecard, Key Performance Indicators (KPIs), Jobs to be Done (JTBD), Personas and Goal-directed Design, and Mission Orders/ Commander's Intent (or *Auftragstaktik*).

Section I, Introducing Fitness for Purpose (Chapters 1–3), uses real-world examples to familiarize the concept. Section II, Understanding Fitness for Purpose (Chapters 4–7), presents our system— the Fit-for-Purpose Framework. Section III, Managing Fitness for Purpose (Chapters 8–10), provides our pragmatic, actionable guidance on using the Fit-for-Purpose Framework in a real-world business. Finally, the concluding section of the book (Section IV, Chapters 11–14) identifies gaps and weaknesses, points out occasions where it isn't appropriate, and then shows some integrations of the Fit-for-Purpose Framework with several popular approaches, concluding with our final call to action.

What Are the Benefits of Adopting the Fit-for-Purpose Framework?

Understanding fitness-for-purpose will enable you to find, satisfy, and keep customers in a manner that is more robust and more efficient than perhaps you have been achieving until now. Understanding fitness-for-purpose is the first step toward long-term survival for your business in the complex markets of the 21st Century.

About Your Authors

Both of your authors own and run businesses. Neither are classically trained marketing or strategic-planning people. Since 2008, David has run a management-training, event-planning, publishing, and consulting business that operates globally from its headquarters in Seattle. Alexei has a more modest consulting and training business based in Waterloo, Ontario. While delivering his expertise as a contractor was a reasonable career choice, he opted for a more difficult path to build a more robust business delivering to different types of clients, diversified across industries and geographies.

Some Choices We Made

In the first two sections of this book, all of the examples are from physical, tangible goods product and service companies such as restaurants, airlines, and wineries. These examples are intended to be easily accessible and communicate sometimes difficult concepts in a simple manner. However, we intend to apply this to intangible goods and professional services businesses, which becomes much more explicit in Sections III and IV.

Particularly in Section III, Managing for Fitness-for-Purpose, we made conscious choices to use examples taken from our own businesses—management training, consulting, and event planning. This candid and transparent approach comes at the risk of offending some of our current clients, business partners, and existing consumer market, but we have been careful never to breach any client confidentiality. We are, however, explicit about the market segmentation for David's licensed training business, and this will doubtless cause some channel partners to wonder which segment they've been grouped into. We made a conscious decision to be transparent in the pursuit of authenticity because we want you to believe that the techniques described in this book actually work, that they are tried and tested, and that they are in regular use. We use the concepts covered here to manage our own businesses and we felt the best way for you to understand that was to tell it like it is.

The book also features some fictitious scenarios, often inspired by actual experiences we've had first hand, observed second hand, or had relayed to us by individuals who will recognize a vignette or two. There are composite fictitious characters inspired by a collection of real people. The Neeta character is a composite one, although Neeta was originally inspired by a woman in our professional network who actually does work for the WSIB in Toronto. The life of Neeta that we depict is in no way intended to reflect on the life of any real person, either living or dead. Where we have used fictional stories to illustrate concepts, we have done so to simplify and provide greater clarity. Truth is always so much uglier than fiction and we didn't want the complexity of real life getting in the way of understanding basic concepts.

There are many anecdotes from real businesses, often brands that you will have heard of. In most cases, we have had some personal exposure to elements of these stories or they reflect directly from our personal experience. In all cases, the details of the stories can be researched through publicly available sources. Many references are provided in footnotes for those interested to delve deeper on any specific anecdote. Where details weren't public, we've disguised the source and anonymized the businesses involved.

Acknowledgments

We wrote this entire book during only seven weeks in the summer of 2017. We wrote many small parts of the book quickly: stories, concepts, and examples. We rewrote them, broke them up, moved them to different chapters and dropped them altogether as we strove for the logical and engaging presentation of our ideas and practical guidance. We could do all these things only thanks to our very first readers. The reviewers, as we called them, explored, critiqued, and challenged our writing, literally, on a daily basis.

We are sure this book wouldn't be the same without Mark Leach and Scott Relf, who provided us with regular feedback and suggested many improvements to the manuscript. It was very encouraging to hear from Christophe Louvion, who read our still-incomplete draft and was able to apply our guidance instantly with his executive team. Kaveh Kalantar provided us lots of quick and substantial feedback and also suggested connections to the innovation domain. We also thank a long list of reviewers for their timely, helpful feedback and comments, including: Gabe Abella, Marina Arefieva, Martin Aziz, Andreas and Susanne Bartel, Jesper Boeg, Simon Cockayne, John Cutler, Bernadette Dario, Becky Fitzgerald, Jonathan Hansen, Sudi Lahiri, Kent McDonald, Steve McGee, Jay Paulson, Fanny Pittack, Andrei Popov, Bill Sesko, Elin Sjursen, Joey Spooner, Craeg Strong, and Brice Walsh.

We're also grateful to those who helped us with the book's production on a tight schedule: our editor Wes Harris, copy editor and designer Vicki Rowland, indexer Sharon Hilgenberg, and graphic designer Santhosh Kumar.

Finally, we want to thank the participants who attended Lean Kanban conferences and leadership retreats worldwide in recent years and the hundreds of students in Alexei's training classes who helped refine some of the techniques presented in this book.

1 The Best Taxi Service in the World

"MORNING, GUV'NOR! WHERE TO, THEN?"

David pulls the handle to close the door and falls back into the bench seat in the rear of the black taxi. "The Hilton Tower Bridge, thanks!"

"Is that the one off Tooley Street?"

David is groggy. He's just off a red-eye flight from Seattle. After collecting his luggage, he rode the Heathrow Express train into central London. He knows the game. Of course, the cabbie knows the answer to the question he's just asked; he wants to know if David does.

"By London Bridge Station," David replies.

"Yeah, Tooley Street, right." The cabbie engages gear and David hears the familiar low rumble of the diesel engine as the cab pulls out of the stand at London Paddington and up the exit ramp to the traffic light. David puts his feet up, pushing his suitcases against the dividing wall between him and the driver to prevent them moving around and falling over inside the cabin.

"We're going to have to go through the park, around the Palace, and across the river over by Victoria. There's a protest march and the whole area around Fleet Street, St. Paul's, and into The City will be closed off."

"Sure, no problem," David replies.

"So, where'd you come in from, then? Glasgow?"

"No, Seattle. Overnight flight. I'm a bit jet-lagged."

"Oh, right then, so this is home for you?"

"No, I live in Seattle. Been there fifteen years."

"You work for Bill Gates, then?"

"No, but I used to!"

"You've got the right idea. This country is going to the dogs, Guv'nor. If it's not one thing it's another. This government has no idea. Really, no idea at all."

David smiles. A grumpy, opinionated cabbie is all part of the service. This is London and there is no better way to get around than in an iconic black London taxi. Of course, nowadays they also have Mercedes minivans. Those have six seats—one more than a classic black cab—but seriously, what visitor to London wants to ride in a Mercedes minivan? You can find that anywhere. The taxi driver continues his monologue on the state of the country as the cab rounds Buckingham Palace and heads south to cross the River Thames.

The taxi stops at a light entering a roundabout on the south side of the river. "Guv'nor, it's all backed up here." The driver gestures to his left, pointing out traffic at a standstill exiting the roundabout toward the east. "We'll need to try another way."

"Okay." David trusts the driver implicitly. There is no GPS in a London taxi. The "knowledge" of the streets is quite literally wired into the brain of the driver. London cab drivers have an enlarged hippocampus as a consequence of their two- to four-year training to earn a taxi license.[1] The training is known as the Knowledge because they must learn the entire map of London, including every lane and alleyway. The cab moves forward and continues south.

Suddenly the taxi makes a left down a narrow street of tidy, brick-built terraced homes, then a right, a left, and another right into an impossibly narrow lane. It's a back alley, lined by high brick walls and regularly spaced, solid wood doors painted in a variety of colors. The cab pops out onto a main road and makes a right, still heading south. It's the wrong way, but a barrier there acts as a central reservation preventing left turns. At the earliest opportunity, the driver veers the cab into a sharp U-turn. "We'll be all right from here, now," he offers. "Try doing that in an Uber, eh! Oh, and have you heard the latest?"

"No. I'm out of touch."

"Well, first it was whether or not their drivers were employees. And the court said they were. So that was a blow for them. It means they are liable for all sorts of stuff. Next, this latest case is because

---

1. www.wired.com/2011/12/london-taxi-driver-memory/

some of their drivers have been refusing to take service animals. You know, as cabbies we're not allowed to refuse blind people with guide dogs. We are obliged to help them."

"I didn't realize Uber was in London."

"Well they are, and they are a menace. They're operating without a license. The prices they charge aren't sustainable. They're trying to buy market share with low prices. But the mayor, he's on our side. He understands the value of the black cab service."

"Boris?" David asks, referring to Boris Johnson, London's then-mayor.

"Right, Boris! Mind you, he doesn't get everything right. Look at the traffic running down this street here. Look how busy it is, on a Sunday morning. I mean, really. That never used to happen. But see the bike lane? You have to be a bike to ride up this street nowadays. It used to be two-way traffic but now it is one way, except for bikes. That's Boris for you—Boris and his bloody bikes!"

The cab comes around London Bridge Station, now on Tooley Street and just a couple of hundred yards from the hotel. Despite the traffic and the alternative routes, the fare comes to just over fifteen Pounds. David pulls a twenty out of his wallet. The taxi pulls in to the hotel entrance on the north side of the street. The doorman opens the taxi's door. "Welcome to the Hilton Tower Bridge. Good to see you again, Mr. Anderson. Can I help you with your luggage?" To the driver, David proffers the twenty through the hole in the glass partition. "That's all for you. Have a good day."

The cabbie is mildly surprised at such a generous tip—at least he pretends to be. "Thank you very much, Guv'nor. A true gent, indeed. Enjoy your stay in London." Perhaps he's just surprised that a Scotsman, with their canny reputation, is tipping him over 20 percent. David smiles. The entertainment on the journey was worth every penny of the tip. Welcome to London!

Why Are London Taxis the Best?

London's black cab service is truly fit-for-purpose. The service has two key elements to it: the iconic black cab—the product—and the driver—the London cabbie—the means of service delivery. Both have evolved to be uniquely suited for their environment.

The black cab itself is made in the United Kingdom by a firm called The London Taxi Company,[2] which, by rights, shouldn't even exist. It is one of the smallest-volume vehicle manufacturers on the planet. It has no economies of scale. In terms of basic functional specifications, the black cab is a seven-seat, diesel-powered utility vehicle. The front passenger seat is optional and usually omitted, leaving five seats in the rear cabin for paying passengers plus one for the driver in front. A London Taxi Company cab costs about twice what a typical seven-seat diesel-powered family SUV would cost, and yet London cabbies accept this extra cost. Why?

Partly, it is regulation, but the regulations allow for limited competition amongst suppliers. And regardless of regulation, the taxi business has to work economically. The purchase price of the vehicle can't be prohibitively expensive. So why are London's black cabs worth the money?

The design has evolved to be ideal for its purpose. The vehicle has an incredibly tight turning radius that enables U-turns in very narrow streets. The wide doors, low floor, and large interior floor space are designed to enable passengers to load their own luggage into the vehicle without the driver getting out to assist. Luggage travels in the cabin with the passengers instead of in the boot at the back of the vehicle. This makes loading and unloading faster and facilitates stopping to pick up passengers in situations where parking would be illegal. Even the diesel engine was, once-upon-a-time, a differentiating and important part of the design. Compared to petrol (gasoline)-powered models, diesel engines are simpler and cheaper to maintain, and they have a far longer life expectancy. Even forty or fifty years ago a London taxi was good for perhaps 500,000 miles. Today's models can be expected to last a million miles.

The taxi driver, or cabbie, also is uniquely evolved for the purpose. London taxi drivers are not only licensed but they are members of the Licensed Taxi Drivers' Association (LTDA). To become a member of this club, they must have studied for at least two years and passed a difficult exam. London cabbies are very proud of their

---

2. London Taxi Company is now a wholly owned subsidiary of the Chinese automaker Geely, better known as the owners of Volvo. Geely now makes London taxis in Shanghai for sale in the Chinese market, where the London cab is positioned as a premium service offering. en.wikipedia.org/wiki/The_London_Taxi_Company

professionalism. The LTDA is a tight-knit clan—a highly cohesive social group. To become a member, a high standard had to be achieved and the members expect one another to live up to those standards throughout their careers. Consequently, London taxis are very safe and fraudulent behavior is uncommon. The cabbies, being human, exhibit "requisite variety" in their thinking—they don't always take the same route from A to B. Unlike a software algorithm in a GPS that would always send, for example, an Uber driver, by the same route, London cabbies mix it up a bit. This—and their Knowledge— makes them extremely adaptable to changing conditions such as protest marches or backed-up traffic due to an accident. And a grumpy, opinioned monologue on the state of the nation, its government, and its dogs is all part of the service. Try asking Siri, "Is the country going to the dogs?" It just isn't the same!

The London black taxi service is an example of something that has evolved to be extremely fit-for-purpose. It is very robust to insurgent competition. It got that way through an evolutionary process over decades—arguably three centuries, as the first Hackney Carriage licenses for horse-drawn "cabs," as they were nicknamed, were issued in 1662.[3]

London actually has two classes of licensed private vehicles for public transport: the black taxis and licensed private hire cars, or "minicabs," which are not metered and cannot be solicited in the street; instead, they must be booked for a journey and a fixed price agreed with the driver in advance. This second category also includes limousines and uniformed driver services such as Mercedes E or S class cars. Into this mix, insurgents such as Uber have recently arrived. Part of the legal dispute between the LTDA and Uber argues that Uber's mobile application is, in fact, a modern-day taximeter, and that Uber operates an unlicensed, metered taxi service, which is illegal in the United Kingdom.[4] The inclusion of the taximeter to tie distance and time to price makes it a "taxi." So far, the black taxi service is proving robust to insurgents such as Uber, with third-party mobile applications such as Gett[5] helping it repel them. The minicab private hire business is under assault, however. It isn't sufficiently differentiated, typically using regular minivans or sedan cars, nor

---

3. en.wikipedia.org/wiki/Hackney_carriage

4. Despite this claim, Ubers are currently considered to be minicabs.

5. www.theguardian.com/technology/2015/sep/05/london-black-cab-drivers-app-uber-taxi

is it sufficiently robust, with drivers often relying on GPS devices—and there is no tight-knit social group of minicab drivers with the Knowledge.

As the prospect of autonomous vehicle technology looms on the horizon, a question mark does hang over manually operated taxi services with human drivers. It remains to be seen for how long a service like LTDA black cabs in London can survive when they compete with automated alternatives. At the time of writing, we suspect that the uniquely evolved capabilities of London's black cabs will enable them to persist despite the arrival of disruptive new technology. The drivers, their Knowledge, their ability to constantly sense the environment, and their information-sharing network are likely to outperform technology for some considerable time to come! Meanwhile, the black cab is iconic—any visitor to London wants to ride in one. And because the opinionated driver with his authentic dialect will remain difficult to replicate with technology, nostalgia is likely to protect the black cab for much longer than many taxi services around the world.

Summary

- The London black taxi cab service, consisting of the product component (the cab) and the service delivery component (the driver), is extremely fit-for-purpose.

- The cab's design has evolved to be uniquely fit to operate on London's streets: quick to get in and out of, tight turning radius, and so on.

- The cab driver has evolved, too: it takes at least two years of learning—memorizing all city streets and alleys—and an exam to become a cabbie. Part of the cabbie's brain even enlarges in the process!

- London's black cabs being fit-for-purpose makes the service robust to new, disruptive technologies. Meanwhile, not so fit-for-purpose transportation services are under attack by disruptive mobile apps.

2 Justin Bieber versus the Storm King

Beliebers in Mumbai Disappointed at *Purpose* Concert

ON THE TENTH OF MAY, 2017, THE 23-YEAR-OLD Canadian pop singer Justin Bieber played his first-ever concert in India, in front of 56,000 adoring fans who'd paid a small fortune to watch his first performance on the subcontinent. The following morning, his fans, known collectively as the "Beliebers," were clamoring for an apology.[6] Bieber's performance had left them unimpressed, even insulted. They felt let down. They felt disrespected. What had gone wrong?

At the time of this writing, Justin Bieber has the second-largest following on Twitter, with just under 100 million followers. He is by any measure a huge star, with a global fan base. He was barely a teenager of 13 when his performances covering others' songs, posted to YouTube by his mother, attracted the attention of talent managers and record labels. Bieber had a musical education and plays several instruments, including piano, drums, guitar, and trumpet. He's capable of writing and playing music, although many of his most famous songs have been written for him. Ten years later, he was on tour with his fourth studio album, *Purpose*.

In the city formerly known as Bombay, the home of India's movie industry (known as "Bollywood") and its rich and famous entertainers, Bieber hadn't lived up to expectations. Evidently lip syncing, at times he had wiped his face with a towel while the lyrics kept on

---

6. www.bbc.co.uk/newsbeat/article/39896338/why-india-wants-justin-bieber-to-say-sorry

playing. Fans were unimpressed. They were listening to a recording, not Bieber singing live. In a city where the expectation is that entertainers are immaculately dressed, with every hair in place and that they perform obviously well-rehearsed, impeccable dance routines, Bieber's appearance was disheveled. He looked like he'd just come from the hotel gym, dressed in a T-shirt, sports shorts and socks, and a pair of sneakers. For those who'd paid the equivalent of $100 to $1,200 (US dollars) for a ticket, plus travel expenses, Bieber's performance, the only India date on his ironically named *Purpose Tour*, simply wasn't fit-for-purpose!

To understand what went wrong with Bieber in India, we need to understand that Bieber and his music are a product and to see three components that contribute to every product or service: its design, its implementation, and its service delivery (Figure 2.1). With his concert in Mumbai, Bieber and his organization failed at service delivery. They failed to meet the expectations of adoring fans and deliver a live performance that respected the adulation of the Beliebers and honored the investment they'd made in the opportunity to watch their idol perform live.

Justin Bieber was born in London, Ontario, Canada and grew up in nearby Stratford. His hometown, located on the River Avon, hosts the annual Stratford Festival from April to October—formerly known as the Shakespeare festival, it was renamed eventually as it included works of other classical as well as contemporary playwrights. It is also home to the somewhat smaller Stratford Music Festival. From a very young age, Justin was immersed in a community that knows how to

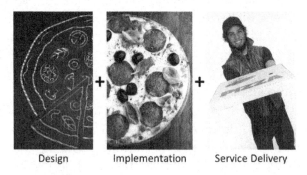

Design   Implementation   Service Delivery

Figure 2.1. Three components of a product or service: design, implementation, and service delivery

spot and nurture performing-arts talent. Bieber fits a typical "design" for a music industry product—a good-looking young man with talent, performing skills, and energy—he's attractive in several dimensions and inspires many other young people for whom he personifies a dream. Bieber's "design" is fit-for-purpose!

Bieber can also play and write songs. Allegedly he isn't the strongest singer, which may explain why in live performances he relies on a backing vocal track to which he can lip-sync if necessary. But he wouldn't be the first pop star lacking a strong singing voice whose performances are enhanced in the studio to provide depth and range for studio recordings. Ultimately, Bieber has still sold an estimated 100 million recordings and his first full album was certified triple platinum in the United States. Bieber's "implementation"—his recorded music—is popular, successful, and clearly fit-for-purpose.

What happened in India is simple—it was a failure in service delivery (Figure 2.2). He and his organization got something wrong! Perhaps his schedule was too tight? Perhaps he was suffering from jet lag? Perhaps his managers overlooked some detail important to the audience in a new country? Whatever it was, he ended up giving a lackluster performance, which sent an arrogant message to his fans.

He appeared simply not to care enough! His live performance—the service delivery component of Bieber as a product, wasn't

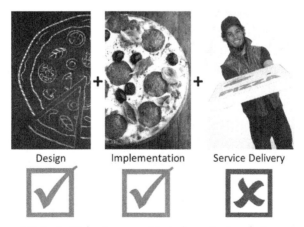

Design   Implementation   Service Delivery

Figure 2.2 Justin Bieber's concert in India: winning design, proven implementation, but something went wrong with service delivery.

fit-for-purpose. Bieber lost some respect in India. If this behavior were to be repeated, it's all too likely he would lose more fans, or at least his live performances wouldn't attract such large crowds or such high prices for tickets. In the modern-era music industry, where artists make very little from recordings and most of their earnings are from touring and playing to live audiences, Bieber showed some vulnerability. It's hard to imagine contemporaries such as Katy Perry, Lady Gaga, or Ariana Grande disrespecting a Mumbai audience in this way. For now, Bieber's image is strong enough and his fan base large enough that his career will withstand one bad night and a few days of bad publicity in a single, albeit very large, country.

What this story clearly illustrates is that customer satisfaction requires attention to all three elements—the product design must be right, the implementation must be right, and the service delivery must also live up to expectations. If any one of these elements isn't good enough, disappointment ensues, resulting in poor reviews and a lack of recommendations. Will Bieber's Mumbai audience show up with such enthusiasm and alacrity next time? Only time will tell.

Storm King Red

Storm King[7] is a mountain in the foothills at the northern end of the Olympic range in western Washington State. It lies in Clallam County, the most northwesterly county in the contiguous ("lower forty-eight") United States. Rising to 2,700 feet, the 1.7-mile hiking trail offers a steep and mildly challenging climb of 2,100 feet in elevation gain, rewarding the hiker with stunning views overlooking Lake Crescent, to the west of the town of Port Angeles. It's a popular day hike for locals and tourists alike.

Camaraderie Cellars is a winery located in Port Angeles where vintner Don Corson makes wines from grapes grown in five vineyards located in eastern and southern Washington. In 2015 Corson introduced Storm King Red,[8] a blend of varietals available only in a 1.5-liter Astro-oPaq, also known as a "satchel," "pouch," or "tote," and featuring a

---

7. www.nps.gov/olym/planyourvisit/mount-storm-king-trail.htm

8. https://store.camaraderiecellars.com/product/Storm-King-Satchel

Figure 2.3 Storm King Red by Camaraderie Cellars excels at all three: design, implementation, and service delivery.

plastic spigot in the bottom-front from which to pour the wine (Figure 2.3). Storm King Red is named after the previously mentioned day hike and packaged deliberately to target hikers who enjoy picnicking without compromise. Corson also envisaged consumers grilling in their yards, barbecuing on beaches, as well as those picnicking on beaches and in parks, forests, and mountains. The package is filled with argon, a neutral gas, to prevent oxygenation, thus spoiling the wine, while the material is recyclable and extremely lightweight. A 1.5-liter pouch weighs the same as a standard 750-milliliter wine bottle, since the glass typically is half the weight of a full bottle of wine. So, Storm King Red is perfect for a backpack, rucksack, picnic hamper, or chill box.

The wine itself is a blend designed to be easy to drink with most foods and to appeal to a broad range of palates. When people are picnicking at the summit of Storm King and enjoying a sandwich and a cup of wine along with their view of Lake Crescent, they don't need to be challenged—they aren't looking for anything exotic. Mouth feel isn't an issue when the mouth is filled with a sandwich. The wine should be well defined on first taste with a simple, smooth finish. Storm King Red is perfect for picnics. Its robust blend is designed to travel well. It doesn't need to sit on a shelf for days "settling down." It doesn't need to be carefully stored. It isn't delicate! Don Corson has shown that he perfectly understands his market segment. The Storm King Red blend simply isn't available in bottles. It is a product perfectly designed for a niche. It was designed with empathy for the consumer and it clearly communicates what it is and is not. If you want a nice, high-quality red wine for a picnic, hike, beach barbecue, or backyard party, Storm King Red packaged in its vacuum-sealed, argon-filled pouch is the perfect solution. It pairs well with burgers, hot dogs, sandwiches, or barbecued ribs. Storm King Red is entirely fit-for-purpose!

Don Corson was the first vintner in Washington State to offer wine in the AstroPaq, in 2015. He was also sharp to recognize that this style of packaging needed to be tailored to a previously unrecognized need. He needed to find customers with a "purpose" for whom pouch-packaged wine would be ideal. The manufacturers of the packaging were promoting its virtues as recyclable and lightweight. Other wineries who've followed Corson's lead, such as Victor Palencia with his La Monarcha Cabernet Sauvignon, have been promoting these virtues of light weight and easily recyclable packaging.[9] However, these aren't exactly compelling messages: "Buy our pouch wine because the package is more ecologically friendly than a glass bottle"; or "Buy our pouch wine because it is lighter in weight than an equivalently sized bottle." How does pouch wine differ from boxed wine? Boxed wine is usually sold as a budget, low-price offering for price-sensitive consumers who aren't wine connoisseurs or who are purchasing for a party where they know people won't be fussy. If the partygoers are the type of wine drinkers who order it as "red" or "white," then box wine fits that bill. Corson worked out that he could put a premium wine in an AstroPaq and tailor it entirely to a specific niche. As a consequence, he retails Storm King Red for $28 per 1.5-liter pouch—the equivalent of $14 per bottle—clearly not a budget wine. While other vintners from Washington State are evidently experimenting with the packaging, their approach is unimaginative and destined to position the pouches as an alternative to boxes—condemning it to the narrow margins in the budget-conscious end of the market—cheap wine, in a bag. The current retail prices of boxed wine in the same market are $16 to $24 per 3-liter box—Storm King Red commands a 130–250 percent premium over these prices! Cheap boxed wine isn't argon filled.[10] Argon isn't used in box or tetra-pak wine packaging. Argon would be overkill to protect the quality of wine costing $4 per 750 milliliters. Corson has demonstrated how to make higher margins from a premium product by understanding a segment—by showing that he knows both why and how his customers drink. He understands their purpose for consuming his wine. Storm King Red has a design—a robust blend of varietals intended to travel and drink

---

9. www.greatnorthwestwine.com/2016/03/01/washington-winery-puts-reds-in-recyclable-pouches/

10. Argon is the element number 18, atomic weight, 40. As argon is heavier than air, air bubbles entering the pouch from the spigot rise to the top and the argon effectively seals the wine from oxygenation, even after opening.

well straight from the spigot. Corson found a market segment and designed a product to serve it. At least in the local market, the name of the wine communicates what it is and why it exists. Corson is also an accomplished vintner and his use of argon in filling the pouches can't be the cheapest option, but this attention to detail shows strong implementation. His wine is designed to satisfy, offering good value for money—mid-priced quality. Finally, delivery in a pouch—ideal for backpacks, lightweight and easy to carry, and available through retail outlets where day hikers are likely to be hanging out in their evening leisure time—ensures the service delivery component. Storm King Red is designed to keep its customers coming back again and again. In all three dimensions, design, implementation, and service delivery, Storm King Red is fit-for-purpose! Its creator, Don Corson, has shown how to find a market and design a product to satisfy and retain his customers.

Introducing Neeta, Zak's, and Westside Pizza

Neeta[11] is a project manager with the Workplace Safety and Insurance Board (WSIB),[12] a public-sector government organization of the Province of Ontario, Canada. She manages teams and coaches process improvement in the delivery of IT services. Like many IT organizations, schedules are unpredictable and employees need to be prepared to be flexible with their working hours and be dedicated to delivery. A deadline is approaching: the new version of their website is scheduled to go live over the weekend. The project team is in a crunch. Deep into testing, there are still many small issues to be resolved. It's clear that the team will need to work some extra hours mid-week if things are to stay on track and a successful, quality deployment of the new software is to happen as planned.

Neeta is determined to ensure that the team can stay focused on work, and she'll use what remains of her discretionary spending project expense account to bring in dinner for everyone who is working late. It's Thursday evening and she's decided to order pizza from a local restaurant. She knows her geeks like gourmet pizza—they are

---

11. Although Neeta was inspired by a real WSIB employee, Neeta is a composite character whose resemblance to any one person living or dead is purely coincidental.
12. www.wsib.on.ca/

fussy about exotic flavors such as artichoke and sundried tomato—and with several vegetarian team members, she needs to ensure a good choice of toppings to suit the tastes of meat eaters and vegetarians alike. Her geeks care about the "design" and the "implementation" of the pizza. There is only one place she knows of that will satisfy her team—Zak's Artisan Pie & Crust. They're located downtown and will deliver. She presses the speed-dial button.

It's a big project. The team is quite large—in geek parlance, they're a "ten-pizza team"—and so she'll be placing an order for ten pizzas—six with meat, four vegetarian, with a variety of different topping combinations. She calls the restaurant to place the order. Sixty to ninety minutes for delivery from a place only a few blocks away? They aren't the fastest or most predictable at "service delivery." No problem! Meanwhile, her team are eyes down, heads full of lines of code, test reports, style sheets, and markup language. Neeta doubts whether they will even notice the time going by.

Eighty minutes later her phone buzzes in her bag. It's the pizza delivery. She goes to the door to let the delivery boy into the building. He's carrying a tall, rectangular, insulated red bag full of pizzas. He's been carefully balancing them on the back of his motorcycle for the past ten minutes, happy it's still autumn and the weather is dry and clear, not yet too cold, but darkness has already fallen. Neeta signs for the delivery and tips him $20. She'd already paid for the order by corporate credit card over the phone.

"Working late, eh?"

She nods. "We have a new version of our website scheduled to go live this weekend. Just a few last teething problems to iron out."

"All right then, have a good one!"

She starts to unpack the pizza in the break area, laying out the boxes and checking the contents. Hmmm. It seems there has been a small mistake—only one pepperoni and a Greek that she didn't recall ordering. Never mind, the team won't even notice. First come, first served for the pepperoni! Otherwise the pizza looks and smells great. The delivery boy evidently took some care, and the restaurant lived up to its reputation—they do bake a good pizza. For Neeta's team of web developers, Zak's Artisan Pie & Crust makes pizzas that are fit-for-purpose. They love the recipes—the "design" of the pizzas—and they love the quality of the ingredients as well as the light, thin crust base, baked to perfection—the "implementation"—and for their "purpose" this evening, the lead time and predictability of delivery—the "service delivery" was adequate. Fancy stuff and prices to match, but it's worth it! This team has worked hard, they deserve something nice for dinner!

The following evening things look like they're on track. All the critical issues are resolved. Neeta announces that the scheduled deployment of the new website will happen as planned in the small hours of Sunday morning. Some team members will work a few hours on Saturday. Others will be on-call and some on-premises for the deployment beginning midnight Sunday morning. She looks around the office. It is almost empty. She looks at her watch and recalls the 5:55 train she needs to catch. Friday night! She's glad to be going home.

About an hour later, Neeta pulls into her driveway after a short drive from the train station, parks, and walks to the front door of her suburban Toronto home. "Mommy's home!" Her two youngest kids come running to greet her in the hallway. The older ones seem engrossed in a TV show and a game on their iPad. The sitter emerges from the kitchen smiling.

"Welcome home! I wasn't sure of your schedule. I've given them snacks but they haven't eaten. Do you want me to help pull something together for you?"

"No, that's fine! Thanks for taking care of them this afternoon. You can take off when you're ready."

"Sure! No problem! I'm glad I could help you out. They've been pretty easy so far."

From the other room, her youngest calls, "Mommy, what's for dinner?"

"I'm hungry," says one of the older ones.

Neeta pauses, eyes drifting upward to her left. What is there in the fridge? The pantry? The freezer? She's been too busy all this week for grocery shopping. And, frankly, she's exhausted. She's at home on Friday evening. Slippers, the chesterfield in the living room, and a glass of red wine sound mighty inviting right now.

"Mommy, I'm hungry. When is dinner?"

"*What* is it?"

"How about we order pizza tonight?"

"PIIIIZZZZZZAAAA!!!!! PIZZA! PIZZA!"

Her six-year-old takes off at top speed toward the family room, "Mommy's getting us pizza for dinner. Pizza!"

"Can we get pop, too?"

"And ice cream?"

"Ice cream! We want ice cream!"

"Let's see what we've got in the freezer. Meanwhile, I'll call for the pizza."

This time Neeta reaches for her phone and selects a local pizza delivery place, Westside Pizza. They're just down the street at the strip mall on the edge of their subdivision. It isn't a fancy place. The menu is basic stuff: cheese pizza, pepperoni, ham and pineapple—the usual. What she likes about this place is the proximity—they deliver quickly, and the price is right, too. This isn't gourmet, it's fast food. Westside Pizza offers a menu with simple "design." However, they are excellent at "service delivery," and in this case, she cares more about that than she does about the design aspect of the service. She orders a cheese pizza. She has some pop in the pantry—hidden at the back. Ice in the freezer and some grocery store–brand vanilla ice cream in a big plastic tub is in there, too.

"How long will it be, Mommy?"

"They said they'd have it out to us in twenty minutes."

"All right, twenty minutes," her six-year-old starts the timer on her iPad. Tick, tick, tick!

Neeta kicks off her shoes, ponders where her slippers might be, and decides she'll find them later. "Now, which bottle of red wine should I open?"

"Two minutes to go!" Three of the kids are now at the front window tucked in front of the curtains watching for the pizza delivery.

"One minute!"

"Why isn't our pizza here yet?"

"What is causing the delay?"

"Patience; he'll be here soon enough!"

"It's here! It's here!"

The young man in a bright green wind cheater just pulled up on his bright green e-bike with delivery trailer—all in matching livery.

The kids run to open the door. "Pizza!"

Smiling, the delivery boy carries a single flat, square box in his hands. "All right then, who ordered a cheese pizza?"

"Me!" "Me!"

"Mommy!"

"You'll be paying the bill then, eh?"

Neeta hands him a $20 note. "The change is for you." She takes the box.

"Thanks a lot. That's very kind of you." He smiles, "Enjoy your dinner!"

The kids run into the house. Neeta opens the box. One cheese pizza, just as she ordered. "The kids are a one–cheese pizza team," she thinks to herself. She sets the pizza down in the middle of the table, pours some glasses of pop. "You can have ice cream after the pizza, okay? And remember, this is a special treat. It'll be a normal meal tomorrow night!"

She smiles, as the kids climb over the table and reach out to tear off a slice of pizza. She can finally relax for a few minutes.

"Now, where did I leave my wine glass?" she thinks.

Neeta didn't order the pizza from the same store as the night before. Why? She had a different purpose. This time she was feeding her four hungry children whom she'd been slightly neglecting this week during a crunch time at work. This wasn't a normal week or a normal Friday. She doesn't usually feed her kids pizza—it's a treat! The kids don't like fancy gourmet flavors and even if they'd eat artichoke and sundried tomato, they wouldn't appreciate it. And why pay extra for something they won't value? Heck, they hardly notice whether the pizza is hot. What they care about is that it is pizza and it is plain cheese pizza. And that it was delivered quickly. They were already hungry. Their patience could have run out. There could have been an emotional meltdown as their empty stomachs gave way to anxiety and loss of control. In this example, "service delivery" trumps "design" and "implementation" (Table 2.1).

Table 2.1 Different selection criteria, yet both vendors fit-for-purpose

	Zak's Artisan Pie & Crust	Westside Pizza
Design	Fancy	Unimaginative
Implementation	To perfection	Mediocre, but passable
Service Delivery	Erratic, but passable	Excellent
Overall	Fit-for-purpose!	Fit-for-purpose!

Different purposes, different selection criteria, different vendors; same product, but at differing quality levels. Neeta's purpose controlled her selection criteria. To understand what your customers expect and what keeps them coming back again and again, you need to understand why they choose your product or service. You need to understand their purpose—the customer's "why." What purpose were they fulfilling when they consumed your product or service?

In this chapter, we've shown examples of how customers select products and services offered to them by businesses in three different industries. In the next chapter, we outline how companies can discover their customer purpose and the selection criteria that matter to their customers. We'll be revisiting Neeta's story several times and will explore how Zak's Artisan Pie & Crust or Westside Pizza might ensure that Neeta is satisfied and remains loyal. For example, in Chapter 10, It's Not Luck, we will explore "what if" they wanted to win more of Neeta's pizza purchasing business. How might they go about it? What changes would be necessary? Throughout the book, we'll introduce many examples from various tangible goods and physical service businesses as well as others from intangible goods and professional services businesses, including those from our own management-training and event-planning businesses.

Summary

- Products and services include three components: design, implementation, and service delivery.
- To be fit-for-purpose for different customers, all three components must be sufficiently good. All three require business owners' attention.
- Customers understand their "why" and their selection criteria intuitively when they choose among the available offerings.
- The same person can have different "whys" in different situations—and different criteria will drive them to different purchasing decisions.
- When running a business, it would be helpful to have a system for understanding your customers' "why," their selection criteria, and how those affect your design, implementation, and service delivery. We will present such a system—our Fit-for-Purpose Framework—throughout the rest of the book.

3 Man versus Machine

New Ways to Identify Your Customer's Purpose

BEFORE YOU CAN EVALUATE WHETHER your products or services are fit-for-purpose, you need to be able to identify your customer's purpose. Over the last few years, we've introduced two ways of learning your customer's purpose:

1. Using humans and narrative
2. Using surveys and data

The first approach relies on the innate human ability to tell and interpret stories. The second approach has the obvious quantitative side—things you can measure, for example, time—but also the less obvious qualitative side. The qualitative is still factual: observations are matched with established categories. The two approaches complement each other. These two approaches, the human approach and the technological approach, are so important that we dedicate Chapters 8 and 9 to fully explaining each.

Focus Groups Explore and Cluster Common Narratives

Who knows why Neeta ordered pizza? Who has the best chance of understanding her purpose in selecting your pizza restaurant and delivery service? And if Zak's or Westside were to introduce a new pizza recipe (design), change their preparation methods (implementation), or vary their delivery schedule, who would be the first to know if customers perceived any of these as improvements, and why? The answer is, of course, their frontline, customer-facing staff. The staff member who takes the order and the delivery boy who delivers the pizza have the most valuable information their business needs for long-term survival—why their customers select them and what they hope to achieve with their product or service.

If you have a social media team providing online customer service, then your staff monitoring Twitter, Facebook, and Snapchat will learn fairly quickly how your changes are affecting your customers.

Interestingly, for many tangible goods physical businesses, the people who know most about the customer "why" are often the lowest paid, shortest tenured staff members. Many businesses don't value their customer interface, their customer-facing staff. They treat these personnel as fungible commodities and accept high levels of staff turnover. There is no institutional memory and little learning. Valuable information—almost impossible to acquire via expensive market research—leaves with every employee's exit.

We encourage you to train your front line to be observant and encourage them to chat up your customers. Use your front line to gather narratives from their experiences interacting with customers. Periodically, hold focus groups with customer-facing staff and have them tell stories of real customers; listen for patterns, listen for common narratives. As clusters of narratives are identified, label them, give them a nickname—you've identified a segment. Now, listen for more: How are people in that segment consuming your product or service? How are they using it? Why did they select it? What is their reason or purpose and how much of that purpose is your product or service fulfilling for them? From these stories, you can start to formulate an understanding of the criteria those customers are using for selection and what their thresholds for acceptable performance might be. This concept is fully explored in Chapter 8, Humans and Narrative.

British Airways has recently been outsourcing their away station gate agents to vendors such as Menzies Aviation. When a passenger checks in with the airline at overseas airports, such as those in Germany, they are met by an agent in a Menzies uniform. Customers flying with British Airways from Germany do not encounter a uniformed full-time British Airways employee until they are aboard the aircraft. Cabin crew are too busy to chat up all but the most elite passengers in the premium cabins. They simply don't have time to hang out with passengers to discover why they fly. The consequences of this are obvious—Menzies staff are likely to know more about why British Airways' passengers are flying than British Airways staff do. In addition, at their home airports, such as London's Heathrow, British Airways is gradually replacing their gate agent ground crew with automated machinery. The flying experience is becoming less and less personal. These changes are being made in the name of cost saving. There is a danger here that, from a marketing perspective, British Airways is quickly shifting to a point where, metaphorically, they are "flying blind"—they simply won't know why their customers are choosing them. The loss of this information may prove much more costly than the immediate out-of-pocket costs saved through outsourcing and automation.

Fitness Box Score
Another way to understand your customer's "why" is to survey for it. We've introduced Fitness Box Score as a shorthand means to report how well customers believe products and services fulfill their purpose.

In evolutionary biology, a species survives and thrives if it is suitable for its environment. If so, it is said to be "fit" for its environment, and the variants or mutations of a species that do best are said to be "fittest" for the environment. Hence, we have expressions such as "survival of the fittest." The level to which a species is "fit" for its environment is its "fitness" level. Hence, Fitness Box Score is designed to measure how fit your products or services are for their environment. The fittest product or service is the one customers like best, whereas a product or service they reject as not good enough to fulfill their purposes is considered unfit.

Using fit-for-purpose cards (F4P cards, for short), as shown in Figure 3.1, you collect micro-narratives describing why customers selected your product or service. "Why did you choose our service?" "What was your reason or the purpose behind your selection?" "Now, how well did our product or service fulfill your expectations given your specific reasons for selecting us?" And finally, "Tell us why you gave the rating in the second question." From this information, clusters of similar "whys" can be compiled and market segments identified. Using the ratings and the answers to the third question, you can identify fitness criteria and their thresholds. We will explore the F4P

F4P Card	(to be filled in by the Customer)	(office use only)
		Service Request Type
Date: Customer's Name:		
Identify your service request or work item:		

Question 1: Tell us *why* you chose our product or service. Select **up to three** reasons or objectives you had when choosing our product or service:	(a) (b) (c)

Question 2: For each reason or objective in Question 1, please indicate how fit for purpose you found our service in fulfilling your expectations. Please score each reason or objective separately using the following scale:

	(a)	(b)	(c)
5. My expectations were exceeded	5	5	5
4. My expectations were fully met	4	4	4
3. My expectations were mostly met but a few minor concerns remained	3	3	3
2. Some significant needs were unaddressed	2	2	2
1. I got some value but most of my expectations were unmet	1	1	1
0. I found nothing useful. It was unfit for this purpose	0	0	0

Question 3: Tell us why you gave the score(s) in Question 2.

(a)
(b)
(c)

Figure 3.1 An example F4P Card

Cards and Fitness Box Score in Chapter 9, Surveys and Data. We delve fully into the evolution of F4P Cards and Fitness Box Score and compare them to the established market survey technique, Net Promoter Score (NPS) in Chapter 12, It's Your Future, Be There.

Evaluating Fitness-for-Purpose

So far, we've seen that products or services have three main elements or dimensions that make them fit-for-purpose: design, implementation, and service delivery. We've also seen that the customer's purpose, or their "why," affects how they perceive the design, implementation, and service delivery. Neeta had two different reasons to order pizza on two different evenings in the same week, which caused her to select a different vendor for each evening. Because of her different objectives, Neeta had different selection criteria: she needed gourmet flavors and high-quality preparation for her office team but she didn't care about minor errors in the order accuracy, nor did she care too much about delivery time or price; for her family, the criteria were different: a simple menu, fast delivery, precision with the order accuracy—it had to be cheese pizza and nothing else would do—but quality in the baking of pizzas wasn't as important. When Neeta and her husband cook dinner themselves, they care to get fresh, organic ingredients from the local farm store. But on Friday evening, Neeta made an exception to ensure speedy delivery.

We call the criteria Neeta intuitively uses for selecting her pizza vendor Fitness Criteria. For each criterion, she has an expectation of what is acceptable to her. We call these expectation levels the Fitness Criteria Thresholds. Every fitness criterion will have a threshold level below which the product or service is considered unfit-for-purpose.

The set of Fitness Criteria may be different for each given reason, each customer purpose, or their "why." Oftentimes, different customers share the same criterion, but their satisfaction thresholds vary. If your market segmentation is based on "why," you should have a set of Fitness Criteria metrics for each segment. The Fitness Criteria set consists of pairs: the criterion and its threshold value.

Table 3.1 shows the fitness criteria and their thresholds for two different market segments based on Neeta's two different purposes.

Table 3.1 Fitness Criteria across design, implementation, and service delivery for given whys

	PURPOSE	
	To feed the project team working late	To feed the hungry children
Criterion	Threshold	Threshold
Design		
Menu	Large, broad selection of gourmet recipes	Simple; a few basic toppings, including plain cheese
Promised quality	Organic, fresh, locally sourced ingredients (when possible)	No one is asking where the ingredients come from
Oven	Wood-fired	Gas- or electric-fired
Price	Up to $30 per pizza	Up to $15 per pizza
Implementation		
Quality	Hand-thrown dough	Pre-prepared crusts, potentially from frozen
Preparation	Fresh, hand cut ingredients prepared onsite	Canned tomato sauce; frozen, canned, or bottled ingredients; potentially prepared offsite and simply baked directly from cold storage
Safety (or conformance to regulatory requirements)	Health and safety regulations in the storage and preparation of foodstuffs must be adhered to at all times	Health and safety regulations in the storage and preparation of foodstuffs must be adhered to at all times
Service Delivery		
Delivery time	1 to 2 hours	< 30 minutes
Predictability	$+/-30$ minutes	$+/-5$ minutes
Order accuracy (functional quality)	A few small errors acceptable; failure to supply any vegetarian pizzas would be unacceptable	Total precision; mistakes are unacceptable
Quality on delivery (non-functional quality)	Hot and tasty; thin, light crust; quality ingredients, appropriately cooked	Not important; lukewarm is acceptable; microwave reheat at home if necessary
Safety (or conformance to regulatory requirements)	A blind eye will be turned to minor traffic law violations providing accidents are avoided	A blind eye will be turned to minor traffic law violations providing accidents are avoided

Fit-for-Purpose and Emotional Motivation

Fit-for-purpose is established in each of the three product dimensions of design, implementation, and service delivery as having minimum thresholds. Below these threshold levels, the product or service is unfit-for-purpose and the consumer will reject it. If a consumer has an emotional attachment or loyalty to your brand, she may choose to wait in the hope that your product or service improves to an acceptable level rather than switch away to another brand. Customer loyalty, an emotional, identity-related attachment to your brand, or some other form of customer lock-in such as bundling or network effects within a suite of related products or services, may be an antidote to a lack of fit-for-purpose. Firms with an exceptionally loyal following and a strong emotional attachment to their brand may be able to offer products that aren't truly fit-for-purpose and get away with it for some time. A product or service that both enjoys customer loyalty, or customer lock-in, and meets or exceeds fitness criteria thresholds in each of the three dimensions is well positioned for long-term success.

Fittest among Peers

Given a motivation to purchase—a customer purpose or need— and neutral position in terms of emotional selection, how might a consumer select one product over another in an environment where more than one vendor offers suitable products or services? Fit-for-purpose is either a good *blend* in the absolute of the three elements—design, implementation, and service delivery—or a strong *match* of fitness within those elements to the consumer's purpose or why. Once a product or service meets the minimum threshold levels to make it fit-for-purpose for a given customer's "why," then it competes to be fittest among a group of peers that are all fit—each of which meets the threshold levels. Selection tends to come from a combination of design, implementation, and service delivery—for which the vendor may have had to make tradeoffs—and from emotional reasons such as affinity with a brand. We'll revisit this in Chapters 8 and 9 in a discussion of managing and taking action based on fit-for-purpose assessment and review.

We explore the missing emotional element in greater depth in Chapter 11, Blind Spots. David also intends to explore it yet deeper in the third book of this series, provisionally titled *First Who, Then Why!* which will look at identity-related motivation for selection and decision making.

Segment Your Market Using Customer Purpose

This is the big new idea in market segmentation—segment your customers based on their purpose—the "why" they select you. When you understand your customers' purpose, you can tune your product and service offering to best serve that purpose. For each product or service, you should be able to explain how its design elements serve the customer's purpose. You should be capable of providing an implementation of the product or service at the required quality levels based on your understanding of the customer's fitness criteria thresholds for each purpose. If your current capability isn't well matched to your customer's expectations, you are likely to fail in that segment. You may want to reconsider: Do you want to invest in improving your capability? Or would it be better to avoid that segment rather than serve it poorly? Ideally you want to achieve positive Fitness Box Scores in each segment you serve. If you do this, you'll have high customer satisfaction and you will likely retain these customers, hopefully making them both loyal and active advocates who promote your business to others. Positive Fitness Box Scores should correlate with high Net Promoter Scores.

Neeta doesn't represent one customer segment—she exists in two segments because she has different purposes for ordering pizza in different contexts. This is an important lesson that can be missed in traditional market segmentation exercises. In Chapter 10, It's Not Luck, we explore how to exploit this knowledge and how to design a service offering for pizza that can win Neeta's business in both of her contexts.

Beyond Net Promoter Score

Net Promoter Score (NPS) has become popular in recent years as a means of sampling customer sentiment and assessing customer satisfaction. *Forbes* writer Stephen Denning, in his 2010 book *The Leader's Guide to Radical Management*, described NPS as "the only metric you will ever need." We respectfully disagree with Steve on this one. In his context—writing for *Forbes*, an investment guidance periodical—there is evidence that high NPS scores correlate with high stock prices for public companies. Hence, as a *Forbes* writer, providing advice such as "Buy stocks of companies with high NPS scores" is probably useful. However, some of our clients have complained that NPS isn't actionable; it simply tells you whether your customers like you a bit more or a bit less than they did a month ago—or three months ago. It is hard to know what to do if, for example, the score is declining and the indications are that customers are increasingly dissatisfied. It was such a complaint from a client in the winter of 2013 that led David to start exploring alternatives, ultimately leading to this book.

While reviewing this manuscript, a former client likened NPS to a general health indicator, a concept we explore in Chapters 4 and 5. A general health indicator is something that you need to monitor but that doesn't come with a threshold or a target. You don't necessarily have a target pulse rate or blood pressure, although you might have a defined range within which you'd be considered healthy. Dramatic changes in a general health indicator may indicate something significant, however. Senior executives at a large retail bank in central and eastern Europe complained that it is hard to know what to do based on month-to-month fluctuations in a score. Whereas actionable guidance may be one issue with NPS, we believe there are other issues, which we'll discuss in Chapter 12, It's Your Future, Be There. Meanwhile, we believe that adopting an understanding of a customer's purpose, their "why," segmenting your market based on "why," and building an understanding of the criteria customers use to select your product or service is a far better way to ensure satisfied customers, repeat business, and future recommendations.

Why Customer Purpose Matters

Without a capability to identify your customers' purpose, you run the same risk that British Airways is taking—you may be flying blind! If yours are unfit-for-purpose, your customers will select your competitors' products and services. Unable to sense why they've done this, your strategy will flail around, randomly seeking the new formula to win back business. You'll waste vast sums of money guessing and speculating while your competitors use data to stay focused on superior customer satisfaction. The fittest will survive. Survival is not essential, it's a choice! If, as a business, you value survival, now is the time to develop the capability to know whether your products and services are fit-for-purpose.

As long ago as 2004, American Airlines adopted the slogan, "We know why you fly!" This was a commendable direction but we don't believe they did "know why [we] fly." In their traditional TV commercials produced for the campaign, such as the 2009 one-minute spot,[13] the straw-man scenarios were intended to resonate emotionally but failed to make compelling reasons to explain "why you fly." Their reasons were: seeing your niece turn five years old, beating your brothers at touch football, reminding your family what you look like, Grandma's cobbler, moving to a new city (for your significant other), and having lunch with a client and dinner with your spouse on the same day. To explain the purpose of a trip, that cobbler at Grandma's must be one hell of a dessert! The campaign ran for more than eight years—until American's rebranding following their merger with USAirways, begged the question, "What exactly does American do to know why we fly?" Which leads us to the conclusion that if they truly knew why we fly, they would be designing their product and service offerings specifically to our needs. Having identified niches and designed products and service offerings for those niches, we'd expect communications that have a narrow message, show empathy, and clearly resonate with the target audience rather than the exotic edge cases that their advertising agency concocted for the campaign. We'll explore this in greater depth in Chapter 7, We Know Why You Fly.

Understanding Customer Purpose Should Be a Core Strategic Capability

Segmentation based on customer purpose—based on "why"—should be your new go-to-market strategy, and correctly identifying your customer's fitness criteria is core to your success. An ability to correctly identify fitness criteria and respond to them with appropriate designs, implementation, and service delivery is what will make your business robust in the coming years.

---

13. https://www.youtube.com/watch?v=_RtpszbxaoE

Summary

- For each fitness criterion, customers have some level of expectation that is acceptable to them.

- You should segment your market based on your customer's purpose. Each market segment will have not only a different purpose, but a different set of fitness criteria and thresholds.

- The people who know your customer's "why" and understand their criteria are your frontline staff. These are often the lowest-paid employees with the highest turnover rate.

- Emotional motivation and brand loyalty can sometimes compensate for a lack of fit-for-purpose.

- Fitness Box Score and F4P Cards are new tools to understand your customer's "why." They have evolved to give you actionable information. These techniques also offer substantial improvements over the popular Net Promoter Score (NPS). We present them in detail in Chapter 9.

- Without understanding its customers' various purposes and fitness criteria, your business may be challenged to satisfy or retain its existing customers or to find new ones. Therefore, understanding your customer's "why" and their fitness criteria should be your business's core strategic capability.

SECTION II

Understanding
Fitness-for-Purpose

Section I introduced fitness for purpose with examples of products and services both fit- and not-so-fit-for-purpose, as well as their fitness criteria. In Section II we present the Fit-for-Purpose Framework and the theory behind it.

Are you familiar with the concept of Key Performance Indicators (KPIs)? Chapter 4 will challenge your understanding of KPIs. It analyzes several examples in which there was no shortage of data, indicators, or criteria, but only a few of them mattered to selection. And in the few that mattered, the thresholds of customer satisfaction and happiness turned out to be not where the companies expected them. Chapter 5 challenges the multitude of data and metrics collected by many companies: are these useful for selection? Are they better for some other purpose? Are some of them completely useless? Chapter 6 presents several common fitness criteria found in many different—seemingly unrelated—industries' product development and service delivery processes. Chapter 7 shows how different fitness criteria and thresholds play out in different market segments, then presents the complete Fit-for-Purpose Framework.

Section III, Managing Fitness for Purpose, provides our pragmatic, actionable guidance on introducing the Fit-for-Purpose Framework in a real-world business.

4 On Base Percentage, the Boston Marathon, and the Car of Your Dreams

IN ORDER TO THINK CONSTRUCTIVELY about what makes a product or service fit-for-purpose, it is helpful to have a model, a framework, or a system with which we can reason about it and make meaningful decisions for our business. We'll pull all the theory together and present the Fit-for-Purpose Framework at the conclusion of Chapter 7, but first a story about how Billy Beane and the Oakland ATHLETICS changed baseball. . . .

"But Does He Get on Base?"

"If he can hit, then why doesn't he hit good?" Billy Beane, general manager of the Oakland Athletics baseball team throws the question across the table to the assembled group of scouts in a scene from the movie *Moneyball*, based on the book of the same name by Michael Lewis. *Moneyball*, starring Brad Pitt as Beane, tells the true story of the 2002 season when the Oakland Athletics pioneered the use of statistical methods for player analysis and game strategy. Beane had hired a new assistant, Paul DePodesta, who is portrayed in the movie as the composite character Peter Brand, played by Jonah Hill. DePodesta was a fan of the work of Bill James, author of *The Historical Baseball Abstract*. He combined his passion for the game with his top-notch education and training as a statistician.

For context, the Oakland Athletics are based in the city of Oakland, California, a blue-collar, working-class town on the eastern shore of the San Francisco Bay. Despite being closer to San Francisco than many suburbs, Oakland maintains a unique identity as a city, part of which is its beloved "A's." The Athletics are a "small market team." They don't have as much television revenue from broadcasts on local stations as do the teams from large cities with large television markets, such as the New York Yankees or even as their rivals across the bay, the San Francisco Giants. Oakland has also fallen behind richer teams that have upgraded or rebuilt their stadiums to optimize their game-day revenue.

Throughout the late 1990s and early 2000s, the Oakland Athletics were one of the poorest teams in Major League Baseball, playing in their old ballpark, the Oakland–Alameda County Coliseum. The team focused on developing young players, eventually producing Rookie of the Year outfielder Ben Grieve and the great trio of starting pitchers, Mark Mulder, Tim Hudson, and Barry Zito. While the A's could still afford to pay their contracts, they started finishing higher in the standings and finally, after a long break, appeared in the playoffs. In 2001 they made the playoffs for the second year in a row and—for the second year in a row—lost in the first round, effectively the quarterfinal, to the richest team in the league, the New York Yankees. To add to their troubles, at the end of 2001 three of the A's' star players reached the end of their contracts: the speedy centerfielder Johnny Damon; their best hitter, first baseman Jason Giambi; and the closing pitcher Jason Isringhausen. All three were moving to big market teams. If the A's were to stay competitive in 2002, Billy Beane had to replace all three with low-cost, equally talented alternatives. The situation was a good illustration of the precarious life of small market teams: even if they develop good young players, they can still become victims of their own success as the market value of those players eventually reaches unaffordable heights[14] and the players move on to richer teams that can pay them more.

Advising on which players to choose for the 2002 season roster, Peter explains to Billy, "Your goal shouldn't be to buy players. your goal should be to buy wins. In order to buy wins, you need to buy runs." To buy runs, you need to get players on base.

---

14. Mulder and Hudson left Oakland after the 2004 season; Zito, the youngest of the three, after 2006.

For our readers outside North America, a period of play in baseball is called an inning. It continues until the defending team gets three opposing players out. The defending team tries to get the three outs as quickly as possible and then take their offensive turn. The offensive team tries to avoid outs for as long as possible. How do you not make an out in baseball? By getting on base, thus extending the inning and letting more teammates take turns at bat. The players already on base may advance from base to base and eventually score runs if they return to "home plate," where they started.

The best way to get on base is, of course, to hit the ball well and out of defenders' reach. Hitting the ball is one of the core baseball skills and it was as early as the 19th Century that the game developed a statistic to measure it: the batting average. It is the percentage of at-bats in which the player hits the ball well enough to reach at least the first base. Historically, the batting average has been one of the key criteria to identify the game's best hitters. It also provides endless entertainment to many fans, who track it and compare their favorite players.

Paul DePodesta—Peter Brand—however, spotted an important flaw of the batting average. Although it's a good measure of a player's hitting prowess, the batting average doesn't give a player credit for various other ways of getting on base and helping his team generate runs. Such ways include walks (free passes due to not swinging at bad pitches), getting hit by a pitch, taking advantage of fielders' errors, and so on. The rules of calculating a batting average exclude walks from the count of at-bats, count reaching base on error as no-hit, and so on. Peter recommends to Billy that the key performance indicator they should be using for player selection is the on-base percentage (OBP). OBP is a simpler metric that incorporates all times a player reached base, hit or not, and all plate appearances, whether or not they count as "at-bats" for batting average purposes. Peter contends that although the batting average may be useful for comparing the best hitters, the OBP may be much more useful for determining whether a player helps the team win, and hence, for choosing the team's roster of players.

Baseball statisticians have tracked OBP for all players for decades. It just had never occurred to anybody to use it as a criterion for player selection. To someone unfamiliar with baseball or its history, it may seem terribly obvious and intuitive to use OBP to select players whose job it is to get on base instead of making an out. But the concept that OBP should be used in place of the revered batting average (or several other offensive statistics with a long tradition) was revolutionary and controversial at the time.

When selecting young or reserve players lacking long-enough statistical records at the major league level, scouts had to resort to using other, more qualitative and subjective measures for player selection. This is illustrated in the movie with a discussion among the scouts, reporting their qualitative observations of players: "He's got a beautiful swing. The ball explodes off his bat." Or "Can't hit the curveball." But more often they simply looked for real or imagined similarities with successful players of the past: "He looks like a Mantle or a Mays, quite frankly." The quest for looks could lead the scouts to make recommendations based on appearance characteristics that didn't have anything to do with athletic ability: "Clean cut, good face, good jaw" and "He passes the eye candy test, he's got the looks, he's ready to play the part." Or even: "He has an ugly girlfriend. Ugly girlfriend means no confidence. His girlfriend is a six at best!" Feeling confident of their assessments, one scout speculates: "Give this kid 400 at-bats, he's gonna get better." Social affinity played a role too: "He's one of our guys." And some of the scouts' criteria aren't even printable in this book! While the state of baseball scouting in 2001 may have been overdramatized in the movie, Peter and Billy sense an opportunity.

Peter and Billy now realize that OBP is perfect for arbitrage. They look at some players' OBP and believe "they will get on base." Managers of other teams look at other performance indicators and overlook the same players. Peter and Billy believe OBP will help them make the most out of their limited budget and settle on it as the key performance indicator and fitness-criteria metric to use for player selection.

Oakland's 2002 season has ups and downs and Billy Beane has to make some changes. He trades a number of players, including, in one of *Moneyball*'s dramatic moments, a very promising rookie first baseman, Carlos Pena. Beane wants Scott Hatteberg to be the team's everyday first baseman. Hatteberg is a former catcher near the end of his playing career. Moving to first base is his only chance of extending his career because his elbow is damaged and he can't throw the ball from home plate to second base to defend against advancing base runners.[15] Hatteberg has a decent career batting average, but Billy spots his unusually high OBP.[16] Hatteberg walks a lot and hence gets on base more often than his batting average might suggest. He is the player that can help the A's win *now*. The team rallies in the second half of the season and reaches the playoffs again.

The A's' strategy helps them maximize the number of games won over the course of the very long 162-game regular season, when they play good, average, and weak teams. They have done well relative to their limited resources. But playoffs are different. Now the A's have to contend, in absolute terms, in high-stakes elimination games with only the best one-fourth of the teams in the league. The A's are optimized on the offensive side of the ball, where they found the undervalued players. But now they have to bat against much better pitchers—the quality of pitching, more so than of hitting, goes up significantly in the postseason. Most of the playoff teams have much deeper pockets and can afford deeper rosters. They're ready to exploit others' weaknesses and they have few weaknesses of their own. Their very best players also tend to step up their performance levels in the playoffs—the Yankees' Derek Jeter, Mariano Rivera, and Bernie Williams are examples.

The A's used OBP to fill their batting order with undervalued players and did well in the long regular season, but their weaknesses on defense and pitching (beyond the first three starters) left them vulnerable in the playoffs. In 2002 the Oakland Athletics lost in the first round of playoffs for the third year in a row, this time to the Minnesota Twins.

Even so, Billy Beane is approached by John Henry, owner of the Boston Red Sox, who is interested in hiring him as the new general manager in Boston. Henry explains to Beane why he wants him as his new GM. "You won just as many games as the Yankees. You lost Damon, Giambi, Isringhausen, and Pena and yet you won more

---

15. For our non-American readers: the distance from home plate to second base is 39 meters. The catcher must be able to make a strong throw from his knees or a squat position and hit a small target— his teammate's glove. Any delay in releasing the ball, a lack of velocity, or an inaccurate throw that forces the teammate to move will give the opponent's baserunner precious split-seconds to advance into scoring position.

16. Hatteberg's career on-base percentage of .364 is a very high threshold. At the time of writing, only twenty active Major League players (out of approximately 400 hitters, and less than one per team) have an equal or greater career OBP.

games without them than you did with them. The Yankees paid $1.4 million per win, and you paid only $260,000."

Henry gives us the metric he is using as an owner—how much is he paying per win? This makes some sense as a benchmark against other owners. However, Billy Beane replies, "I don't know, John, I just lost in five in the Division series." Later, talking to Peter Brand, he says, "If you don't win the last game of the season, nobody cares." This is a theme throughout the movie, mentioned in an early scene with team owner Stephen Schott, "My bar is to take this team to the championship." He wants to play in the World Series and win it!

For Beane, the fitness criterion and key performance indicator is defined by where his team places in the tournament. The fittest team is the one that wins the World Series, and to do so is his career goal.

To summarize, key performance indicators (KPIs) should be used as fitness criteria to make selections. The A's used OBP to select players and determine their value for trade and pay. John Henry was willing to use dollars per win as his selection criterion to pick Beane as his new GM. However, Beane had a different value system. His was more aligned with the fans; the finishing position in the tournament is his fitness criterion—fans want their team in the playoffs, ideally every year, and they want to win the championship at least once every generation, once every twenty to twenty-five years. It is performance like this that makes a local sports team fit-for-purpose and encourages the fans to buy season tickets and keep showing up, week after week, year after year.

Fitness criteria are used to make selections. Fitness Criteria are KPIs—they indicate the likelihood of a desirable outcome that will satisfy the customer. We believe many companies are using the term "key performance indicator" for metrics that do not reflect selection and do not predict desirable outcomes and satisfied customers. As a result, these businesses are optimizing for the wrong things—they are like the teams playing against Oakland in 2002, selecting players based on criteria that do not directly relate to winning.

The Boston Marathon

The Boston Marathon is the oldest marathon in America, running every year continuously since 1897. Its first running was inspired by the revival of the marathon in the first modern Olympics held in Athens, Greece, the previous year. The Boston Marathon is, however, very different from all other annual big-city marathons in another very important respect. When someone describes their running accomplishments as "I ran Boston," it instantly says a lot more than if they reported finishing a marathon in another city. Why? To enter the Boston Marathon, you have to run another marathon and finish it within a certain time limit. Boston is the only marathon in America to have such a requirement, and it's part of what makes Boston so special. At the time of writing, the so-called Boston qualifying time is three hours, five minutes for men and three hours, thirty-five minutes for women.[17]

The Boston Marathon has fitness criteria for its participants: time at the finish line is what matters. Finish time is a Key Performance Indicator (KPI) and the key word in "KPI" is "key." In other athletic events, such as track and bicycle or swimming races, the finish times and the athletes' placement are the key performance indicators. We can use the finish times to directly compare the athletes' performance and select the winner.

Besides their finish time at each distance, athletes track many more indicators as they train for competition. But they make no mistake which few of them are key. And we want leaders responsible for bringing their products and services to customers to think like athletes.

Let's consider a few examples:

- Body fat percentage
- Resting heart rate
- VO_2Max (the volume of oxygen the lungs can process per minute)
- Monthly training mileage
- Calories consumed with food and burned during workouts
- Paces and repeats of various interval training workouts (minutes / seconds per unit of distance, interval, or track lap)

17. These qualifying times are for runners aged 18 to 34. For ages 35 and up, the Boston qualifying times increase gradually for each five-year age group. The Boston Athletic Association trusts only certain certified marathon courses, and only the finish times measured on those courses are considered for qualification.

- Cadence (steps or other motions per minute)
- Elevation gain while on a training run or bicycle ride

It is true that many top athletes have a low body fat percentage. Many endurance athletes have a below average heart rate—their heart muscles are very strong and pump greater than average amounts of blood with each stroke. Great swimmers have a lot of lung capacity. The best marathoners log a lot of training miles. Many athletes watch what they eat and maintain steady levels of calorie intake and training volumes to keep their body weight optimal. Stronger athletes run their interval workouts at faster paces or with more repeats. Better athletes have more consistent technique—they maintain a certain healthy cadence when they run, bike, or swim that helps them move faster with the same effort, maximize their training benefit, and minimize the injury risk. Athletes training for mountain races also make sure that many of their training runs take them uphill and that certain amounts of elevation gain show up in their training logs. But no one would think of deciding a contest based on any of these measures. These metrics aren't KPIs. They're general health indicators. They don't indicate selection. They don't have threshold levels. They don't have targets, but they do have an indicated range that represents "healthy," and often more or less or a trend in a direction indicates better health. For example, a low body fat percentage is better than a high one, but there are limits—too low would be unhealthy.

We believe that too many companies measure general health indicators and treat them as key performance indicators. They are then puzzled when their performance is not market- or industry-leading. They are like cyclists with very low resting heart rates who simply can't understand why they aren't winning races. There are no medals for lowest resting heart rate!

The Car of Your Dreams

In 2010 Fiat chairman Luca di Montezemolo was demoted to president of their Ferrari business unit.[18] Di Montezemolo, a former racing driver, joined Ferrari in 1973 as assistant to founder Enzo Ferrari

---

18. In January 2016, Ferrari became fully independent of Fiat following a restructuring and IPO (initial public offering). en.wikipedia.org/wiki/Ferrari

and in 1974 became the manager of the Formula 1 racing team, the Sportivo division of Ferrari, known as *Scuderia Ferrari*. In 1991 he was appointed president of Ferrari for the first time. Thirteen years later di Montezemolo was promoted to become the chairman of Fiat. So why, six years later, was he being demoted and put back in the Ferrari business where he'd spent so much of his career?

While the truth may be complex, nuanced, and political, the roots of the change lie in a decision to increase production at Ferrari. In 2009 Fiat had acquired a large holding in the American car maker Chrysler as part of Chrysler's restructuring and exit from Chapter 11 bankruptcy protection. Fiat would go on over the course of the next five years to acquire all of the remaining shares in Chrysler, which is, at the time of writing, a wholly owned subsidiary of Fiat. So, for context, in 2009 Fiat needed money to fund its acquisition of Chrysler stock and to invest in synergies between the two firms. This led to, for example, the sharing of some technology and vehicle platforms and the reintroduction of Fiat brands to the retail market in North America, where Chrysler dealers started to sell the Fiat 500 subcompact car. Fiat needed money, and one source of cash was its profitable Ferrari unit.

Di Montezemolo had always believed in keeping Ferraris exclusive—small volume production and high prices. Demand for Ferrari cars was buoyant and rising, even in the harsh economic times of 2009. Di Montezemolo was under pressure to push Ferrari to make more cars and generate cash that could be put to good use in other parts of the business. He refused. A Ferrari guy, he stuck to his beliefs that Ferraris should be exclusive and that there should never be too many of them in circulation. If you take a few moments to research prices for used Ferraris, you will observe how strongly they hold their value. This is due to the scarcity of examples of any one model. However, Di Montezemolo lost the argument, and his stubbornness over it undermined his position as chairman of Fiat. As a consequence, he was asked to step down and resume his leadership at Ferrari but on the basis that production would be increased. This time, however, he had a genuine business justification for agreeing to increase production. In 2009 the waiting time for a new model had risen to twenty-seven months. This had caused some interesting and unusual behavior—the rate of order cancellations was rising. It seems that some Ferrari buyers weren't patient enough to wait twenty-seven months to take delivery. There is always a residual level of order cancellations—some buyers die before they can take delivery of their new vehicle, others suffer business setbacks or job losses and are unable to pay for the vehicle when it is eventually manufactured. However, the cancellation rate in 2009 had reached an unusually high level, a level that was considered unacceptable within the firm.

So, production at Ferrari was stepped up in 2010 and the waiting list gradually shrank as the delivery time slowly declined from twenty-seven to twenty-one months. At this time, the order cancellation rate returned to historical residual levels. Di Montezemolo had done his bit to increase production and generate cash for Fiat, and he ordered that production should be paced at the rate of new orders and that the delivery time should remain constant at twenty-one months. After all, Ferrari wanted their customers to be passionate about Ferrari, and one way they could prove their loyalty was to show patience while waiting twenty-one months to take delivery of their vehicle.

To put this story in the language of this text, a lead time of twenty-seven months wasn't fit-for-purpose! Ferrari discovered their customers' lead time threshold level to be twenty-one months. This is how long loyal Ferrari followers were prepared to wait for the car of their dreams to be delivered. So one of their fitness-criteria metrics is lead time, and its threshold value is twenty-one months.

Ferrari used the cancellation rate as their improvement driver. They monitored the cancellation rate while they increased the production rate. When the cancellation rate fell to an acceptable level they then paced production to the new order rate to stabilize the delivery wait time (the lead time) to twenty-one months. When David visited the factory in 2011, the production rate for eight-cylinder models, such as the California, was one every forty-five minutes, or twelve per eight-hour shift. The factory was operating two shifts per day for a total of twenty-four eight-cylinder model cars each day. The production rate (of cars) represents the factory's capability and is a general health indicator—faster is healthier. The cancellation rate is the improvement driver. Until the cancellation rate falls below a certain threshold, the factory must strive to produce cars faster in order to shrink the waiting list and waiting time for delivery. The cancellation rate has a target that is defined by the historical residual rate of cancellations. Lead time is the fitness criterion, or KPI, with a fitness threshold of twenty-one months. Cancellation rate (and meeting its target) is the improvement driver motivating faster production.

As a postscript to this story, five years later, in 2014, di Montezemolo was again asked to increase production at Ferrari. Once again, he pushed back against this pressure. Perhaps there wasn't a logical business reason, from a Ferrari perspective, to agree to the increase? Perhaps Ferrari customers were satisfied and di Montezemolo considered their product and service levels fit-for-purpose? His refusal eventually led to his dismissal from the firm he had joined forty-one years earlier.

Another Car of Your Dreams

On August 2, 2017, the great entrepreneur, innovator, and Tesla CEO Elon Musk reported that 63,000 customers had cancelled their Model 3 reservations.[19]

Soon after Model 3 was unveiled in the summer 2016, many customers rushed to place orders, even knowing the production would not begin for more than a year. The cancellations still left Tesla with a backlog of 455,000 orders (a cancellation rate of 12 percent so far). Tesla expected to start production in December 2017 at the rate of 20,000 cars per month. Musk expected the first six months of manufacturing the Model 3 to be "production hell."

Mr. Musk made a self-critical statement, suggesting at the same time there was a blessing in disguise: "It's like if you're a restaurant and you're serving hamburgers, and there's like an hour-and-a-half wait for hamburgers—do you really want to encourage more people to order more hamburgers?" (It's interesting how Mr. Musk equated approximately one month of waiting for a car to about three minutes of waiting for a hamburger. Does this tell the reader something about Mr. Musk's own selection criteria when he is in the mood for pub fare?)

Assuming the backlog is still 455,000 units at the start of production, that the "production hell" resolves quickly, and the production rate is 20,000 per month, the lead time of the order currently last in the backlog will be twenty-three months from the start of production.

---

19. www.businessinsider.com/elon-musk-tesla-model-3-cancellations-hamburgers-2017-8

We have to add only another few months still remaining until the production start (August to December 2017), resulting in twenty-seven months of lead time. All of a sudden, this contemporary Tesla story starts to sound like Ferrari in 2009. It also begs two questions: Is Tesla's brand as strong as Ferrari's to let the company get away with unsatisfactory service delivery? And for how long?

This Tesla story is a warning to many product developers in various technology fields who are overly obsessed with the design of their product features and who don't pay enough attention to implementation and service delivery. It is also a lesson to those technology companies whose brands are certainly not as strong as Ferrari's or Tesla's and who hold design in higher regard—elevating their product designers and managers ("innovators") to a higher social status—at the expense of implementation and service delivery.

Approximately 400 miles south of Tesla's production facility in Fremont, California, is San Bernardino, the original location for McDonald's, the world-renowned hamburger chain. While McDonald's originally prided itself on its narrow, focused menu and family-friendly concept, the quality of their product and the speed of their service delivery was always a key to their success. They called it the "Speedee service system."[20] We have to ask, do we think the McDonald brothers, who created the concept, would have been proud of a ninety-minute wait?

Mr. Musk's hamburger analogy suggests what's on his mind right now. It is not figuring out, figuratively speaking, a tastier hamburger recipe. His cars already delight drivers. They capture the public's imagination. The focus is likely to be on implementation, ensuring the production quality at the factory in Fremont, and on service delivery, reducing the delivery time to be in line with the expectations of the growing population of electric car drivers. The company's recent history suggests it is likely to be up to these tasks. Tesla cars drive by wire, controlled by a computer. The computer software can be updated frequently, over the air. The frequent wireless updates are the service delivery component complementing the design and implementation of software code. Tesla already knows how to excel in service delivery.

---

20. en.wikipedia.org/wiki/Speedee

To summarize the current state of the Tesla Model 3: the cancellation rate (currently 12 percent) is the improvement driver, the production rate (estimating 20,000 per month in December 2017) is a general health indicator (the greater the healthier, hopefully, in 2018), and the lead time (approximately twenty-seven months currently) is a KPI and a customer fitness criterion. When the cancellation rate reaches negligible levels, the then-current lead time will indicate Tesla 3 customers' real fitness threshold.

The delivery lead time of two years (give or take) appears to be acceptable to car collectors and enthusiast drivers, such as those who drive the exclusive Ferrari or who are the first in their town or neighbourhood to drive a Tesla. And it only works for companies with very strong brands such as these two. The satisfactory delivery time for the so-called early adopter market, which follows after the enthusiasts, or the mainstream market, which comes much later, is much shorter by far. Mainstream buyers might be prepared to wait one month, maybe two, but certainly not twenty-seven. Ferrari's niche strategy includes enthusiast drivers only, so the company can afford the long delivery time. Tesla, however, clearly aims for the mass market, therefore it still has to significantly improve its implementation and service delivery if it is to remain fit-for-purpose with mainstream buyers. The change of fitness criteria as the products enter different phases of their lifecycle is discussed further in Chapter 14, Be Paranoid. The evolution and transitions of a company as its products go through such phases will be analyzed in detail in the second book of this trilogy, *Built To Last*.

The Streak

So far in this chapter we've provided examples of fitness criteria: the key performance indicators that indicate selection, improvement drivers that motivate change, and general health indicators that should be monitored because they may give early warning of problems that will eventually manifest in a failure to be fit-for-purpose. For example, a falling production rate is a leading indicator for a lengthening lead time, and eventually dissatisfied customers who cancel orders. There is one more category of metrics that we must describe before leaving this chapter—vanity metrics—and to do so we return to where we started, the Oakland–Alameda Coliseum, and Billy Beane's Oakland Athletics.

In the second half of the 2002 season, after Billy Beane made some dramatic changes to the Oakland Athletics' player roster, the team started to turn around their losing season. They went on a twenty-game winning streak that set an all-time record for consecutive wins in the American League.[21] Scott Hatteberg hit the winning home run to secure the twentieth victory in a dramatic game with the Kansas City Royals that was tied at 11–11. Pitt as Beane in the movie remarks, "It's hard not to be romantic about baseball. . . . These things are great for the fans." However, Beane knows that a twenty-game winning streak and the all-time record for consecutive games won is merely a vanity metric. "It doesn't mean anything." Vanity metrics make us feel good. Vanity metrics are often mistaken for key performance indicators, though. Firms that use vanity metrics to drive behavior focus on the wrong things. They become addicted to the self-medication of feeling good while their actual performance is inadequate. We'll examine vanity metrics in greater depth in the next chapter.

Four Types of Metrics

We believe that a company's metrics can be classified into four categories:

- Fitness criteria, with a threshold, used for selection (by customers)
- General health indicators, with a range, used to monitor capabilities, or aspects of the business
- Improvement drivers, with a target, used to motivate improvements, and generally linked in a causal fashion to fitness criteria
- Vanity metrics, which make us feel good, where more is always better

Many so-called key performance indicators are more likely general health indicators, though some will be improvement drivers—

---

21. This record stood until just this year, when the Cleveland Indians' 22-game winning streak ended with a loss to the Kansas City Royals on September 13, 2017, two weeks after we completed the writing of this book. www.usatoday.com/picture-gallery/sports/mlb/2017/09/11/2017-cleveland-indians-winning-streak/105498840/.

important, but they don't indicate selection, nor do they have a direct relationship with customer satisfaction. Yet more may be vanity metrics—they make us feel good but do not correlate to improved business performance or stronger customer satisfaction. In the next chapter we'll explore all four types of metrics in detail.

Summary

- Fitness criteria indicate selection.

- Key Performance Indicators (KPIs) should be fitness criteria.

- The 2002 Oakland Athletics used the on-base percentage (OBP) as a KPI to select their offensive players.

- The A's won twenty games in a row. While the fans were impressed, the general manager Billy Beane (as portrayed in the movie *Moneyball*) saw the winning streak length as a vanity metric.

- The Boston Marathon uses the finish time of another certified and qualifying marathon as a KPI for selecting the entrants.

- Runners trying to qualify for the Boston Marathon and other competitive athletes know the finish time is their KPI. They track many other indicators, but they make no mistake about which of them is "key."

- Ferrari discovered at some point that their lead time of twenty-seven months was unsatisfactory to their customers and increased the production rate to shorten it to twenty-one months. Lead time is the KPI, the production rate (cars per shift) is a health indicator, and the order cancellation rate was the improvement driver.

- At the time of writing, Tesla finds itself with a similar lead time as Ferrari for their Model 3, which is aimed at a much broader consumer market. Already having a winning design, the company will try to improve its implementation and service delivery to be fit-for-purpose on the broader market.

- We've identified four types of metrics:
  - Fitness criteria (KPI) with thresholds
  - Health indicators
  - Improvement drivers
  - Vanity metrics

5 The Expanding Universe

The Expanding Universe of Metrics

MANY COMPANIES ALREADY COLLECT a lot of data and measure and track many metrics. They track their sales and profits, employees' time, quantities of various materials, inputs, finished goods inventory, and so on. Our clients tell us what they track, and it's usually a long list. Some of their metrics are very straightforward; they describe the company's performance and are used in many businesses. These include:

- Sales (dollar amounts)
- Return on investment (ROI)
- Number of customers served
- Revenue per customer
- Same-store sales

Some metrics are about quality of products and services, for example:

- Number of defects (often broken down by defect category or severity)
- Number of customer complaints
- Customer satisfaction scores

Other metrics focus on the workforce, such as:

- Contractor/employee ratio
- Employee satisfaction scores

- Staff attrition rate
- Percentage of billable hours

Some other metrics concern customer engagement, or are attempts to measure customer engagement, such as:

- Conversion rate
- Churn rate
- Average lifespan of subscription
- Percentage of opt-ins following marketing campaigns
- Website visits
- Time spent on the website per visit

Still other metrics are process oriented, and many of those are specific to certain industries, for example:

- Server uptime (important to an information technology company, obviously)
- Multiplier (what a law firm bills its clients per hour versus what it pays its associates for the hour)
- Service-level agreement (SLA) conformance rate

We've also discovered some quite creative metrics. One company asks its employees to report the approximate number of hours they spend on volunteer activities in their community. The company sees volunteering as an indicator of a healthy workforce. Reporting is voluntary and nobody verifies the reported hours with a clock. As one of the company's executives explained to us, if the reported volunteer hours were to decline, that could be because their staff are overworked or stressed out. The leaders would see it as an early warning sign.

Some metrics become popular following broad societal trends and the introduction of new technology. Many companies currently track social media likes (retweets, reactions, Facebook page fans, and the like), Net Promoter Score (NPS), and so on.

Modern technology enables the current trend toward collecting more data and justifying business and operational decisions with data. We observe this trend in many industries. A reasonable near-future prediction is that many companies will collect even more data and track even more metrics as they try to make better business decisions.

The metrics universe is vast already and it continues to expand!

More isn't necessarily better. As we saw in Chapter 4, the sport of baseball is rich in metrics, but very few of them are truly key performance indicators that have a causal relationship with winning and should be used for player selection. So which metrics in your business provide high leverage, resulting in good decision making? And which are merely noise getting in the way of good decision making? How would you determine which metrics you should pay attention to?

Are Our Metrics Fit-for-Purpose?

Why do we collect metrics? What is their purpose?
And are they fit-for-purpose?
Let's consider examples from Chapter 2. How did Neeta decide on and choose pizza? How would pop music fans in Mumbai select a concert worth investing a month's salary to attend? How would Olympic National Park day hikers choose a beverage for their mountain summit picnic? Based on what fact, quality, or advantage? What would indicate to a company competing for these customers' business that the customers are more—or less—likely to choose them? What would tell the company leaders that they indeed run their company in ways that are likely to keep these customers satisfied?

Recall how Neeta chose pizza for her colleagues and for her children. Did she need to see Zak's Artisan Pie & Crust's P&L statement? Did she care about Westside Pizza's same-store sales trend? Was it important to her to know how many pizzas they bake per employee shift? Would she even think about the current levels of inventory of various pizza ingredients? The prices of those ingredients? Mileage logged by pizza delivery vehicles? Staff overtime hours?

Yet each pizzeria probably tracks all or most of these indicators one way or another, each for its own good reason. They just don't factor into their customers' decisions. Neeta's choice for her kids was based mostly on delivery time, its predictability, and functional quality.

Key performance indicators (KPIs) are those few metrics with direct links to customers' decisions—direct links to market selection. Have you ever met a manager who boasted about tracking fifty different KPIs? Probably. Well, even if those fifty measures are all performance indicators of some kind, at least forty-five of them most likely aren't *key*! The implication of a "key" performance indicator is that it is highly influential in predicting a desirable outcome. As we saw in Chapter 4, on base percentage is a key performance indicator; and although having an attractive girlfriend may correlate with a player's self-confidence, and confidence may correlate with performance on the baseball field, attractiveness of a player's girlfriend is not a *key* performance indicator. It may not even be a performance indicator. There may not be a correlation. It may, in fact, be mere superstition. OBP, on the other hand, is a predictor of runs scored, which in turn predicts wins, which in turn predicts qualification for the end-of-season playoffs and the chance to win the championship.

We need to learn to use metrics appropriately and to understand how to classify and categorize them.

Classifying Metrics

Companies have different purposes for tracking different metrics. We broadly categorize those purposes four ways: vanity metrics; fitness criteria (KPIs), health indicators, and improvement indicators. All four were illustrated with anecdotes in Chapter 4. Let's start by analyzing the category that got the least attention previously, vanity metrics.

Vanity Metrics

Vanity metrics are often mistakenly categorized into one of the other three categories, but their main—or even sole—purpose is to make an individual, a team, a department, or a business unit feel good. Vanity metrics are the magic mirror that make the organization look good in reflection. The reality, however, is that they aren't useful for anything beyond an emotional crutch and the psychological wellbeing of the staff. We know they are vanity metrics because they don't predict desirable outcomes or customer satisfaction, so they aren't fitness criteria. They aren't key performance indicators. They don't drive improvement and don't have a target, and they don't indicate general health. Metaphorically, vanity metrics are the corporate equivalent of measuring waistline or bicep size. David may have a target range for his waistline of thirty-three to thirty-five inches, but this is because he has a large investment in chinos and trousers with a thirty-four-inch waist. There may be some instances in which waistline size may be used as an improvement driver but only in specific weight-loss scenarios, because relative changes in waistline are known to correlate to weight. Bicep size may be measured by a personal trainer as an indicator that the training is working. If a client is paying for personal training that includes lifting weights and eating a high-protein diet, we might expect an increase in bicep size. However, there is unlikely to be a target size, so it isn't an improvement driver. It's merely an indicator that other measures are working. The goal is likely physical strength, or endurance, perhaps to compete in a triathlon. Greater upper-body strength should correlate with improved performance at swimming and cycling (holding a suitably aerodynamic position for a time trial requires a cyclist to have a lot of upper body strength) and hence, a better overall finish time for the race. It is highly unlikely that bicep size is a fitness criterion used for selection, even though some body builders may feel that way about it.

Unfortunately, obsession with body shape is a popular distraction in society, so obsession with body size metrics is all too common. Businesses also suffer from the metaphorical equivalent of tracking their waistline, for example, the popularity of a leader. Strong leaders will tell you that great leadership isn't about popularity, instead it is about respect. Reporting a popularity statistic is a vanity metric for a leader; it doesn't indicate effectiveness, improvement, or general health. Anyone who's tracked global politics in recent years should know this to be true—popularity of a political leader doesn't indicate effectiveness. Indeed, the opposite may be true: a popular but highly ineffective leader may stay in office too long, because popularity does indicate ability to get re-elected. In corporations, a popular leader may simply linger too long as others turn a blind eye to ineffectiveness, and the leader fails to see his own shortcomings while he obsesses over his popularity.

Vanity metrics make people feel good. Is the culture of your business such that "feel good" metrics are actually needed? If so, perhaps you do need to keep them around but you have deeper cultural problems. If your employees don't feel good about themselves, if your business as a social entity doesn't feel good about itself and exhibits low self-esteem, then you need to be asking "why is that?"

The more vanity metrics you have in regular use, the less healthy your business and its culture are. Eliminating the need for vanity metrics and then eliminating those metrics is good for your business. Go after the culture problems that are causing you to need vanity metrics. Address those first, then eliminate the metrics.

Both of your authors are the fathers of daughters. David's and Alexei's oldest are already teenagers. If you want your daughters to avoid obsessing about the size of their waist, or their body shape in general, you bring them up to appreciate diversity in body shape and to reject the societal idea that there is an ideal body shape. And although there may be optimums for some applications—great tennis players tend to be taller, great gymnasts smaller—this is because the physical requirements of some sports favor certain body shapes over others. The flipside is also true. David's younger daughter and both of Alexei's dropped out of gymnastics because they became too tall to perform at a level that met their own satisfaction. Instead they pursued soccer. When Alexei's youngest didn't feel quite right in her own body on the soccer pitch, she switched to dancing and pursued it more seriously than anything before it. When there is no judgment about whether a recreational interest in playing soccer is better or worse than pursuing gymnastics or dance, then there is no notion of a preferred height or body weight. It's a matter of personal choice. Addressing cultural issues eliminates the need for, and potential obsession over, a vanity metric such as bicep or waist circumference.

A particularly insidious example of a vanity metric is the airline industry's on-time departure percentage. This has been in use for at least twenty-five years, and airlines treat it as a fitness criterion. It is used as a key performance indicator for the airline—for their performance on a given route—and for the ground crew, especially the supervisor, who is the flight dispatcher responsible for the departure paperwork. These individuals are often directly incentivized and rewarded based on their personal on-time departure percentage. The problem is that on-time departure isn't a fitness criterion for passengers. There are two metrics that matter: the passenger's time spent waiting at the airport and on-time arrival. The first is important to passengers because they have something better to do. If a flight is significantly delayed, a text message from the airline advising them to arrive later to the airport will free up wasted time and improve satisfaction. On-time arrival is important because of related dependencies:

connecting flights, meetings, planned social or recreational activities, and so on.

When a Delta Airlines' routine flight departed on time, Alexei's Atlanta-based client was not impressed. His criterion was on-time arrival and the replacement flight one day after a cancellation was already one day too late—on-time departure is a metric that can be gamed by canceling flights that will leave late or rescheduling them for future times when they're likely to depart on time, whether that meets customer needs or not. Fortunately, Alexei was already on the ground and well into the meeting with this client after rebooking with a different airline the previous evening, following the cancellation of his initial departure. This saved the purpose of his trip from a complete defeat. On the day of writing, our social media channels have lit up with posts from Erik-Jan Kaak, the 2013 Austrian CIO of the Year, who, along with fourteen other passengers, was delayed for eight hours at Berlin's Tegel airport by Air Berlin because a dispatcher wouldn't hold a connecting flight back for just five minutes to accommodate those arriving on a delayed flight.[22]

And as this book was about to go to print, Ryanair announced cancellations of many of its flights across Europe.[23] One reason for the cancellations was a shortage of crew members, specifically pilots. New competition for their services, mostly from Norwegian at Ryanair's home port of Dublin, caused some to switch their allegiance, while a change in company vacation policy caused a squeeze in the latter half of 2017.[24] In what appears to be a deliberate misdirection, Ryanair issued a press release stating that flight cancellations were necessary to improve punctuality, which is plain language for on-time departure rate. They claimed their punctuality had fallen below 80 percent and flight cancellations would help it achieve its annual punctuality target of 90 percent. What is "punctuality," exactly? If you look at this from the passengers' perspective, the on-time arrival percentage for those on a cancelled flight is zero. Passengers who don't get on

22. On August 15, 2017, just before we finished writing the book, Air Berlin filed for bankruptcy.

23. "Ryanair to cancel 40–50 flights per day for six weeks." Source: BBC; www.bbc.com/news/business-41291483

24. "Ryanair faces over 20m euro compensation bill over cancellations." Source: BBC, www.bbc.com/news/business-41304456

planes because their flight was cancelled don't arrive on time. You can't increase the on-time arrival rate by cancelling a flight. The airline can optimize for on-time departure because only flights that leave the airport are measured. Analogously, passengers want the airline to "get on base"—they want Ryanair tracking on-base percentage, while instead the airline reports batting average. We believe Ryanair may be discounting the intellect of their customers. We believe their customers are smart enough to work out that a canceled flight wasn't a punctual flight at all.[25]

Both of us have observed how on-time departure rate has driven undesirable behavior with airlines. Jet Airways in Toronto begin boarding for long-haul flights on Airbus A330 twin-aisle jets ninety minutes prior to departure. Alaska Airlines starts boarding short-haul flights at Seattle Tacoma International Airport forty minutes prior to departure. Alaska needs forty minutes to board a Boeing 737-700 with only 124 passengers seated in two cabins. By bizarre comparison, British Airways can defer boarding a Boeing 777-300 ER with 300 passengers seated in four cabins until just thirty-five minutes prior and still depart on time. Alaska Airlines is a very good short-haul, full-service airline that regularly wins awards for customer service. However, in this instance they have it wrong. Commencing boarding forty minutes prior to departure is for Alaska's own vanity and not a factor in superior customer satisfaction.

Can you think of any metrics in your organization that clearly aren't used for selection by your customers, aren't used internally to drive meaningful improvements, and don't indicate the general health of a line of business or of the firm as a whole? If so, what is it about your culture that drives you to measure, report, and obsess over this metric? Is it simply that you measure it because you can? Because you need to be seen to be measuring and reporting something and acting upon data and statistics? What additional instrumentation do you need to measure valuable metrics as an alternative? What cultural

---

25. As this book goes to press, Ryanair executives have been called to a meeting by the UK regulator, the Civil Aviation Authority (CAA), which is displeased with Ryanair's treatment of customers who have been affected by the cancellations. Additionally, its chief operations officer resigned amid the turmoil: www.theguardian.com/business/2017/oct/07/michael-hickey-ryanair-chief-operations-officer

or social elements need to be addressed to obviate the need for a metric that isn't driving desirable behavior?

Fitness Criteria

Fitness criteria are your KPIs. They affect customers' choices directly. For each fitness criterion (KPI), you have to know what level of performance you need to win customers in each customer segment, that is, what levels they deem acceptable or exceptional.

A three hours, five minutes finish time could send a male runner to Hopkinton, the starting line of the Boston Marathon. Three hours, six minutes won't do. But three hours, five minutes won't be remotely fast enough to qualify for the Olympics—the qualification threshold is much higher. And that Olympics qualifying time is not enough to win an Olympic medal—that level is still higher. The finish time is a marathoner's KPI.

When Neeta ordered pizza for her office, one to two hours was a sufficiently good delivery time. Beyond two hours, she would have had to call another restaurant. One to two hours was not nearly good enough when she was ordering pizza for her children, though. It had to be no more than thirty minutes. Waiting thirty minutes for a pizza slice at lunchtime at a food court near Neeta's office, however, would be unacceptable—Neeta can't waste that much time on her lunch break. The delivery time from taking the order to handing off the pizza to a customer is every pizzeria's KPI. In the case of the food court pizza concession, the pizzas are baked in advance; in this case, the queuing time is a critical selection criterion. Neeta won't want to wait in a long queue, so the concession must design its implementation and service delivery to minimize queuing time.

The Storm King Red wine pack weighs only three pounds.[26] The weight makes Storm King Red a unique product, hugely satisfactory to a small group of recreational day hikers packing wine and sandwiches for their picnic. The same amount of Saint-Émilion in traditional glass bottles weighs five and three-quarters pounds.[27] Would hikers be thrilled to add nearly three pounds of weight that provides no value to them to their backpacks? If Storm King Red were this heavy, it would lose its differentiation—hikers could choose

---

26. 1.4 kilograms
27. 2.6 kilograms

from the multitude of wines of the world. The package weight is a KPI for Camaraderie Cellars when selecting a packaging supplier for their Storm King Red product. In addition, the package design is important: that it comes with its own spigot makes it clean and easy to use and the seal is reliable—you don't want it to leak all over the inside of a backpack; and the recyclable nature of the package may also be important to the values of the buyer, while the handy finger holds make it easy to carry. Many aspects of the design make it fit-for-purpose, but the overall weight of the container is a key performance indicator. By eliminating the weight of the glass, the package can be larger—1.5 liters—which offers enough wine to provide two or three glasses for four to six people in a hiking party.[28]

A strikingly good example of a correctly chosen fitness criterion is one that shows how Alaska Airlines has emerged as a leader in the North American aviation business—their twenty-minute baggage handling guarantee. For several years now, Alaska has guaranteed that the first bags will be delivered to the carousel within twenty minutes of the moment the aircraft door is opened on arrival. If not, you can instantly claim a $50 discount on your next flight or 2,000 miles credited to your frequent flyer account. Alaska and their service partners are remarkably good at achieving the guarantee. Alaska's baggage handling is sufficiently fit-for-purpose that David no longer carries a roll-aboard bag when flying with them. Instead, he always checks baggage. This makes his in-airport experience less stressful and yet affects his total journey time only negligibly. Alaska flights are generally direct, so the chance of lost baggage is minimal.

Alaska has pursued this model to encourage fewer bags in the overhead space, and a faster, less stressful boarding experience for all passengers. If this works well, then, in theory, the spread of variation in time to board an aircraft would shrink and they would be able to tighten their current, forty-minutes-prior boarding criterion to something more acceptable such as twenty to thirty minutes.

For a major rival such as American, Delta, or United, which operate a hub-and-spoke model, a delivery guarantee may not be enough to encourage passengers to change behavior and check bags rather

---

28. At the time of writing some vintners have started to offer 0.75 liter astropaqs: the equivalent of a single bottle of wine at almost half the weight. Not everyone has a lot of friends or desires to drink a lot of wine.

than carrying them on. Passengers would have to trust that the transfer in the hub always works correctly and that bags don't go missing. When asked why customers don't check bags, most cite a fear of lost baggage or of pilfering by baggage handling staff as their reasons for keeping baggage with them in the cabin. Fit-for-purpose baggage handling must be trustworthy baggage handling. The level of trust in the system is a key performance indicator for the traveler.

Alaska exploited their point-to-point service and struck contracts with baggage handling services at every destination airport. It's unclear exactly how the improved service has been achieved, and perhaps Alaska doesn't care. Our guess is that baggage handlers are told, "When you see that smirking Eskimo on the tail fin, you high-tail it out to that aircraft double-quick and get that first hold of bags onto the carousel pronto." In other words, we suspect service for other airlines may be suffering to prioritize Alaska's bags. Regardless of the implementation, the twenty-minute baggage handling guarantee is a commendable example of a fitness criterion done right.

Embedding Fitness Criteria into Contracts

Since 1986 Spain has pursued the development of high-speed rail services to connect its major cities. The first line in the Alta Velocidad Española (AVE) network between Madrid and Sevilla opened in 1992. But it wasn't until 2008 that Spain's two largest cities, Madrid and Barcelona, were finally connected by an AVE line constructed by Siemens, running Velaro E S-103 trains carrying up to 400 passengers and capable of speeds exceeding 300 kilometers per hour. A total of twenty-six complete trains were supplied as part of a contract that also included a fourteen-year maintenance contract. The maintenance contract has a service level agreement based on percentage on-time arrival of each train, with eighteen services running each day. Although we haven't seen the full terms of the contract, reports suggest that a sliding scale of penalties is due—with a complete refund on the cost of operating the train—if delays due to mechanical or signaling issues on the line exceed thirty minutes. By tying the payments on Siemens' maintenance contract directly to a passenger fitness criterion, the Spanish government has ensured that Siemens is motivated toward the best interests of the taxpayers who funded the line and subsidize its operation. In general, Spain's AVE rail network is regarded as the most punctual in Europe, with almost 100% on-time arrival. It's worth noting that in Spain, and for rail transportation, "punctuality" appears to mean on-time arrival, not merely on-time departure.

It is almost ten years since the opening of the Madrid–Barcelona high-speed rail line, and yet contracts tied directly to consumer fitness criteria remain very rare. It may be counter-intuitive, but such contracts are in everyone's best interest. Living up to an on-time arrival contract challenges Siemens to maintain its fitness-for-purpose and surely enables it to win new business over rivals. At the same time, on-time arrival pleases passengers, generates repeat demand for the AVE service, maintains passengers' numbers, and reflects well upon the politicians who advocated for it and the civil servants who wrote the contract and oversaw the project. Everyone wins when contracts are constructed around fitness criteria.

Fitness Criteria Should Have Defined Thresholds

Suppose we've identified the fitness criteria (KPIs) that matter to the customers of our product or service. We should be able to identify the threshold performance level at which the customer will be satisfied and a subsequent threshold beyond which they'd report that we had exceeded their expectations and potentially over-served the market.

David's firm organizes each year a number of leadership retreats around the world. The retreats follow a format called Consultants' Camp originally attributed to Gerald M. Weinberg, a respected author and pioneer in the field of software engineering and management of technology businesses. The retreats are primarily intended as a social gathering of David's business partners around the world—those who conduct licensed training or who run consulting practices using the methods promoted by David's firm. Retreats are, however, open to a wider audience, including corporate change agents and consultants who aren't yet part of the global network affiliated with David's firm.

The purpose of the retreats is multi-dimensional. At a simple level, retreats create a forum for people in the network to get to know each other. Leadership retreats knit the social fabric of the community. Once individuals who previously didn't know each other well have gotten lost hiking in the mountains and had to call out the emergency services to "rescue" them, or once they've all gotten soaking wet and freezing cold rafting together in the chilly snow-melt rivers of the Alps and warmed up in the van home with a swig of local, farmer-distilled *hausgemacht* (homemade) schnapps, they have a stronger bond with one another. Retreats have a format that allows for a five- to six-hour afternoon break for recreational activities. Retreats are about enabling David's clients and his partner network to have fun together and bond. They are always held in vacation destinations within two to three hours maximum transfer time from a major airport such as Munich, San Diego, Los Angeles, Denpasar (in Bali, Indonesia), Barcelona, Lisbon, and so on. There is a fitness criterion that the transfer should never be more than three hours and ideally not more than two. To mitigate the transfer delay, David's team arranges for attendees to share shuttle buses or chauffeur-driven cars. This gives them more social time to chat and share their experiences. They don't notice the transfer time so much while deep in conversation with other attendees. Elevator manufacturers put mirrors in elevators of high-rise buildings for similar reasons. Apparently our vanity ensures that we don't notice the passing of time while we admire our reflection—or perhaps that of others. So, it's the perceived transfer time that matters more than the absolute amount of time.

While building strong social fabric is an important and valuable aspect of these retreats, their main purpose is to advance the state of the art in both intellectual property—the management ideas and training and consulting being offered—and the knowledge, understanding, and state of development of the market from which most attendees derive their living.

There is a danger that a retreat attended only by insiders in a fairly closed group of vendors will become an echo chamber, so diversity is encouraged and sometimes proactively engineered. In 2016 David's firm gave away around ten places at these events (valued at about $1,800 per person) to lucky winners of raffles at local meetup groups around the world. This enabled corporate employees—who perhaps had only a professional development interest in David's management ideas—to attend the event free of charge, including bringing along their spouse or partner, provided they or their employer covered the travel expenses to the nearby hub airport.

Participants in 2016 retreats were asked to complete F4P cards in order to develop a Fitness Box Score and provide valuable insights into market segmentation and customer purpose for attending the retreats. This technique is fully described in Chapter 9. It was clear from the results that the retreat had overserved some of the attendees who reported that their needs and expectations had been exceeded. Further analysis showed that this result correlated to the attendee cluster who had won tickets as door prizes at local meetup groups. In other words, the outsiders, included to add diversity and fresh insights and opinion to spice up the events, had been the ones taken aback by the quality.

To illustrate this, the 2016 North American Leadership Retreat was held at the Estancia resort in La Jolla, California, about ten miles north of San Diego. It's an upmarket property sprawling on several acres, just inland from the Pacific Ocean and its beaches, and just to the south of Torrey Pines, famous for its world-class golf courses used on the rotation for the US Open. Retreats always start with a social event on the first evening, and on this occasion, it opened with a five-course wine-paired dinner, with table service, featuring regional wines chosen from California's Central Coast and southern region, as well as one from just across the nearby border in northern Mexico. All of this was accompanied by live Spanish guitar. For retreat regulars, such an opening evening is expected. It's all part of the engineering of the event to promote social fabric. It's an event populated with the business partners of David's Lean Kanban Inc. and some of their best clients. It is worth doing properly.

However, the segment of attendees who won the opportunity to participate were used to much simpler fare at small regional conferences, often organized by local volunteers and affiliated with professional organizations such as the Project Management Institute (PMI). Such events are generally run on tight budgets, using premises that have been donated by a benevolent local business, and the ticket prices are often very low because individuals pay for them with their own money rather than expensing them to their employer. It isn't unusual for the catering to be a "make your own sandwich" buffet.

The results of Fitness Box Score surveys weren't surprising, but they served to illustrate that there are two thresholds for fitness criteria: the first threshold is the minimum level of performance that represents fit-for-purpose; the second is where performance exceeds customer expectations, perhaps delighting them unexpectedly, but indicating that we may have overserved the market. Therefore, results indicating that we've exceeded expectations may reveal opportunities to trim costs without a loss in satisfaction. There may be opportunities to remain fit-for-purpose while improving margins and profitability.

In summary, fitness criteria have two thresholds:

- The threshold of acceptable performance, below which we are unfit-for-purpose
- The threshold of exceptional performance, beyond which we have overserved the market segment

General Health Indicators

Lots of metrics already tracked by companies are health indicators. They don't affect customers' choices, but they may be the businesses' vital signs. They tell us whether we have a pulse. They tell us if our business is healthy enough to pursue its strategy. Sometimes they give us advance warning if we're in danger of missing our fitness criteria. A sudden change of a health indicator—an upward or downward trend—should cause the business to re-evaluate its strategy or operations. They are performance indicators, but not key ones!

What if we detected a change in a runner's VO_2Max (lungs' oxygen processing capacity) or interval workout pace? That could affect the realistic goals for the upcoming race, possibly change the training plan or the race tactics, or even affect the decision on which race to enter. These are obviously health indicators in running. They matter! They affect strategy! But they are not the same as the finish time, which we learned in Chapter 4 is the fitness criterion used to determine qualification and selection for inclusion in the Boston Marathon or the Olympic Games.

Even for non-athletes, basic health indicators include heart rate, blood pressure, and weight. For this reason, your general practitioner or a nurse at your family health clinic will measure and record these metrics. Sudden changes can indicate the appearance of a new medical condition. For example, a sudden and unexplained drop in weight was a signal that David's father had contracted prostate cancer. Alexei's father's urine test showed unexpectedly a high concentration of protein, signaling an advanced stage of kidney disease.

General health indicators tell you that your business is alive, and changes in them indicate that the business is doing better or worse or that something may have changed in the environment that is affecting performance.

What if the staff attrition rate increased at Westside Pizza? More orders would have to be taken, implemented, and delivered using newer staff members who have less on-the-job experience. This could lead to an increased number of mistakes during order taking— increasing the chance of delivering the wrong pizza to the customer, who might be Neeta's picky kids with a low tolerance for errors. It may also increase the number of cases in which a delivery person took the wrong route to the delivery address—and Neeta's kids don't have their pizza by the time their iPad timer ticks down. Mistakes made by less-experienced staff while baking pizza would have less impact, because Westside uses a lot of pre-prepared, canned, and frozen ingredients. But that would be a different story at Zak's Artisan Pie & Crust—preparing their gourmet pizzas takes much more skill! Staff turnover is an important health indicator in the pizza baking business—or any other business, for that matter.

Improvement Drivers

One of the trends in the computer software industry over the last two decades has been the code test coverage metric. Methods and tools appeared during this time to measure it quickly and accurately. What is this metric about? Computer program code contains a lot of logic— if this, do that, else, do something else. When computers run, they take some of these logical paths and not others based on user input, stored data, time, status of various devices, and other circumstances. Test coverage is the percentage of these paths that the computer programmers working on the software can execute quickly, with a push of a button, by running all their existing automated tests. For a long time, test coverage across the industry remained shockingly low. Most testing was done manually at the end of the development process. This process enabled too many defects to "escape," earning the industry its reputation for low quality. Consumers came to associate software with frequent crashes, unexpected errors, and "bugs."

Increasing test coverage seemed like a worthy goal that would be likely to influence customer satisfaction, as we would expect greater test coverage to correlate to lower escaped defects. The customer should therefore experience fewer faults, outages, and unexplained weirdness from their technology products and services. However, many software development managers treated test coverage as a KPI for their programming teams, often setting high targets such as 90–95 percent. This approach backfired. Given aggressive test coverage targets, many programmers wrote a lot of code as well as many accompanying tests to produce the high number so they could report their programming assignments complete. Such programming efforts often produced much greater amounts of code than what was truly necessary to solve the software users' original problem. Covering the last 20 percent (and presumably the least critical) of logical paths in the code produced a diminishing return on investment—effort better invested elsewhere. The inner workings of software code became more complicated than truly needed, eventually slowing down software delivery and leading to other quality problems. Managers created a KPI and their employees "achieved" it. At the same time, some software groups produced very high-quality software and test coverage close to 100 percent. But their high number came about as a side effect of other quality practices done right, not because individuals were given a metric with an aggressive target.

It thus became possible to have a high percentage of test coverage and have either a very healthy code base or a very "sick" one. Percentage of test coverage was not a fitness criterion, it did not always correlate to desirable outcomes, either in the short or longer term. This illustrates that incorrectly defining an improvement driver with a target as a fitness criterion—and selecting for it—can produce undesirable effects.

A team of scientists have recently put these software industry observations to test.[29] In the largest test coverage study to date, they included 31,000 test suites, each containing thousands of test cases. Their conclusion? The test coverage percentage correlates weakly with test suite effectiveness when controlled for the sheer number of test cases. This leads to several practical recommendations.

The software industry already has true customer fitness criteria, such as escaped defects reported by the customer per release, impact of defects on customer objectives, frequency of updates delivered, and lead time for specific updates delivered. If current test coverage is

---

29. Laura Inozemtseva and Reid Holmes. Test Coverage Is Not Strongly Correlated with Test Suite Effectiveness. www.linozemtseva.com/research/2014/icse/coverage/coverage_paper.pdf

low, say, 10–20 percent, and there is motivation to increase it, then use test case count as an improvement driver and set an initial target to, for example, double it. Once the target is achieved, consider whether you need to continue on this path and if so, set a higher target. After one or more such cycles, downgrade the test case count and test coverage metrics to health indicators and set a reasonable range within which they can vary without intervention. Beyond a certain threshold, test coverage may become a distraction or a target for gaming. This is undesirable. Treating it as a health indicator is the solution to prevent this dysfunction. Meanwhile, continue to monitor the true fitness criteria metrics that relate directly to customer satisfaction.

When John Henry reports dollars spent per win to Billy Beane in *Moneyball*, he appears to be using it as a selection criterion. Billy Beane is fit-for-purpose as his new GM because he has achieved such a low ratio of cost to wins. Henry offers Beane $12.5 million to take the position. At the time, it would have made him the highest paid professional sports team manager in the world. However, dollars per win isn't a fitness criterion—or it shouldn't be. It shouldn't be a KPI. Instead, it is an improvement driver. After Billy Beane establishes on-base percentage as the fitness criterion for selecting players, and this knowledge becomes apparent to the other teams in the league, the values of players will start to normalize based on OBP instead of on other statistics. Both trade prices and salaries will align with OBP and hence it will be impossible to maintain a low dollars-per-win ratio using only OBP as the player selection criterion. If Beane had been measured on dollars per win as the selection criterion by his boss, the team owner, then every year since 2002 his performance would have deteriorated and he might have been deselected, that is, fired, because he couldn't maintain his cost-to-win ratio.

To maintain a low dollars-per-win ratio from season to season, it is necessary to keep innovating, to keep finding new ways of discovering value in players that other teams do not see. If innovation and new insights don't occur, then over a short time of perhaps two to three seasons, values and wages will normalize around the new fitness criteria, and any advantage will be lost. In other words, dollars per win is actually a metric for measuring the health of an innovation or continuous improvement program. Maintaining a low dollars-per-win ratio will drive improvements. For Steve Schott,[30] owner of the Oakland Athletics, it makes sense to track this metric. He owns a small market team that has less money at its disposal than big market teams. If his team is to make the playoffs consistently, they need to maintain a low cost-to-win ratio. They need to be constantly innovating.

This is indeed what has happened with the A's over the past fifteen years. Despite losing Paul DePodesta, as he moved on to sign with the Los Angeles Dodgers and, eventually, as general manager of other teams—now effectively Billy Beane's peer and competitor—they have continued to find value in players that others don't see.[31]

In the 2014 season the A's were the fourth-poorest team in the league, but again fared much better than the fourth from the bottom in terms of wins and losses. Traditionally, baseball teams liked to have two catchers, one as their everyday starter and one as a backup. Oakland, however, had two young catchers split the duties more evenly. They'd start one or the other and substitute them to exploit favorable matchups with opposing pitchers. The A's created, in the aggregate, the league's best catcher. The team also unlocked the potential of Josh Donaldson, and turned him into a star, by moving him from catcher to third base.

The A's continued to innovate to stay ahead of other teams in the league that were adopting and developing their own *Moneyball* strategies. By mid-season 2014, they had the best record in the league, eventually finishing second in the American League West and qualifying for the playoffs. Dollars per win is an improvement driver ratio and for the Oakland Athletics continuous improvement is necessary in order to compete against much richer teams.

How Walgreens Went from "Good to Great"

In his 2001 book, *Good to Great*, Jim Collins compares Walgreens with Eckerd/CVS. Traditionally, drugstores used "profit per store" as the metric for selection. This encouraged them to create larger and fewer stores, often in less expensive, perhaps suburban locations. Walgreens adopted a different metric, "profit per customer visit." This new metric

---

30. Note: Ownership of the team has passed to Lewis Wolff and John Fisher.
31. http://bleacherreport.com/articles/
2106007-2014-oakland-as-proving-theyre-still-the-kings-of-moneyball

aligned better with convenience. The choice of customer visit as the denominator shows that Walgreens recognized that convenience was a factor in consumer selection. Convenience was a fitness criterion! As a consequence, more stores in more convenient, often more expensive locations would be necessary to outperform their competitors.

Profit per customer visit plays the role of an improvement driver, but also a health indicator. If it were negative, then Walgreens would be unhealthy. Profit per customer visit aligns staff, from store manager up to senior marketing and revenue executives, on how to keep the business healthy and improve it. Profit per store had a tendency to focus competitors on cost reduction. Profit per store has the potential to become a vanity metric. It would be possible for the number of stores to be falling, the total revenues for the firm to be falling, and market share to be in decline, yet profit per store continues to be healthy.

What is required is to choose a number, or frequency, of customer visits as the general health indicator, and find a means to track that, such as a loyalty card or a payment card number. In this way, profit per customer visit becomes the improvement driver. This is based on the assumption that convenience is a customer fitness criterion and that customers select their drugstore based on convenience, preferring to make more frequent visits to a convenient local store rather than fewer visits to an inconveniently located store that may have slightly lower prices.

Using Metrics to Drive Change at Sungard

Amit Kaulagekar[32] is a management consultant and financial services industry process improvement expert, based in India. For the past six years, he's been working with FIS Global,[33] a Fortune 500 company based in Jacksonville, Florida, which, among many other products and services, provides management consulting to financial services clients such as Sungard, the pensions and insurance management firm. Amit engaged with Sungard in January 2014 to help them improve service delivery for new enrollments and for changes to existing retirement plans. Teams based in the Central time zone of the United States and

---

32. edu.leankanban.com/users/amitkaulagekar
33. www.fisglobal.com/about-us/about-our-company

in Pune, India, would receive scanned images of paper forms completed by consumers and mailed to Sungard in the United States. In the winter of 2014 their capability was being overwhelmed by an increased volume of new enrollments. There is a usual seasonal surge in January, but on this occasion there was also an overall increase in the volume of business. This motivated an examination of how they were working and whether their efficiency could be improved. Amit was asked to step in and advise them on how to make improvements with the ultimate goal of hitting their service level agreement (SLA) of 99.5 percent of forms processed within five days of receipt. In January 2014 the on-time performance against their SLA was only 61 percent. Roughly 40 percent of requests were processed late against customer expectations.

In this case, the paying customers are companies, on behalf of whom, Sungard, for example, administers an employee retirement savings plan. The forms being scanned are coming from end consumers, typically employees of Sungard's customers who are opening a retirement plan or making changes to an existing plan. This current service level was unacceptable and Sungard wished to decrease processing times and improve the on-time percentage against the SLA. Amit was inspired by techniques he'd learned from us[34] and he set about applying these ideas at Sungard. The existing KPI for the approximately thirty people in the processing department was productivity per individual per day, measured as tasks processed per day. A "task" referred to the processing of a single scanned form, for example, one for a new enrollment in a pension savings plan for a specific individual. This choice of metric was dysfunctional. It led to staff grabbing and hogging tasks for themselves, later leaving large numbers of them open—assigned yet incomplete—overnight. There was too much work-in-progress and as a consequence, processing times were long. There was also a complete lack of collaboration among staff and team members. Those with better knowledge or superior techniques for processing changes faster were unwilling to share their knowledge with their colleagues. Sungard was using a general health indicator, productivity per person per day, as a fitness criterion and

34. David is known for his work on improved service delivery in professional services such as software development and IT operations, using the Kanban Method and Enterprise Services Planning.

key performance indicator. The result was poor customer satisfaction and unsatisfactory service delivery.

The KPI was changed to percentage of on-time tasks, within the SLA, as a team. This directly aligned to the customer fitness criteria. The consequence of the change was greatly improved collaboration, increased functional quality on processing (up from 97 percent to 99.3 percent), and on-time percentage against the five-day SLA rose to 84 percent in only two months. This change was one of several over a fifteen-month period that ultimately led to 99 percent on-time delivery against one-day and three-day SLAs based on different types of requests. We'll revisit Amit's story of improvement at Sungard in Chapter 7. By aligning team and individual metrics to customer fitness criteria and correctly selecting a fitness criterion as a key performance indicator, Sungard dramatically improved their business performance. The improved service delivery led directly to new business, increased market share, and better economic performance. Percentage on-time delivery as a team was a fit-for-purpose metric; throughput of tasks per individual was unfit-for-purpose and had to be changed.

Call to Action

How can you use the insights from this chapter to improve your business performance?

Try this exercise with your executive team—list the metrics you report now. Can you classify them as fitness criteria that affect customer selection? What are the thresholds for acceptable performance? If you are Walgreens, how far will people walk or drive before your drugstore is no longer convenient for them? If you are Starbucks, how far will people walk to get a cup of coffee before your café isn't convenient enough and the customer seeks an alternative? If you can't describe and validate a threshold, it probably isn't a fitness criterion.

Which of your metrics are health indicators? Health indicators won't have an ideal level or a target, but you should be able to identify a reasonable range. With health indicators, a significant change in the reported number would indicate a change in your environment and business conditions. How do you use this information?

And which of your metrics are driving changes? Do these have a secondary effect intended to influence a fitness criterion or key performance indicator? For example, profit per customer visit at Walgreens encouraged them to open more stores in more convenient locations.

And which of your current metrics just don't belong in any of those three categories? Why do you collect them? What do you do with them? How many are there as a percentage of all the metrics you track? Are they truly vanity metrics that make you feel good but don't influence economic outcomes, customer selection, or customer satisfaction? Are you measuring your winning streaks and then failing to qualify for the playoffs? If so, what are you going to do about them? Can you remove the metric? Do you need to drive cultural changes first in order to eliminate the need for it?

For your metrics to be fit-for-purpose, you need to be able to identify their purpose and categorize each accordingly as a fitness criterion, an improvement driver, or a general health indicator. You should be able to identify thresholds for fitness criterion, targets for improvement drivers, and ranges for general health indicators. Can you align your improvement drivers with fitness criteria? Can you align general health indicators with improvement drivers? For example, production rate was a general health indicator for Ferrari that aligned to order cancellation rate as an improvement driver because delivery lead time was a fitness criterion for the customer. If you can categorize your metrics and show alignment between them, then they should be driving effective behavior and directly contributing to your economic performance.

Correct classification and alignment shows that your metrics are truly fit-for-purpose! Correct classification should help you eliminate the expanding universe effect—it should help you boil things down to just a few numbers that truly drive your business success.

If you can't show alignment of your metrics and classify them correctly, what needs to change? For example, a drugstore that measures profit per store would be unable to show how that relates to convenience as a customer fitness criterion. If you don't know that customers value convenience and select you because of it, your other metrics are unlikely to be driving you in the right direction. Correct selection of metrics stems entirely from understanding your customers, segmenting your market based on their purpose, and correctly identifying their selection criteria—the fitness criteria that determine your business success. In Chapter 6 we look at commonly recurring fitness criteria that will give you a good starting point, and Chapter 7 will help us understand how to segment a market based on customer purpose and design our business, our products, and our services to satisfy these segments.

Vanity or Productivity?

A final footnote to this chapter: during the writing of this book, David would from time to time post updates to social media channels such as Twitter or Facebook communicating our progress as "average words per day." This idle boasting is pure vanity! In fact, as we write this close to the completion of the manuscript, we've averaged just over 2000 words per calendar day—not every single day was a writing day, but we haven't specifically tracked days when neither of us was available for any writing. While this sounds productive, David's 2010 book was written in a mere twenty-two writing days, for an average of 3,275 words per day. However, this text was written with a lead time of only six weeks in July and August of 2017, while David's 2010 book took nine calendar months to complete, working in short bursts of four or five days in between other engagements.

Average words per day feels like a productivity measure. It feels like it is a general health indicator. In fact, it isn't—it doesn't say much about whether you'd select either of us as a writer in the future, nor does it say much about the quality, and it doesn't tell you anything about the lead time to complete the work.

On the other hand, actual words produced each specific calendar day as a time series is a general health indicator. If word count for specific days fell to zero, then we no longer have a pulse—the book project has lost momentum and there is a danger that it might get abandoned or overtaken by other events and forgotten as a low priority.

Note the subtlety of this difference, average words per day is a vanity metric, whereas actual words each day as a time series is a health indicator. Both would typically be displayed on the same chart. It's so easy to communicate average words per day in text as a single number, while actual words each day needs a chart to show the trend over time. The lure of vanity metrics is powerful. It is easy to be sucked in to their simplicity and consequently drive undesirable behavior in your organization.

Summary

- Companies already collect many metrics and the amount of metrics and data is projected to grow. "The metrics universe is vast already and continues to expand!"
- Call for action: question why you collect metrics, their purpose, and whether they're fit-for-[that]-purpose.
- Vanity metrics:
  - Often are mistaken for one of the three useful types.
  - Have no meaningful impact on decision making but serve a "feel good" purpose.
  - Generally reflect some cultural issue that should be addressed first in order to remove the pressure to track the metric.
- Fitness criteria:
  - Should be your KPIs.
  - There are good examples of how companies in various industries apply them.
- Fitness criteria have thresholds:
  - Minimum thresholds below which the product or service is unfit-for-purpose.
  - Exceptional performance threshold that would be differentiating and perhaps an enabler of market disruption.
- General health indicators:
  - Have a guide range but no ideal value, threshold, or target.
  - Can be allowed to vary within a defined healthy range without intervention.
  - Many of the metrics you're already tracking are more likely to be general health indicators than KPIs.
- Improvement drivers:
  - Have a target value to be achieved over time.
  - When the target is reached, consider deprecating the metric or changing it to a health indicator and establishing the healthy range.

- Industry examples:
  - ○ Airlines' on-time departure percentage is a particularly insidious example of a vanity metric mistakenly used as a KPI.
  - ○ Some software companies have misused test coverage as a KPI. Treating it as a health indicator and the count of test cases as an improvement driver is a better solution, avoiding dysfunction.
  - ○ The Oakland Athletics baseball team continued to innovate even as the rest of baseball caught up to their *Moneyball* ideas. Cost-to-win ratio is an improvement driver showing they continue to innovate.
  - ○ Walgreens pharmacy chain used profit per customer visit as an improvement driver.
  - ○ Sungard realized how they were using a general health indicator as a KPI and how that resulted in poor customer satisfaction. They turned their service around by getting rid of the false KPI, finding their customers' fitness criteria, and using those as KPIs.

6 From Valentine's Day to Vertu: The Universal Fitness Criteria

WHEN NEETA ORDERED PIZZA, she cared about the lead time to delivery. She also cared more or less about predictability of delivery. She cared about the quality of the menu and ingredients to varying degrees. She cared about order accuracy, although she had different tolerance levels for mistakes. She cared about tastiness and quality of the pizza and its condition upon delivery. She trusted that the restaurant conformed to health and safety standards in food preparation, and she cared about price in relation to the quality of the pizza she was ordering. She had differing levels of elasticity for pricing levels depending on context. She was less price sensitive when purchasing for the office than she was when purchasing for the children at home. It turns out that these fitness criteria that determine Neeta's selection of restaurant are representative of commonly recurring selection criteria that determine whether a product or service is fit-for-purpose. When you don't have deeper insights into what is driving customer selection, these commonly recurring fitness criteria are a very good place to start.

Commonly Recurring Fitness Criteria

There are four categories of commonly recurring selection criteria that provide us with measures for determining whether a product or service is fit-for-purpose:

- Lead time and its predictability
- Quality and its predictability

- ○ Functional
- ○ Non-functional
- Safety or conformance to regulatory requirements
- Price or affordability—although price may require some special treatment

Let's consider them one by one.

Lead Time and Its Predictability

Lead time is the time from accepting a customer order until delivery, for example, the time from when Neeta placed her pizza order until it was delivered to her doorstep. In some contexts, lead time is called time-to-market, meaning the time from when we decided to do something until it was ready for launch. Lead time is almost a universal, ubiquitous criterion in product or service selection. It matters in many different businesses, whether they are a tangible goods (physical) business or an intangible goods (professional services) one. Why? Customers' purpose, whatever that might be, is very often linked to their timeline and the impact of other events or lost opportunity over time. This is sometimes called the "cost of delay." For Neeta, cost of delay may have resulted in temper tantrums and emotional behavior from her younger children, so at the very least, delay in delivering her pizza for the children on Friday evening would have driven up her stress levels.

If a product is delivered way too early, the customers may not appreciate it or have any use for it. A marketing campaign for a Valentine's Day promotion that is ready to launch in November has no value until after New Year's. On the other hand, if our business delivered a product to our customers way too late, the customers' purpose, and their need or use for our product, may have already expired. If our Valentine's Day promotion wasn't ready until early February there may be little point in announcing it, because our customers will have already made a purchasing decision or simply won't have enough time to see and react to our promotion. The customers, in this case the marketing department, waiting for our internal ad agency and content marketing team to deliver the campaign can't—and won't—wait forever. In general, if our delivery is too late, customers may have given up on our product or service, bought it from our competitors, or found alternative ways to satisfy their needs. In a corporate setting, this may result in pressure to outsource to a vendor rather than rely on an unpredictable internal service that isn't fit-for-purpose.

Not too early and not too late! Therefore, every product or service has a time window when the customer's purpose for choosing it (preferably from us rather than our competitors) has both validity and value. Depending on what business we're in, such time windows may vary widely in duration as well as how far into the future they are. For example, David has worked with Olympic Broadcasting Services (OBS) and their Olympic Channel TV service. A business such as this is constantly driven by the dates of the events they service and cover, and often windows of opportunity are short and the consequences of late or unpredictable delivery are severe. Alexei has worked with a biotech company, some of whose products are generic drugs. The whole industry knows the expiration dates of patents on various original drugs. The companies developing generic drugs race against the clock to bring their products to market near the date they all know many years in advance. Those arriving on time divide the market, others find very little market share left. Not every business is like this, however. The consequences of a delay in Microsoft's release of the latest version of Windows or of their Office suite products is relatively minor because of their monopoly position and customer lock-in. The high cost of switching means that cost of delay is relatively low and the need for predictability is mostly psychological rather than economic. However, no matter what business we're in, it's important to have a delivery capability with understandable, measurable lead time. Without an understanding of our delivery capability, we may not be able to continue taking customers' orders with any confidence that we can deliver within their expectations or acceptability thresholds. Lead time is such a universal fitness criterion that every business should be measuring it.

As a metric with which to manage our business, lead time is not a single number. There are several components to it. Let's examine them using Neeta's commute as an example.

Neeta considered commuting by train, bus, or car. One of the commuter train lines runs through her suburb, the nearest station only a few minutes' drive from her house. Her office also is only a few blocks from the downtown train station. The train ride is forty minutes, with trains departing every ten minutes during the rush hour. Even if Neeta somehow were to miss a train, she would simply take the next train ten minutes later. The total trip time would be about one hour. Not ideal, but still a pretty good deal in a big, growing city. What's better, though, is that the travel delays, should they occur, would be short and controllable. The train service has high predictability! Trains can be busy in peak times, but the smoothness of the ride should allow her to do some reading, email, or even more serious work. It's a relatively low-stress option.

Neeta eliminated the bus commuting option quickly. The best she could find was a combination of several bus lines with a total one-way travel time of two and a half hours. A bus might be fine for a short trip within town, but for a commute across municipal boundaries it is not at all fit-for-purpose.

Neeta thought about driving to the office. The route, a combination of expressway and city streets, would take her about forty-five minutes in the best case. But what if there was a jam on the expressway or one of the streets was closed for construction? Then the trip time could exceed an hour, or even, on a bad day, an hour and a half. What if Neeta had an important meeting at nine o'clock in the morning? How early would she have to leave her house? As a train commuter, she could take an earlier train to be on the safe side, but with the car, no early hour seemed early enough! And if there were tie-ups at the end of the day, Neeta worried about having to pay the sitter extra to watch the kids after school or being late for an evening soccer practice. These represented tangible impacts of a delay. The car is faster in the best case, but it's not predictable. This lack of predictability in traffic conditions means that sometimes Neeta would either have to compensate by leaving work early or accept that she'd have to pay extra for babysitting—and that in some cases her kids wouldn't get to soccer practice on time. Driving is also stressful. She has to drive, pay attention to traffic, and if she were to multitask, at best it would be a hands-free conference call or listening to an audio book or a podcast. Neeta considered the potential penalties of driving to work unacceptable and hence, she chose the train, of course. She believed it to be more reliable, and she trusted it more than she did the uncertainty of driving.

Considering Neeta's choice analytically, both transportation modes are fast enough for her in the average case, but the train has greater predictability. If we measure its predictability by variation in trip time, it is within ten or fifteen minutes. This amount of variation, not the travel time itself, was Neeta's fitness criterion and the satisfaction threshold that she used intuitively when choosing her transportation mode. The city planners most probably understood it—that's why they designed the train service!

The Table 6.1 shows the summary of lead time and predictability for Neeta's commute options.

Table 6.1 Comparison of commute times

	Commute Options and Times		
Criterion	Car	Train	Fitness
Best case	45 minutes	55 minutes	Satisfactory. Both transportation modes are fit enough.
Typical or average case	60–65 minutes	60 minutes	
Worst case	90–120 minutes	70 minutes	The train service is fitter. The car's varia-
Variation: the worst-case delay using the best-case scenario as a baseline	45–75 minutes	15 minutes	tion in travel time—its worst-case travel time—exceeds her fitness threshold.

This comparison shows us that we need to consider at least two criteria related to lead time: (1) the duration of time in the average, or typical, case; (2) the variability of time, measured not by typical or average cases, but by those closer to the best and the worst cases. We need the average time and the range from shortest to longest. In other words, ask not one question about time, but two: how fast? and how predictable? Customers may care sometimes for one, sometimes for the other, or sometimes both.

Companies in regulated industries and businesses with short windows of opportunity for a given market may find another time-related criterion useful: timeliness. In what percentage of opportunities did they hit their regulatory deadlines and dates just prior to short market time windows? Being more reliable at hitting them often requires measuring and understanding lead time, both its average and its predictability.

A more sophisticated quantitative understanding of this may be necessary in higher risk businesses or in regulated environments. The use of probability distribution functions (PDFs) for lead time, often constructed as histograms of historical lead time occurrences, is recommended but we've chosen to spare our readers from quantitative mathematics and statistical analysis in this book.

Quality and Its Predictability

Some of our readers may be familiar with the art and science of defining specifications for products. If your professional background includes product management, business analysis, or system analysis, you are familiar with the terms used below and don't need them explained to you. For the rest of our readers, the terms "functional quality" and "non-functional quality" may seem strange and alien. These arcane terms are often criticized, but in perhaps 50 years no one seems to have improved upon them, so first, a brief explanation with a few examples to help you comprehend the confusing difference between functional and non-functional quality.

If the product is an electric car, the key part of its functional quality is that it has a rechargeable battery powering its electric engines. The non-functional quality includes the range, that is, how far you can drive on the fully charged battery, and the battery recharge time.

If the product is a car of any kind, part of its functional quality is that it has a steering wheel made precisely to the specification, for example, with diameter of 18 inches. The non-functional quality of the steering wheel is how it is made or implemented, its substance or feel—vinyl covered, leather covered, wooden, and so on.

If our product is a diamond, its functional quality is the size and weight in carats. The non-functional quality is the color and clarity of the diamond, how bright and sparkling it is.

If our product is music, the functional quality may include playing a tune on the violin with every note at the correct pitch, at the right time, of the right length, and with the bowing technique indicated by the composer. The non-functional quality is how the violin sounds—the acoustics, the dynamics, and timbre of the instrument—how beautiful it sounds as it is played.

If the product is an online social network, the functional quality includes features to help you find and add friends, make posts visible to your friends, and see their reactions. The non-functional quality may be how many concurrent users it can support, whether the network is reliable 24/7, and so on.

If our service is an online trading system, the functional quality includes executing market and limit orders. The non-functional quality includes low latency of the market information available to the trader and the speed of order execution.

If our service is testing samples of biological material for presence of various chemicals, the functional quality is whether we can detect a particular chemical. The non-functional quality is the smallest quantity or concentration of this chemical we can detect.

This problem of functional versus non-functional quality is echoed in almost all business problems—the "how well" is often harder than the "what."

Consider how much the demand for electric cars increased when their range increased from 50 to 100 kilometers to 400 kilometers. Or when it became possible to supercharge the car battery in a little more than an hour instead of overnight. A social network that can support a billion daily users is much more valuable than the one capable of supporting "only" fifty million monthly visitors. It is also more valuable if it gives you reliable 24/7 access instead of daily "fail whales." Diamond per-carat prices vary more greatly based on the clarity and color than on the size of the diamond.

Or consider selection of orchestra musicians based on the quality of their playing. For musicians, such as Alexei in his younger years, or David's younger daughter, functional quality is a core selection criteria. If you can't play at the technical difficulty level required by the orchestra's repertoire, you simply aren't selected for the orchestra at all. The quality of your playing—the lightness of your hands and the timbre of your bowing—determine your seating position. The better your non-functional quality, the closer you sit to the conductor.[35]

David's elder daughter recently started playing several Chopin nocturnes on the piano after ten years of practicing the instrument. She could have attempted these pieces five years earlier, however, as

---

35. Prestigious professional symphony orchestras may have more qualified candidates wanting to play than the seats in the orchestra. The orchestra conductor can then turn to non-functional criteria for selection.

she tells her father, "Chopin has to be played beautifully." It takes many years of developing the fingertip feel to master the dynamics of playing Chopin. Chopin's compositions are, in business analysis terms, highly challenging in non-functional quality, whereas the functional nature of them is relatively straightforward. To translate this into business analysis terms, the difference between non-functional and functional quality of performing Chopin's compositions is quite significant. It was equal to, in this case, five years and thousands of hours of deliberate practice by a dedicated young pianist.

In summary, the concept of functional versus non-functional quality is this: functional is the "what"; non-functional describes "how well" the "what" is implemented. In some domains, such as music, the word "fidelity" is used to describe non-functional quality. In some analysis literature, elements of non-functional quality are referred to as "the -ilities"—that is, predictability, reliability, durability, and so forth.

Non-Functional Quality

We might consider a Rolls Royce a quality automobile, but the functionality it offers has no greater utility than a much cheaper vehicle. We could find an alternative car that carries the same number of passengers and luggage and has similar speed and performance capabilities. It isn't difficult to find similar vehicles with the same number of doors, seats, windows, steering wheels, gears in the gearbox, and so on. We perceive a Rolls Royce as having high quality because its quality is non-functional—the substance of the vehicle is substantial, and the craftsmanship exceptional. Perhaps we like the real wood trim in the interior with its finely polished grains. A cheaper vehicle might feature a fake plastic alternative. We would consider that finely polished wood trim has greater non-functional quality than a cheaper, manufactured, printed, plastic alternative. Non-functional quality is a term that refers to the substance, durability, finish, reliability, solidness, weight, and so on.

Neeta has a tolerance for the condition of her pizza on delivery. She has expectations for what "normal" looks like from each restaurant, or perhaps as a convention or standard in the industry or across Toronto as a metropolitan area. She has expectations for how hot and tasty it is and how fresh the ingredients are. She also has a tolerance for how these might vary from her expectations. If the pizza arrived badly burned, for example, this would be unacceptable and would put her off ordering from that restaurant again.

Recently, David has stopped eating lunch at a Thai restaurant close to his office in Seattle. The problem is the variability in the spiciness of their food. David has previously lived in Asia and is used to eating spicy food, particularly chili-spiced Malaysian/Indonesian food and Indian-spiced food. However, there were days when the three-star (out of five, indicating spiciness) Pad Kee Mao at this restaurant left him in tears, mouth burning, and unable to finish half the dish. On other occasions, it seemed like they'd forgotten to spice the dish at all. The restaurant has an open kitchen and therefore total transparency. David tried to correlate spice levels to which member of staff was cooking that day, but was unable to do so. It appeared to be completely random. The restaurant wasn't fit-for-purpose: David couldn't rely on having a tasty and filling lunch and then being able to return to work in a healthy condition for the afternoon.

The recipe for Pad Kee Mao tells us "what" it is and gives us the functional specification; the quality of the ingredients, the preparation, and the cooking define how tasty it is and give us the non-functional quality. Regardless of non-functional quality, it would still be a Pad Kee Mao if the recipe was followed. Whether we find it an acceptable Pad Kee Mao depends on the implementation by the chef and the capability of the restaurant. Non-functional quality—and its predictability—are key fitness criteria in selection and in our willingness to pay a quoted price. For exceptionally high (non-functional) quality Pad Kee Mao we would pay a premium.

Functional Quality
Functional quality refers to specification accuracy. If Neeta ordered a cheese pizza, was it a cheese pizza that arrived, or a pepperoni? If it was a pepperoni, we had a failure in order accuracy—a failure in functional quality. If David ordered a Pad Kee Mao and a Pad Thai arrived, we'd have had a similar failure in functional quality. If an ingredient such as garlic was missing from the finished dish, then the recipe for Pad Kee Mao hasn't been followed accurately and we have a minor failure in functional quality. Variability, or the predictability in functional quality, is a matter of degree of variation from

specification. Garlic missing is a minor variation; Pad Thai rather than Pad Kee Mao is a major variation.

As we saw with Neeta, tolerance for failures in functional quality differed depending on whether she was ordering pizza for the office or for her children. This tolerance to variation is what we call predictability. How often, as a percentage, does the pizza restaurant deliver exactly what was ordered? And when they don't, how badly do they get it wrong? Neeta has a threshold for both frequency of mistakes and the magnitude of the mistake. Functional quality and predictability is a fitness criterion for Neeta. It has two components: the frequency of a mistake and the magnitude of a mistake. When ordering for her "ten-pizza team" at the office, mistakes could happen frequently so long as they are small, such as a pepperoni being mistaken for a ham and pineapple. However, a larger mistake—for example, no vegetarian pizzas were delivered—would be unacceptable. Neeta's tolerance for the impact of an error would have been exceeded.

Safety and Regulatory Conformance
Neeta cares whether her food is prepared in accordance with health and safety standards for food preparation. She lives in a developed country and she trusts in the systems of local government in the province of Ontario and the cities of Toronto and Mississauga. So she doesn't need to verify safety and conformance. However, if Neeta heard some rumors about health and safety standards being violated, or saw a local news report that a branch of Westside Pizza had been closed by an inspector for code violations, it might cause her to think twice about doing business with them.

On the other hand, does Neeta care whether her pizza delivery boy broke any traffic laws when delivering her pizza? Although she probably should, the reality is that she doesn't. In the highly unlikely event that the pizza boy or others were killed in an accident as a result of reckless endangerment in the speedy delivery of pizza, maybe she would feel some guilt. What if she'd offered a bigger tip in exchange for faster delivery and this had led to recklessness? We think everyone can understand this, but really it is a strawman—it is speculative. The reality is that Neeta cares about the quality of the pizza upon delivery and not whether traffic laws were broken. It may be necessary to drive carefully to ensure quality. Neeta's tipping based on quality on delivery rather than on aggressive speed of delivery may drive the best behavior.

If there is a lesson here, it is that consumers adopt safety and regulatory requirements as fitness criteria when it affects their consumption of the product. When the regulations relate to an aspect of the service that they don't consume and view as an overhead, or non-value-added aspect of the product implementation or service delivery, the regulations won't be a fitness criterion for them. It is the role of lawmakers and regulatory authorities to make these fitness criteria in order to protect others—to protect third parties not directly involved in producing, delivering, or consuming the product or service.

Regulated Industries

In regulated industries, meeting the regulations is table stakes for entering the game. In the United States, the Food and Drug Administration (FDA) regulates the food industry, the Federal Communications Commission (FCC) regulates the telecommunications industry, the Federal Aviation Administration (FAA) regulates the aircraft industry in both the design and construction of aircraft and the operations of air travel and freight services, including air traffic control. If you want to operate a business in one of these industries you have to meet the regulations. All mandated law-enforced regulations are fitness criteria. The regulator is a stakeholder in one respect, a customer of the product or service, and its needs must be met. In many cases the regulator represents the needs of customers when the customers are not at liberty, or qualified, to make safety inspections for themselves. By enacting safety into law, a level of trust is created that enables commerce on a large scale. Of course, the flipside of this is that it creates many opportunities for corruption; many readers from lower social capital countries will recognize that were Neeta in their local market, perhaps, she shouldn't trust that health and safety standards were met in the preparation of her pizza.

Price Isn't an Independent Criterion

Neeta took the 5:10 train from work, got into her car at the train station's park-and-ride lot, and made a stop at a local running store on her way home. It was time for a new pair of running shoes. She joined a gym and took up running after her youngest was born. Several months and about 1,000 kilometers later, replacing the shoes after some mileage became her regular routine and an injury-preventing tactic.

"There will be a local 5K race in a few weeks," the saleswoman said to Neeta while ringing up her purchase. "I've run it every year for the last five years and had a blast every time. Would you like to register to run it?" The saleswoman was a running enthusiast herself. Neeta had never competed in a road race before. She wasn't sure what to say. "I'll think about it."

The saleswoman placed a leaflet with the road race information and registration form in Neeta's shopping bag.

Neeta had sticker shock back home when she opened the leaflet. The race registration fee was $40! It included running the race, measuring her time "officially" with an electronic chip strapped to her ankle, a commemorative T-shirt, and some snacks after the race.

"You could run on a sidewalk around the subdivision and time yourself with a stopwatch for free!" said her husband.

Neeta had a feeling there was more to the race experience than the stopwatch timing. She recalled she spent $40 on pizza tips a couple of weeks ago, so she thought she wasn't risking much and reluctantly decided to give it a try.

The race day exceeded all of Neeta's expectations. After finishing the race, she met and chatted with several local running enthusiasts who spoke about their quest for healthier lifestyles and freely shared their challenges and training tips. Some of them had achieved what they never thought was possible and had inspiring stories of how this sport helped them accomplish more in their lives or careers.

Neeta looked at the race as a project manager, maybe for a minute. It was quite a complex event that must not have been easy or cheap to put on. Several police officers providing road safety cost something, at overtime rates, no doubt. The race T-shirt was made of nice "technical" moisture-wicking fabric (could be useful for a run on a hot summer day, she thought). The finish-line "snacks" included tasty and pretty much all-you-can-eat barbecue—and quite a lot of food was needed to feed the hungry runners. There were also many volunteers along the race course who had to be there early to help make it a great experience for the runners. They had to be instructed, uniformed, and fed. And what about marketing? Even the small things like registration leaflets—what would it cost to design and print them?

Neeta realized that even if everybody paid $40, that might still not be enough to pay for everything. Just at that moment, the race director took the microphone.

"We'd like to thank our generous sponsors, many of whom are local small businesses." And one of them was . . . Westside Pizza!

Neeta spotted the Westside Pizza tent soon after she caught her breath after crossing the finish line. As the race director spoke, she recalled how different the pizza was from the one she ordered for her kids not long ago. Instead of lukewarm cheese pizza, she had a slice of a bubbling hot pie topped with spicy fajita chicken, bacon, onions, and instead of the usual tomato sauce, this was smothered in a ranch sauce. Delicious! Of course, the kids wouldn't like it. It turned out that Westside Pizza wasn't a one-trick pony—they knew how to deliver product that would appeal to other customer segments. For the hungry 5K runner this was more than fit-for-purpose. So nice, in fact, she'd have to try it again! What other recipes might they have? She'd need to check that out.

Neeta realized that none of the 150 or so people at the event was there for a wrong reason. Everybody paid $40, had a good time, and was likely to come back next year. People who would not appreciate such an experience would surely find the price of $40 (that didn't even cover all the costs) way too high. They would balk at it and not participate in the event. Trying to attract them with deeply discounted prices could make the event bigger, more expensive, more difficult to organize, less attractive to its core customers, and ultimately, unsuccessful and unsustainable.

She would gladly pay $40 to run her local 5K road race again, realizing that a $15 price tag (and the experience that would come with it) would make the product much less attractive, less worth her time and effort. At $15, she may as well run around her subdivision with a stopwatch and save her money. The experience at the $40 race made it worthwhile. Changing the price tag changes the market segmentation! Cheaper isn't always better if it comes at the cost of quality (of experience).

When we advise our clients on creating products and services that are fit-for-purpose, the price or affordability of products and services often comes up as a potential criterion. In the strategic planning workshops we run with clients, they often want to list price as a fitness criterion. It is well understood that price has an elasticity to it—there is often a maximum price that consumers are capable or willing to pay for a product or service. If you break that elasticity, then you lose the customer. For them, your product or service isn't fit-for-purpose. However, the limit of elasticity isn't entirely everything we need to consider. Price is rarely an independent variable as part of a set of fitness criteria. It is much more likely that the threshold for price varies with the other criteria and the blend of performance against them. Our recommendation is not to treat affordability as a KPI or price as a fitness criterion in its own right. Instead consider:

1. What kind of customers would be attracted to your product or service at different price levels?

2. What would these customers' purposes be for buying your product or service at these price levels?

3. What would your market segmentation picture look like at each price level?

4. What (non-financial) fitness criteria would matter to customers in each market segment at these price levels?

This begins to sound like old-fashioned socioeconomic class segmentation, but it isn't. It isn't simply about how much disposable income people have available. Price affects the cost and cost affects quality. Quality measures are fitness criteria and affect selection. So price often isn't the fitness criterion at all, instead it is quality, but the quality must be delivered within the affordability range of the consumer's economic elasticity. For example, we may be willing to pay more for faster delivery because time has a value due to the cost of delay, or because there is value in deferring commitment. If we can afford to pay more to avoid a cost-of-delay impact, then we will gladly pay. Imagine a local authority purchasing construction of a bridge across a river in order to shorten journey times. Earlier delivery produces linear incremental benefits for taxpayers who will use the bridge to shorten their journey times. So perhaps it is worth paying more for a faster construction even when a slower, longer delivery would still be acceptable to us and still considered fit-for-purpose. If only our public sector were trusted enough to select bids based on a blended set of fitness criteria and not simply obliged to select the lowest priced bid.

Vertu

We write this just a few days after the announcement that high-end mobile phone manufacturer Vertu has entered receivership and is closing. Vertu was started by Nokia in the late 1990s. It sold high-end mobile devices costing upwards of $10,000—and one that cost as much as $40,000. These devices, in recent times, offered no more functionality than a standard Android smartphone, while older models were based on earlier Nokia Symbian technology. What "purpose" does a buyer have in spending ten to thirty times more for a device with no additional functional capability? The answer is that such a device signals something about them, about their identity, their wealth, their values, and what they need to elevate their own self-esteem. The purpose and the price go hand in hand. What is important is the relative difference in price to regular smartphones, not the absolute price being asked, though there will be some elasticity in pricing. A Vertu buyer wants to signal that they are richer than someone else. They have a deep identity-related emotional motivation. They want to signal wealth, perhaps because it signals success. Traditionally we associate this type of behavior with *nouveau riche* (or "new money"). For this segment, price doesn't have a threshold, it has a multiplier, within some bounds of elasticity.

Vertu was displaced in the market by cheaper alternatives—after-market bling accessories. Vertu was making phones integrating OEM components from other consumer brand manufacturers but replacing the screens with ones made from sapphire and the plastic enclosures with those made from precious metals and encrusted with diamonds. The customers' purpose, however, was to signal wealth, ostentatiousness, spendthrift consumption. From more than a few feet away, it was impossible to tell an Android phone with a jewel-encrusted cover from a genuine Vertu. In addition, it took Vertu time to bring new devices to market. They were often working as a customer of original equipment manufacturers, one or two models behind the current state of the art. Hence, you could have the latest Samsung Android phone with after-market bling costing perhaps $3,500 or you could have a Vertu based on last year's model costing $10,000. For the segment that wants to signal wealth, that want the flashiness of the bling-encrusted phone, the non-functional quality of a craft-designed Vertu with an indestructible sapphire screen is unnecessary. They don't want, nor do they have the time or opportunity, to tell people, "No, seriously, this is a genuine Vertu, not just a jewel-laden cover for my Samsung." Vertu was the Rolls Royce of the mobile phone market, but a Vertu didn't look different from an imitation. So the same benefits an owner of a Rolls Royce might enjoy weren't so readily communicated with a Vertu. Vertu needed buyers who sought to be discreet about their wealth—old money buyers—and to narrow the segment, old money buyers who didn't mind having a phone that was a model year or two behind the state of the art. There simply weren't enough customers in Vertu's segment to sustain the design and manufacture of their phones. Vertu may have been fit-for-purpose for a small audience, but the business wasn't viable because sufficient economy of scale was unachievable. What might it have taken to sustain Vertu? A price rise of perhaps five-fold, taking a $10,000 device to $50,000 when a comparison product might be a Samsung phone with an aftermarket cover costing $3,500? Presumably the company's owners decided it was too risky to experiment with finding a suitable price and product offering that enabled a sustainable business capable of surviving. Unable to sustain a market big enough to support it economically, Vertu closed.

Fit-for-purpose is one thing, but when alternatives compete in the market, the fittest survive. For the segment that wanted to show off their wealth, Vertu competed with after-market alternatives. After-market bling displaced Vertu as fitter for the environment, and Vertu, as a consequence, became extinct. Vertu's identity as a phone manufacturer and originally a spin-off from Nokia meant they were unable to reinvent themselves as a luxury after-market cover supplier. David will examine identity-related failures such as Vertu in the third book of this trilogy, *First Who, Then Why*.

So price isn't an independent variable. Price varies according to the performance against other fitness criteria. Vertu was unable to achieve superior performance against after-market competitors for most of its customers' fitness criteria. As a consequence, the customers selected the alternatives that gave them everything they needed at a lower price. The sapphire screens and their indestructible, nonfunctional quality weren't part of the customers' fitness criteria. Vertu overserved the market on robustness of their displays and made themselves uncompetitive on price.

Summary

- There are four types of commonly recurring fitness criteria:
  - Lead time and its predictability
  - Quality and its predictability
  - Safety and conformance with regulatory requirements
  - Price and affordability
- If you're unsure what is driving customer selection in your business, these common fitness criteria can give you a good start.
- Lead time is not a single number. It is important to consider not only the typical and average cases, but also the best and the worst. Ask both how fast and how predictable it is and needs to be.
- Customers' purpose is often linked to their timeline, therefore lead time is a ubiquitous fitness criterion. Every business should be measuring it.
- Quality can be of functional ("what") and non-functional ("how well") variety. "How well" is often more difficult to achieve than "what."
- Price is not an independent variable. At each price point, customers have different combinations of other, non-financial, fitness criteria and thresholds.

7 We Know Why You Fly

BETWEEN 2004 AND 2012 AMERICAN AIRLINES was telling us, "We know why you fly." The implication was that they were designing their products and services around higher value customers by emphasizing that they understood them better and offered a superior service tailored to the customers' needs, albeit at a slightly premium price. The campaign was born out of severe pressure on prices and competition from low-cost airlines. American was seeking to increase margins and attract more valuable customers who appreciated their superior service.

We're not convinced that American's "we know why you fly" tagline and campaign was ever much more than a platitude. Their 2008 commercials by TM Advertising from their hometown of Dallas came in for some criticism.[36] The campaign was described as "creepy" and the customers' reasons for flying featured in the ads seemed to be obscure. If American was trying to create empathy, it wasn't working. Good advertising takes real-world situations and amplifies them to a preposterous comic level in order to engage the audience in just a few seconds. Selecting outlier cases and highlighting exceptional service will work with a message like "we go the extra mile" (in order to serve you better)—even when your circumstances are unusual, we offer superior service to take care of you. However, in this case, and with this general, broad market message of "we know why you fly," the examples didn't represent realistic segments. There was no evidence that American was designing its products and services to serve identified market segments

---

36. www.adweek.com/agencyspy/american-airlines-sucks-and-so-do-their-new-ads-from-tm-advertising/3026

and certainly not because they knew why people from those segments were flying.

If American was thinking more about purpose-based segments, they would have had fold-flat beds in their long-haul business class[37] as well as status and class-of-service lounges with complimentary food and nicer quality wine comparable with other OneWorld alliance partners such as Cathay Pacific, Qantas, and British Airways. They wouldn't force premium passengers to suffer overcrowded membership lounges where the food and drink are for purchase and an annual membership costs the price of a single domestic economy class ticket. Equally, they wouldn't expect business class passengers to suffer recliner seats on red-eye flights to large business cities such as Sao Paulo, London, and Paris.

Other airlines have, however, shown some inclination that they know why some passengers fly. Air Canada has created a separate brand called Air Canada Rouge, which offers services tailored to people traveling for leisure. Air Canada Rouge aircraft are painted in different livery and have a different design inside. Even flight attendants' uniforms have different colors and a less formal look. Rouge flies to destinations where most passengers go for vacation. For example, direct flights from Toronto to business destinations such as London and Frankfurt are serviced by regular Air Canada aircraft, while Barcelona and Dublin are serviced by Rouge aircraft. In North America, regular Air Canada planes take people to business meetings in Washington and San Francisco, while Rouge planes take them to holidays in Orlando and Las Vegas. British Airways uses a similar bifurcation for leisure travelers, although they operate it under the same brand. The difference is that vacation destination flights leave from London's Gatwick airport. Gatwick has lower taxes than London's Heathrow, British Airways' home airport, and hence, flights from Gatwick can be priced lower. Compare a London Gatwick (LGW) flight to Barcelona (BCN) on British in comparison to a London Heathrow (LHR) flight to the same airport. Even for economy class there may be several hundred dollars' difference in price. The Heathrow flights to Barcelona often fill up with passengers making long-haul connections. British is trying to

---

37. At the time of writing in summer 2017, American has just introduced fold-flat beds in business class on its transatlantic services to London, some twenty years after British Airways took the lead with this level of comfort for business travelers.

push UK-based leisure travelers to fly from Gatwick. While we might view this as a simple demand-shaping exercise, a look down the rest of the flight destinations from Gatwick shows it is solidly vacation oriented. For example, London to Tampa and Orlando fly from Gatwick; Miami is serviced from Heathrow. Gatwick also services many destinations in the Caribbean, Atlantic, and Indian Oceans such as Madeira and Mauritius. British knows that people traveling on vacation have more time on their hands, are hopefully less stressed, and are willing to accept poorer service in exchange for lower prices. Vacation travelers are paying with their own after-tax income, whereas business travelers are often using their employer's money and the costs are tax-deductible and can be offset against revenues. As a consequence, British flies older aircraft from Gatwick. Often these older aircraft feature older interiors, older entertainment equipment, seats with fewer features, and in general, slightly less comfort than a business traveler would expect when flying on British from Heathrow to a major metropolitan area around the world.

So British "knows why [we] fly" in the crudest of fashions and they've optimized their costs based on assumptions about your fitness criteria tolerance thresholds. At the time of writing, we don't think it goes much deeper than that.

Design Service Levels to Different Customer Segments

Fabio manages the accounting department in a growing image analysis and video surveillance company of more than 800 people.[38] The company's innovative products and custom solutions attract customers from around the world with applications such as queue monitoring in airports and stock shrinkage prevention in retail stores. Integrated solutions include components from a broad partner alliance. The company has offices on four continents, employing sales people, field engineers, and a research and development staff. What does this mean to Fabio? Lots of accounting work. The company operates in several countries, which all require timely filing of various financial statements and remittance of appropriate taxes on

---

38. We're protecting the privacy of this company; however, all three of its employees identified here by their first names are real.

sales, profits, and employee salaries. Partners and vendors need to be paid on time, too. Even though accounting is Fabio's main professional identity, he is also effectively a manager of a shop with many different types of picky customers. The demand on Fabio's shop is dominated by work requiring completion by a fixed date, for example, filing and paying quarterly tax installments by their due dates. Up to a certain point, his department's work items are generally insensitive to delays. It costs the company nothing to delay them by a few days as long as the deadline is met. But they become extremely sensitive to delay around certain dates. Delay those by one day and a government fine or a contractual penalty will result. What's interesting is that the duration of time to complete a work item isn't a fitness criterion for this type of work. Fabio's staff can start a work item late and go fast (possibly delaying other work items). Or they can start early and go slowly (speeding up other items). Even predictability or the variation of the duration matters only so much. As long as the duration range is not too wide and it can fit entirely before the deadline, all is well. What matters absolutely is timeliness. This is Fabio's equivalent of "does he get on base?"[39] Was the work item delivered on time or a bit too late, incurring some financial cost? On base or out? Timeliness is the key fitness criterion for much of the work done in Fabio's accounting department.

From all of Fabio's picky customers, let's consider just two for the moment: Pierre, the company's founder and CEO, and Alain, the chief financial officer. Another financial cycle has just completed and Fabio is tallying up the numbers to compile financial reports for these two executives. He is mindful of their two very different sets of needs. Pierre needs the report on his desk pretty much the morning following the day they cycle closes. It has to be accurate, but not necessarily precise. The latest sales figures may be rounded off to the nearest tenth of a million dollars. That will be good enough for Pierre to see the trends and negotiate another deal with confidence. Pierre is leaving for the airport soon for another long-haul flight. He will hit the ground running and meet with a customer when he lands. To be

---

39. A more perfect baseball analogy of Fabio's fitness criteria would be the fielding percentage. It is a defensive baseball statistic, capturing the percentage of cases that a baseball player had to catch or throw the ball, in which he made the correct play and did not make an error extending the opposing team's attack.

fit-for-[this]-purpose, the time to compile the report must be short, even if it sacrifices some precision (but is still accurate).

Alain's purpose is different. If any financial irregularities were to happen in the company, his professional reputation and his license as a certified public accountant (CPA) would be on the line. He can wait longer for Fabio to complete his work, but then the financial figures must be precise. This is not the only criterion, however. Accountants interpret general accounting principles and the existing rules and still have to exercise their sound professional judgment when deciding how to treat various business transactions. Good accounting work should include notes documenting such decisions and how they conform to the principles and the specific rules. Alain will need those. Alain thus has fitness criteria thresholds in both functional (documentation) and non-functional (precision) quality criteria. And he can trade the duration of time for the functional and non-functional quality.

Table 7.1 summarizes Pierre's and Alain's fitness criteria and their thresholds.

Table 7.1 Fitness criteria and their thresholds

	Customer	
	CEO	CFO
Criterion	Threshold	Threshold
Duration	Very short (next day)	Longer (1–3 weeks)
Accuracy* (non-functional quality)	High	High
Precision (non-functional quality)	Low (can round numbers off)	High (to the dollar)
Key categories of assets, liabilities, revenue, and expenses (functional quality)	Present	Present
Notes, conformance statements (functional quality)	Not needed	Definitely needed

* Accuracy and precision are not the same. "I'll be home for dinner between 6 p.m. and 7 p.m." is an attempt at accuracy without precision. Arriving home at 6:53 p.m. would mean the forecast was accurate. However, it was never precise. "I'll be home at 6:45 p.m." is a communication of precision. For this to be accurate the person must be home for dinner on or before 6:45 p.m. Accuracy generally matters more in trust relationships. However, there are instances where precision is needed. Generally, the need for precision is explicitly understood. When precision is delivered when mere accuracy would be sufficient, the customer is being overserved.

What's interesting is that the level of performance with respect to duration that Pierre finds satisfactory is exceptionally high from Alain's point of view. The level of functional quality satisfactory to Alain would appear exceptionally high, perhaps needlessly so, to Pierre. The challenge for Fabio is to serve both of these customers adequately. If he treats all work requests as equal, he has to respond quickly and accurately all of the time. As a financial controller, this requires excellent implementation and service delivery. His capabilities need to be exceptional because he does not differentiate his customers or his market, and he doesn't treat the risks in each segment separately. When Fabio adequately understands his customers' purpose, he can segment his market and serve them separately with different classes of service. This will likely increase customer satisfaction without needing to provide exceptional capability at implementation and service delivery. It may also relieve his staff from overburdening and ultimately lower his costs by enabling him to provide adequate, fit-for-purpose service with fewer staff. As a general rule, segmenting a market and treating it heterogeneously, with service levels designed for each segment, improves customer satisfaction while relieving pressure on capability of implementation, leading directly to lower costs. Segmentation based on purpose increases Fabio's ability to be fit-for-purpose.

We first met Amit Kaulagekar and his client Sungard in Chapter 5. In January 2014 he was asked to help improve forms processing from a capability of just 61 percent against a 5-day SLA with the aspiration of hitting 99.5 percent as agreed in the terms of the contracts with Sungard's clients. Amit had several available ways to exploit differences in customer expectations. The staff on his team were not homogenous, so there were three pay grades: Admin 1, Admin 2, and Admin 3. Admin 3 level staff had more than twenty years' experience and were capable of processing the greatest variety of task types, and had the seniority to deal with the high-risk tasks that carried financial penalties. Forms were sorted into three streams by type and risk and channeled to staff from each pay grade according to the required processing. Without this initial analysis and sorting, Amit would treat the work requests homogenously. To process them all satisfactorily, he'd either need a team consisting solely of Admin 3 grade employees— which would be expensive and difficult to maintain—or he'd have to accept mistakes and quality problems, potentially leading to financial penalties as a consequence of processing forms with inadequately trained or inadequately experienced staff.

Most tasks with financial penalties were linked to the closure of the New York Stock Exchange at 4 p.m. Eastern Standard/Daylight Time.[40] These were given priority and queued for processing first at the beginning of the day after the mail was opened and the forms scanning was completed, typically before 8 a.m. Amit was able to extend the processing day by staggering shifts for his team in India such that they could start processing tasks as soon as the mail was opened in the United States and before other US personnel started work for the day.

Amit set a goal of achieving 90 percent on-time against a one-day SLA. Through a series of improvements to capability and by smart exploitation of his workforce—sorting tasks by type and risk and channeling them appropriately to the different admin levels—the performance improved to 91.8 percent by September of the same year. This was a dramatic improvement, but customer expectations had always been for 99.5 percent on-time against the SLA—although this was originally a five-day SLA—and by September 2014, the team was effectively hitting it. They had done so by setting themselves a one-day SLA as an improvement driver or "stretch goal."[41]

Amit wasn't finished yet, however. Together with the managers in charge of forms processing, he recognized that same-day processing before 4 p.m. Eastern time was necessary for some financially critical tasks, while one-day (or within twenty-four hours) was good for others, and that they could achieve this using their staff in India who would work at times when their US office was closed for the night. There was another whole category of tasks, though, for which one-day processing was overserving and unnecessarily fast. For this class of work types, the SLA was changed to three days. By November 2014 the team had achieved its 99 percent on-time target for forms

---

40. Depending on time of year

41. Stretch goals are discussed in Chapter 13, Von Moltke's Goal-Directed Balanced Scorecard. In this instance, the stretch goal was motivational because Amit had means at his disposal to analyze the workflow and associated business risks and implement changes. Had Amit been without means, or lacking ideas on methods to improve performance, then such a stretch goal would have been demotivational and would have led to failure. It is recommended stretch goals are used with extreme caution and only by managers who believe they have the means to achieve them.

processing. They were unquestionably fit-for-purpose. Their capability was such that they were able to take on work for two additional client companies without increasing their staffing.

The improvements were enabled by implementing strategies based on a combination of concepts and ideas. Amit introduced greater transparency and visibility onto the work using a kanban board and established strict limits to work-in-progress, which focused the team on finishing rather than on starting more work. He used metrics carefully to create alignment and collaboration around behavior that had a direct impact on customer satisfaction and fitness criteria. He introduced feedback mechanisms with a regular cadence—weekly and monthly—to enable analysis of performance, capability, and business risks at both the line- and general manager level, respectively. By understanding that their "market," that is, the tasks they processed, weren't homogeneous in nature, and that the purpose behind them varied, as well as the impact of cost of delay, they were able to fine-tune service delivery using existing staff. They made dramatic improvements. They became completely fit-for-purpose without increasing costs.

Treating all work homogenously implies you have only one market segment, with one set of expectations, and similarly, homogeneous risks to manage. Thinking that you have only one segment is convenient; it allows businesses to focus on optimizing costs. This often comes at the cost of sacrificing quality, resulting in considerable customer dissatisfaction. A focus on cost cutting is likely to leave you unfit-for-purpose in the eyes of many frustrated customers. A knee-jerk reaction to address dissatisfied customers can result in overserving segments and driving costs up. Understanding your market—knowing what drives your market, what purpose they have when choosing your product or service, and what risks they are managing—enables you to build more effective fit-for-purpose products and services. We'll look more at how to exploit market segmentation by designing products, services, and service delivery levels to appropriately match customer needs and expectations in Chapter 10, It's Not Luck!

Who Knows Your Customers?

In both physical businesses and professional services, it's the frontline staff who know your customers best, with some exceptions. We'll get to the exceptions later.

David started his career in the software business in 1981, as part of the early home computing and gaming explosion. In the very early days, it was a craft-based cottage industry serving an enthusiast market. David's first product was a game supplied as a listing in the BASIC language. It was marketed through small ads in the back of enthusiast magazines, and customers who mailed a cheque received back an envelope containing a neatly folded listing on paper. They had to type the program code into their own machine and save the results to cassette tape if they didn't want to have to repeat the process. In those early days, David knew his customers directly—they often purchased his products with chatty handwritten notes. Some would even write back later with feedback and gratitude. Very quickly the market matured and the service delivery component of the product improved. David's business started mailing out cassette tapes with the code already recorded. By 1984, however, the European home computer games market was maturing and delaminating. In the beginning, each company did everything—they were vertically integrated. They designed and coded the games, printed the packaging, duplicated the materials, and marketed and sold the products directly, often by mail order. But as the market matured, businesses specialized into functions and vertical integration disappeared. In the new world, there were development houses, publishers, distributors, and retailers. The market was said to have "delaminated"—broken into a set of layers, each adding value in order to deliver the product to the end consumer. What had caused this delamination?

Mostly it was that the scale was larger. There was an early adopter market that had swamped out the enthusiast computer hobbyists. These new users were game players, not computer geeks: they didn't care to know much about the machines they used to play the games. The quality of information available to the producer—games development houses, such as David's Platinum Productions, based near Glasgow in Scotland—had fallen to a negligible level. Retailers such as the newsagents John Menzies had no mechanisms in place to understand the buyers of shelved, shrink-wrapped games on cassette. Distributors could tell you what was "selling in" and what was "selling through" (generating reorders), and the publisher could also tell you what was being returned as "unsold," but little additional information was available about who or why.

David attended trade shows, mostly in London, several times per year. At these events, the general public would pay an entry fee to browse stands and booths of home computer manufacturers, peripherals manufacturers, magazines, and games publishers. Publishers would time the launch of new games to these events and the public would attend to get a first look and possibly a discount on the retail price. David learned that the best way to get a crowd at your publisher's booth was to stand at a machine on display and play the game. Crowds would gather to watch. When GAME OVER appeared, he'd drop back through the crowd, someone else would take up the joystick, and then he'd stand, watch, and listen. The greatest value David derived from trade shows wasn't the publicity, the notoriety, the sense of achievement, or the congratulations on the latest title, it was the invaluable consumer feedback gleaned from lurking outside the booth watching how a crowd reacted to his work.

To understand your customers, you need direct customer connection. Your frontline staff provide that mechanism. You need to train them to pay attention, to listen, to chat up customers, to record stories, to look for patterns. If you don't have a connection to your customers because of industry delamination, then you need to get out of the building. We've worked with mobile.de, the DACH (consisting of Germany, Austria, and Switzerland) region's leading source for the resale of vehicles, boats, and anything with an engine. Developers of mobile.de's mobile application found they could learn more by hanging out in Berlin cafés and asking passersby to look at new prototypes than they could from studying usage, downloads, or online reviews.

Nowadays David leads a professional services business focused on management training. His frontline people are trainers and consultants. They are all professionals with university degrees. They are highly literate and well educated. They are also the highest paid people, whether they are full time employees, independent associates paid on a casual basis, or subcontractors from other firms. Many of David's trainers are teaching curriculum containing insights like those in this book. They are trained to sense consumer behavior and trained to give feedback. They teach others how to do it.

David also has a secondary sensing mechanism. The events that Lean Kanban Inc. organizes for their business partners, the Leadership Retreats, are, in part, designed to provide a feedback mechanism.

Retreats provide an opportunity for David's firm to learn from its partners what they are seeing in their regional markets, an opportunity to collect secondhand customer narrative.

Most traditional, tangible goods businesses, on the other hand, suffer like David did as a games developer in the mid-1980s—they rely on distributors and retailers and they hope that consumers will fill in a warranty card or visit their website. They might try to introduce a loyalty program so that they can track consumers. Or they're in an industry such as mobile phones, where the customer engagement happens in the retail stores or via their customer care phone lines. In both cases, the retail stores and the call centers, the staff are the lowest paid people at the company, and they usually have the shortest tenure and highest rate of staff turnover. The same story is true for fast food chains, cafés such as Starbucks, and transport services such as train or bus lines as well as airlines. The customer interface is treated as an overhead, as something without much information value, as something that can be automated or outsourced. We believe that you have to decide how much you value information about customer satisfaction, how customers think of you, and their purpose behind consuming your product or service. If you value this information, either invest in upskilling and retaining your frontline staff—pay them more, train them better, keep them longer—or automate those functions and invest in technology to provide your sensing mechanism. The current situation is neither fish nor fowl—it doesn't add value so you see it as an overhead, a target for cost cutting. Either turn your frontline into a valuable market information sensing mechanism or replace it altogether.

Outsourcing Your Front Line
You've seen the example in which British Airways outsourced their away-station gate agents to Menzies Aviation. Passengers flying British Airways from Germany are greeted and served on the ground by agents in Menzies uniforms and encounter British Airways staff only aboard the airplane. Arrangements differ by airline and location. We've learned by observation—and by asking Menzies staff—that Menzies dresses their employees in airline uniforms for some airlines and in some locations. In other cases they dress in Menzies uniforms. In still other cases they use custom-made third uniforms. (It seems

airlines have different purposes when outsourcing to Menzies, with different functional quality criteria.) When a non-airline employee wears the airline uniform, customers get the impression that they're interfacing directly with the airline. You could debate both sides of the argument as to whether this is better or worse than encountering service personnel quite evidently from a third party. Is it better to be transparent with the customer or not? There are pros and cons. The main pro is that the company brand is reinforced with the familiarity of the uniform; the main con is that the staff are not vested in protecting and serving the brand—the airline will be blamed for poor service and their brand damaged if vendor staff fail to meet expectations. With staff in a vendor uniform, it is easier to deflect the blame to the vendor and promise to demand improvements when service fails to meet customer expectations.

Regardless of specific outsourcing arrangements, the danger of "flying blind"—not knowing why your customers choose your products and services—is tangible unless you implement some countermeasure, such as Fitness Box Score surveys, described in Chapter 9, Surveys and Data.

Automating the Customer Interface

Many airlines currently aspire to fully automate the check-in and boarding experience, completely eliminating their human staff from the process. Different airlines are at different stages in this process. Some require passengers to print out boarding passes themselves before coming to the airport. Others have self-operated baggage tagging machines requiring passengers to print and attach baggage tags to their own luggage. Most have automated check-in machines. The current wave of automation involves automated checks for security lines, and automated boarding. The goal is to reach a position within the next few years where human staff are only required to handle exceptions rather than every customer. Airline chief executives such as Alex Cruz at British Airways see automation as a means to cut costs and increase margins. This choice doesn't come without risks. If automating your frontline and eliminating the customer-facing human element is inevitable in your business, then developing a capability to use Fitness Box Score surveys is essential for the ongoing and future success of your business.

If it isn't inevitable that you replace the human face of your business with machines, perhaps it's time to consider investing more in your frontline presence and developing it as a first-class sensing mechanism for your marketing strategy. How much is that information worth? We believe it provides a high return on investment. You can turn your superior market sensing capability and your richer customer intimacy into a competitive advantage.

Other Exceptions

What if you are reading this as the product manager of a software-as-a-service (SaaS) business, or a mobile application business? Or perhaps you work in marketing for a traditional native software application, such as Microsoft Word, which we're using to write this book.

Shrink-Wrapped Applications

The traditional native application market is an interesting one because its origins are just like David's. Like computer games, applications were originally shrink-wrapped and distributed on disk via channels of distributors and value-added retailers (VARs). Today, these applications are distributed over the Internet as downloads and the distributors and VARs are largely gone, displaced by partner firms that offer application services such as consulting, training, or outsourced development of customized extensions to core functionality. Often application firms formalize these relationships with certifications and official licenses. The consumer buys the software directly and then chooses a third party to provide services.

In this instance, the people who know the customers are the licensed service providers, so a sensing mechanism needs to be put in place. Perhaps as part of their license they would be required to send some customer-facing consultants to a customer advisory council (CAC) meeting once or twice a year. Such a meeting would be attended by product managers, product planners, marketing and communications executives, and strategic planners. This is the equivalent of "back-briefing" in Mission Command, described in Chapter 13, Von Moltke's Goal-Directed Balanced Scorecard. In this case, however, the back-briefing is happening *from* the licensed service providers—the channel partners—to the original application vendor.

Software as a Service

Both of your authors have extensive experience working with vendors of online work-management software, especially vendors who make products that implement the ideas from David's 2010 book, *Kanban: Successful Evolutionary Change for your Technology Business.* SaaS vendors can see how their customers are using the product. They can view what customers do: what they type and store inside the product, how different users interact, and so forth. Often the customer purpose is self-evident from the usage patterns.

Early kanban board SaaS vendors such as Leankit and Kanbanize were able to observe that many users were adopting the product for personal productivity purposes. They were adopting the personal habits advocated by Jim Benson and Tonianne DeMaria Barry in the book *Personal Kanban: Mapping Work, Navigating Life.* This was bad news for the vendors—there wasn't much money to be made in a consumer product used and paid for by individuals. In fact, most of the vendors don't monetize their crimped[42] personal versions—they hope to up-sell the user to a corporate license and a full-featured product. This is the so-called freemium approach to market development, in which a crimped version of the product is free and users pay extra to switch on premium features. However, this freemium approach is largely doomed in this example of Personal Kanban adoption. The individual's purpose is "getting things done" or "relief from personal overburdening" and the free product fulfills this. It is fit-for-purpose. If these companies are to make money and sell premium subscriptions they need to develop new segments with purposes related to corporate goals, productivity, and improved customer service.

It's true that there are stories in the market of Personal Kanban adopters who later infected their workplace with the concept. Another collaborator of Jim Benson's, Maritza van den Heuvel, based in Cape Town, South Africa, is a prime example. The entire South African market for adoption of David's Kanban management method can be traced to Maritza's personal usage at home in her kitchen. However, when Maritza's employer adopted the idea, they did so with their

---

42. Product crimping is a practice whereby features are included or automatically manufactured into a product but then disabled. With software products, so-called soft switches can be used to turn on "crimped" features if users pay extra or upgrade their subscription.

own purposes in mind. Her bosses represent different segments, and it is not a certainty that they will choose to adopt the same tool she might be using on her iPad or mobile phone.

Crimped products work for upsell within a segment: do more of the same, use it at larger scale. But always the purpose is the same. For example, imagine workflow visualization board software that is crimped to a single workflow per instance. Imagine that a company such as Vistaprint has implemented the software to manage the flow of work in its internal advertising agency. At the highest level, the work items are requests for campaigns that come from business owners launching products or services for Vistaprint. The internal ad agency in turn uses other professional services such as graphic design, copy writing, copy editing, photography, stock image editing, and so forth. Imagine that each of these departments was also using the software to manage their workflow and provide better customer service—shorter lead times and greater predictability. Imagine that each department individually is paying $15 per month per user for the subscriptions and that each department has its own instance of a workflow visualization board. Each workflow visualization board works independently and you can't see or link work between boards. Now imagine that if we upgrade to the premium version, all six departments, all six professional services, can now run in a single instance in which the work is linked and tracked between boards, and features are available to facilitate the true end-to-end workflow. The premium product enables system-wide, enterprise-level improvements experienced directly by the consumer—the business owner who ordered an advertising campaign—while the entry-level product enables only local optimizations that may have little impact on the true consumer experience.

In this example, the purpose hasn't changed, merely the scale of what is under management and the scale of goal—to improve workflow management for faster delivery with greater predictability, end-to-end across a network of interdependent professional services—has changed.

So, you can upsell within a segment for greater scale or scope. You can't upsell across segments where the purposes are different. In the latter case, you do have advantages: brand awareness, customer relationship, customer recommendation. Maritza can recommend the product she is using at home to her employer, but Maritza isn't making the purchasing decision on behalf of the employer. Maritza's adoption of our software at work isn't a case of upselling, it's at best referral marketing. Freemium isn't the right model to break open the corporate market. Meanwhile, we've provided consumers with a personal use tool for free. It's hard to see how that remains sustainable.

Personal Kanban relieves individuals of overburdening. It keeps them from starting too many tasks. It helps them get things done. It enables them to "stop starting, and start finishing." At the enterprise level the purpose is often faster, more predictable delivery and improved customer service. Different purposes—different segments—and quite likely a procurement process leading to selection of a rival product. So use the "freemium" marketing strategy wisely within segments, for common purpose. If your free product is fit-for-purpose and your premium version is for another purpose, your strategy is flawed!

Mobile Applications

Mobile application vendors can assess whether their apps are fit-for-purpose in part through ratings and reviews left with the download service such as the Apple App Store. However, it doesn't paint the full picture for them. One mobile app vendor we've worked with finds that they also have to rely on press coverage. One recent application they delivered serves a scientific purpose to map the geographical spread of a number of European languages. It received extensive favorable press coverage, including a piece on BBC Radio. They were very proud of the reception for the app and assessed that it must be fit-for-purpose. In another instance, an app for an Australian fast food chain was quickly replaced by the client with a simple mobile interface for their website. The app had clearly failed to impress the client and was not fit-for-purpose.

Some mobile applications also provide social network type functionality, connecting people with shared interests such as fashion or athletics. Because the users are uploading text and images to their accounts, this allows for some assessment of the users' purpose—the "why" they are using the app—and provides benefits similar to the SaaS market. However, our friends in the mobile application development market feel that it is still necessary to survey to truly understand why customers are choosing them and their purpose behind doing so. At the time of writing, a complete answer to the metaphorical question, "Why do you fly with us?" remains elusive for the general case of mobile applications.

Is "Old School" Human Customer Interaction Truly Necessary?

Throughout this book we strongly emphasize high quality, direct customer interaction and the value that a human face on your front line can bring to your business. Of course, today we allegedly live on the cusp of the artificial intelligence "singularity,"[43] so isn't all this talk of direct human interaction and getting out of your building to know your customers better all a bit "old school"? Are we two Generation X geeks who don't quite understand the 21st Century and should go back to hacking assembly language on retro-computing 8-bit gaming simulators?

In Chapter 11, Blind Spots, we look more closely at the blind spots—underdeveloped areas and weaknesses of the Fit-for-Purpose Framework—and how you can compensate for a lack of human touch, particularly at large scale. Given the state of the art at the time of writing, we are still skeptical, but we do see some companies making interesting headway. For example, Delta asks all of its elite frequent flyers (Platinum/Diamond levels) to rate every call to customer care with a single automated question . . . "If you owned a customer service company, how likely would you be to hire the person you just talked to . . . on a five-point scale where five is definitely would hire and one is definitely not?" This is clearly a pretty good proxy for a fit-for-purpose assessment. It is minimally intrusive and injected at a point in the customer interaction when they are most likely to get a response. What it doesn't tell us is what the customer's purpose for the call was in the first place. To get that, we'd need to go back to old-school analysis of the call recording. When you are informed "this call may be recorded for training purposes," the vendor is telling you that they might just learn something that will enable them to serve you better in future and maybe that's worth trading against some personal privacy.

---

43. en.wikipedia.org/wiki/Technological_singularity

Fit-for-Purpose Products and Services:
The Three Dimensions You Need to Care About

As described in Chapter 2, all products and services have three aspects, or dimensions, that affect the customers' evaluation of whether they are fit-for-purpose: design, implementation, and service delivery. We examined Neeta's delivery pizza purchasing experience: The design is represented by the menu—the style and flavors of pizza. The implementation consists of the nature of the ingredients and how the pizzas are prepared and baked. The service delivery is represented by the speed and predictability of the delivery service—by bike or van—the condition of the pizza on arrival, and the demeanor of and interaction with the delivery staff. The person making the delivery is the customer face of Zak's and Westside Pizza. These concepts of design, implementation, and service delivery can be a little abstract, so let's consider some more examples to help you develop a more natural feel for this categorization of business elements.

Computer Games

When David worked in the games industry it was well understood that first there was the game's design, such as its concept, whether it was for one or more players, whether it was collaborative or competitive, and so forth. Then there was technical implementation: the code and its quality with respect to the speed of execution, the frame-rate of screen refresh, sprite animation, 3D graphics rendering, and all the rest. Finally, there was the service delivery element—how the product was taken to market—mail order and fulfillment, quality of cassette duplication, packaging, instructions, and exotic historical technology quirks such as did the game use a turbo-loader[44] to speed up installation into the computer.

Airlines

For an airline, which is a service rather than a product, the design begins with the routes—departure and destination airports, direct flights or stop-overs. It also includes the terminals at each airport and the equipment, or aircraft model, flown. The design decisions also

---

44. Turbo-loader technology was typically sourced from a third party that specialized only in data-compression technology and digital signal processing. In later years, games companies would, for example, override the disk driver or CD-ROM–controller software in machines like the Commodore Amiga to speed up the rate of fetching pre-rendered graphics or data tables.

extend to the layout of the aircraft itself, including the number of cab-ins and the density of passengers within them; the seating configu-ration and design, which includes seat width, reclining ability, and installed entertainment systems; and the ratio of passengers to toilets. Beyond that, airlines must design the classes of service offered—the service levels, including food and beverage menus, seating choices, number of attendants per cabin, and so forth.

Then there is the implementation: most airlines are pretty good at this because the industry is so heavily regulated. However, not all the implementation is done by the airline—they rely on third parties for things such as baggage handling and, typically, food preparation. Otherwise, implementation such as operating and flying the aircraft is conducted by airline staff—qualified pilots, service engineers, and cabin crew, who are well trained and certified on safety procedures. Both flight and cabin crew must be recertified periodically and attend training and examinations from time to time.

Service delivery describes how the customer experiences, or "consumes" their journey: the speed, efficiency, and competence of the check-in and baggage tagging service; the airport security lines; airport services, including shopping, restaurants, bars, toilets, air-line lounges, and perhaps even showers or hotel rooms. Additionally, there is the on-board experience, such as interaction with flight atten-dants, whether the entertainment or on-board Wi-Fi services work properly, the speed and frequency of food and beverage service, how soon the debris of a meal is cleared away, and so forth.

Management Training
In our management training business, the design is represented by the curricula—the topics covered and types of classes offered as well as their design and format, including number of days, style of delivery, whether there are group exercises, or long afternoon breaks. We must define the target audience, the learning objectives, whether a certifi-cate of attendance or some form of professional credential is included, whether completion involves taking and passing an examination, and so forth.

The implementation includes the competence and experience of the trainer and the nature of where and when the class is offered, such as open registration at our management school in Seattle, a fly-away class at a temporary facility in another city, or on-premises at a private client site. The quality of the training materials and supporting materials such as books, games, simulations, and videos are all aspects of the implementation.

And finally, there is the service delivery—how a class participant experiences consuming the class. Service delivery elements include the quality and comfort of the seat, the spaciousness of the classroom, the temperature in the room, the accessibility of the venue, the location, the catering, and the demeanor of the event planner, office manager, classroom assistant, and trainer(s).

All Three in Balance

Successful businesses deliver products and services in which all three elements—design, implementation and service delivery—are kept in balance, and all three are fit-for-purpose. To achieve this, the leaders of the business must respect all three elements. In some fields within the technology sector, the design element is often held in greater regard—the idea, the innovation, the ingenuity, the mathematical or scientific prowess is celebrated—and implementation is considered a boring detail, while service delivery isn't even a consideration.

Imagine for a moment that we use pizza delivery as a metaphor. If a typical Silicon Valley tech company was in the pizza delivery business there would be 1,024[45] (or more) choices on the menu, some of which would be extremely complex and sophisticated in nature, but the implementation would include frequent failures in both functional quality (order accuracy) and non-functional quality (taste) because the ovens would be over-burdened, ingredients wouldn't have been properly stored, or the preparation would have been performed by a poorly trained, junior staff member. And finally, the service delivery would frequently fail, with vast spreads of variation, missed deadlines, and disappointed customers. Nevertheless, the geeks would be immensely proud of their superior, highly innovative pizza menu! Geeks often overvalue intellectual ingenuity and treat

---

45. 1024 = 2 to the power of 10. It is also known as "1K" in technology parlance. You need 10 toppings available in any combination to produce 1024 menu options. Typically, you wouldn't provide a menu with 1024 entries; it would be described as "design your own" with 10 checkboxes (one for each topping) and you choose the combination that you desire. The psychology and sociology of such a culture would reward this ingenuity and value the flexibility of how the many combinations are guaranteed to suit any and all tastes.

implementation and delivery as mere details to be enacted by less intelligent or less well-educated individuals. They often fail to form sufficient empathy with their customers to recognize the value that the other two elements bring to the picture.

Leaders who value customer satisfaction, who believe they "know why [we] fly," need to value design, implementation, and service delivery in equal measure. They need to elevate the importance of all three elements within their firms. They can do this by using the Fit-for-Purpose Framework and by developing individual capability and management talent in each of the three dimensions. Leaders need to celebrate great achievement in implementation and service delivery and not just the intellectually seductive design element.

Chapter Summary

- Identify different customer segments and design different service levels to match their different fitness criteria.

  o Treating your market homogeneously can lead to a focus on cost cutting and customer dissatisfaction.

  o Treating different market segments differently can make your products and services fit-for-purpose while relieving staff from overburdening.

- It is still important to get out of the building to know your customer's purpose.

- If your business doesn't value the market-sensing ability of its frontline staff, you can outsource your front line or automate your customer interface. This involves certain risks and countermeasures.

- In the SaaS business, upselling, or "freemium," strategy works within the same segment (identified by purpose), not across segments with different purposes.

- In the mobile application business, surveying users is still necessary to understand the customer's "why."

- Business leaders should ensure that all three product or service components get equal attention in their organization: design, implementation and service delivery.

Summary of the Fit-for-Purpose Framework

Here is a summary of the main concepts presented so far in this book. We call this the Fit-for-Purpose Framework. It's here to help you put our ideas to use. It's a framework for constructing your product and service designs and framing your go-to-market and strategic planning decisions.

For each of your products, you should be able to describe your market, segmented by customer purpose. For each segment, you should have fitness criteria and threshold levels defining what represents an acceptable level of performance for your customer to be satisfied. You can survey customer satisfaction using F4P Cards and determine your Fitness Box Score. You can monitor this regularly. Each of your products or services has three dimensions to it, and you need to pay sufficient attention to all three if you are to be truly fit-for-purpose.

- Three dimensions of product or service
  - Design
  - Implementation
  - Service delivery
- Market segmentation based on customers' purpose
- Fitness criteria are the criteria the customer (implicitly) uses to select your product or service.
- Each market segment will have its own fitness criteria.
- Use these commonly recurring fitness criteria as an initial template until you know a segment better:
  - Lead time and its predictability
  - Quality and its predictability
    - Functional
    - Non-functional
  - Safety or conformance to regulatory requirements
  - Price or affordability—although price may require some special treatment
- Fitness Criteria have thresholds:
  - Minimum acceptable level, below which the product or service is unfit-for-purpose
  - Exceptional level, beyond which customer expectations are exceeded
- F4P Cards are used in a survey method designed to facilitate both understanding a customer's purpose in consuming a product or service and identifying segments and fitness levels within each segment.
- Fitness Box Score is a means to report survey results and evaluate fitness-for-purpose of a product or service within each segment.

SECTION III

Managing Fitness-for-Purpose

This section gives pragmatic, actionable guidance on introducing the Fit-for-Purpose Framework in a real-world business.

Chapter 8 focuses on the human approach, using the innate human ability to tell and interpret stories. It shows how to connect the front-line staff, who know the customer stories, to the executives making strategic decisions. It also teaches how to sense and respond to situations when customer segments are over- and underserved. Chapter 9 gives a more technological, data- and fact-driven approach, also connecting insights to action. The two approaches to existing customer segments complement each other. Further, Chapter 10 is dedicated to discovering and expanding into new customer segments.

The closing section of the book, following this one, will integrate and compare the Fit for Purpose Framework with several popular approaches and provide the final call to action.

8 Using Humans and Narrative

Identifying Segments Based on Customer Purpose

IN 2013 DAVID GATHERED some of his key team members and a few carefully selected business partners for a company retreat at a house he'd rented on a hilltop resort in the suburbs of Phoenix, Arizona. The purpose of the meeting was to set company strategy for the coming few years and to refine existing materials and product offerings. At the time, David's licensed training business was still in its infancy—less than two years old—and the organization was only just beginning to get a feel for varying behavior among partner firms around the world. Some of these partners were quite active and proactively developing the market for David's training in their region, while at the other end of the spectrum, some had already dropped out of the program. Lean Kanban Inc. wanted to better understand its market for its licensed training business branded as Lean Kanban University (LKU).

Everyone at the meeting had direct customer-facing experience with business partners who had contracted to become licensed training organizations. Some attendees at the meeting represented some of these partners. The task was to better understand companies who had paid to develop some of their personnel as licensed trainers. Why did some of them simply stop at the initial investment in training their trainers and not take it further? Most of those at the retreat also had experience teaching these classes—both open registration, public classes and private, on-premises classes for specific clients. Sitting around the living room coffee table in the house one afternoon, the group began to tell stories about the partners they had encountered.

This was a fun exercise behind closed doors—the stories were candid, opinionated, and humorous. From the emerging narrative, one of the team summarized each story, writing it on a large sticky note and sticking it to a flip chart. Perhaps an hour passed as each person told stories of the partners they knew, while others might chime in with embellishment or reinforcing experience. Patterns began to emerge. The sticky notes were moved and grouped on the flip chart to represent stories clustered by affinity—stories that had similar narratives.

The number of partner firms wasn't extensive and by the second hour of the session, the group was beginning to talk about how to label the clusters. Nicknames began to emerge: the "all-ins," the "long-term committeds," the "aspirationals," the "corporate boy scouts/girl scouts," the "bet hedgers," and the "get-rich quicks." These represented the six initial market segments for David's licensed training business.

The next problem was to understand the partners better from our frontline personal experience with these people and their companies. What was motivating them? What was their purpose? And what did they need from us? Which of these segments fitted with our goals, objectives, and purpose? And from this, how would we form our strategy? Which segments did we want to encourage, and how? With which would we take a neutral stance? And were there any we'd actively want to switch off?

The core identity of Lean Kanban Inc. (LKI) is a management training company, primarily but not solely focused on bringing David's and his collaborators' intellectual property, management concepts, and ideas to a broad audience around the world. The positioning is simple—all professional services, intangible goods, and knowledge worker businesses are in scope and are potential targets for the training offerings. Lean Kanban Inc. does not offer training for traditional physical industries. In addition to offering training, LKI has 4 other lines of business—publishing, events, consulting, and software tools and games. Currently, all the other lines of business are there to support the management training business. Management training is its core identity, and adoption of its management techniques on a global scale is the mission and purpose of the business.

The mission and purpose, the "why" Lean Kanban Inc. exists, is a belief that the professional services sector is poorly managed and that this is causing often-invisible injury to the workforce while leaving huge economic benefits on the table. The late Peter Drucker agreed with this line of thinking. Before his death, he laid out Drucker's Challenge, saying essentially that in the 20th Century manufacturing industry had increased its productivity by 200-fold, so the challenge was to improve the productivity of professional services, intangible goods, and knowledge worker industries by a mere 50-fold. Drucker believed that modern businesses were not being effectively managed, and your authors agree with this. It appears that business schools are not serving the market effectively with their MBA curricula largely based on theories from manufacturing and physical goods industries from the first half of the previous century. There are plenty of MBA graduates running highly inefficient professional services businesses that simply aren't fit-for-purpose. The Lean Kanban curricula seek to plug the gap—to offer clarity and guidance where what was learned in college simply isn't working. The mission of Lean Kanban Inc. is to make strides forward in achieving Drucker's Challenge by providing modern managers with new models, new tools, and new decision-making frameworks, thereby enabling them to make better decisions. If implemented properly there should be a win-win-win: customers should get better products and services that are fit-for-purpose, the workforce and their family members should be relieved of the invisible injuries caused by too much stress in the workplace, and the economic performance of their employers should improve significantly.

Filtering with this understanding of LKI's identity and its mission and purpose, which of the segments we identified through the storytelling exercise fit with that mission?

The "all-ins" were usually one- or two-people businesses for whom David's work, primarily with Kanban, had changed their lives and they'd built their entire business around it, for example, Russell Healy from New Zealand, who was present at the meeting in Phoenix. This segment was loyal, dedicated, proactive, and fully vested with real skin in the game. We clearly wanted to encourage and amplify this segment. The downside is that small, one- and two-person training firms do not create a global revolution unless you have a huge number of them. Building and servicing such a network would be extremely challenging. In addition, larger firms often don't buy their training from very small one- and two-person vendors, so we'd be excluded from large sections of the market we sought to affect. So this segment alone wouldn't be enough.

The "long-term committed" segment was filled with medium-sized businesses that behaved like the "all-ins" with loyalty, commitment, proactive market development, and skin in the game; they were simply larger firms and had other lines of business. In many ways, this scale was better, as these were risk-hedged businesses—much less fragile than the tiny "all-ins." This segment needed to be encouraged and amplified.

"Aspirationals" was an interesting segment. These were people who attended classes such as "train-the-trainer," but not because their current employer wanted to become a licensed training partner. These people would take the coaching masterclass, the most advanced of David's training offerings, not because their employer wanted to pursue an improvement initiative, but because they intended to quit, set up an "all-in," join a "long-term committed," or simply expand their career options. Some of the "aspirationals" were using their current employer to pay for their career switch; others used their own savings to fund it. In a few cases, "aspirationals" handed in their notice on the first working day after completing the training class.

Many businesses have customer segments they won't admit to publicly, or in some cases, even privately. Often, they don't actively encourage these segments, even if they know they exist. Prepaid mobile phone services sell phones not just to those with poor credit ratings and teenagers too young to sign a post-paid contract, but also to drug dealers, pimps, call girls, and other criminal elements. Spa hotels operating within two-hours' drive of a major city offer "romantic getaways." That some of the couples enjoying these romantic weekends may, in fact, be married to other people is something that is well understood, and discretion is a core part of the service that makes the hotel fit-for-purpose.

So LKI had a segment of customers that needed to be encouraged, even amplified, but no direct, explicit marketing could be done to make this happen. It wasn't a good idea to send the message, "Ready to quit your job? Take our training, then find better, more fulfilling employment elsewhere. Let us help you!" The flip side of this is also well understood. Corporations often think twice about sending personnel for training if they believe those people will then be poached away because their new skills make them attractive targets for competitive recruitment. In Dublin the competition between a local online gambling firm and one of Ireland's leading banks got so strong that eventually a handshake agreement at a senior level of management was reached to call an end to the poaching. The unforeseen side effect was that the bank had to start training its own people, which actually led to more business than before.

"Corporate boy/girl scouts" was so named because all of the example stories indicated that the clients, like scouts, were "badge collectors." LKI has a training offering in which people already knowledgeable and experienced in our methods can learn to be trainers and earn a license to deliver our training internally within the company where they work. Some of the people who showed up for this training were badge collectors. These people were loyal to their employers and generally loved their jobs. However, they wanted to boost their own status within their firms as well as their own self-esteem. As internal corporate trainers, change agents, or coaches, it was likely they would train only a handful of people each year and generate almost no revenue for LKI. At the same time, their training, delivered internally, could benefit LKI indirectly by generating demand for conferences, other training classes, and books. This was a segment on which a neutral stance was appropriate. We certainly didn't want to switch it off.

"Bet hedgers" looked like "long-term committed" if you compared corporate profiles—similar sizes, similar lines of business, similar revenues, and so forth. Traditional market segmentation wouldn't differentiate them. However, they differed in behavior. A "bet hedger" took no proactive market development initiative. "Bet hedgers" expected LKI to do all the marketing and demand generation. "Bet hedgers" were "rain catchers"—they expected LKI to make the rain fall and they were ready to catch it if it fell in sufficient quantity. "Bet hedgers" were always complaining that not enough money was being invested in marketing, and their expectations of that investment far exceeded what they had paid to join the program. The partnership was fragile. They could be expected to drop out quickly, and they were costly in terms of time and emotional investment. At best, there should be a neutral stance on this segment and it would be better to turn it off altogether. Turning it off, however, was extremely tricky, because of the similarity with the "long-term committed" segment. We wouldn't want to turn off a valuable segment as a consequence of actions to reduce the number of "bet hedgers." Ultimately, a more neutral stance makes sense, while implementing some stricter policies to make it harder for "bet hedgers" to be disruptive[46] once they are part of the program.

Finally, the "get-rich-quick" segment were entirely rain-catchers. They already believed the rain must be falling in large quantities and they wanted in on the action. They wanted to start catching it and they assumed all they had to do was join the program and then hold out a bucket to catch the rain. Meanwhile, the market reality was that there was slow but steady growth and benefits to be accrued by firms that put in the hard work and proactively developed their local market. The "get-rich-quick" segment was impatient, and the churn rate on an annual basis was close to 100 percent—these partners didn't last long. Ultimately, this segment went away when an alternative offering, in the IT project management space, became the latest pyramid scheme from which they could "get rich quick." LKI retired this segment from its strategic plan in 2016, as its population had dwindled to a negligible level.

Implementing Focus Groups of Frontline Staff

So how would Westside Pizza implement this technique or narrative clustering to identify segments?

They should hold a frontline staff focus group, perhaps once a month. Make it a social event. Cater the meeting, maybe with something other than pizza. It should feel like a tribal gathering around the campfire—breaking bread, chewing the fat of life—but with a purpose, an agenda. Just like the LKI retreat near Phoenix, sitting around the living room coffee table on the couches and armchairs, it should be a cozy, friendly gathering of frontline personnel. Have delivery staff and order takers tell stories of who they've been meeting. What is the customer's story? Some earlier investment in staff training may

---

46. The nature of the disruptiveness was sometimes very direct in terms of their impact at partner meetings, but often it was hidden. It manifested as a very high number of requests for support, overwhelming staff at the LKI office and detracting from work needed for broader market development.

be needed to encourage staff to pay attention, remember stories, and gather the right sorts of information.

We've noticed that some businesses, for example, the clothing retailer and outfitter Thomas Pink, have trained its retail staff to chat up the customers in the store. Thomas Pink retail staff are now proactive about approaching customers and having a conversation with them. No longer is it, "Can I help you?" which was always shorthand for, "Can I sell you something?" It isn't transactional any longer; it's about building a relationship with the customer. Establishing an emotional connection for them with the brand and perhaps the specific store and its staff. It's not about selling a single shirt, it's now about selling to that customer for years and years, again and again. It's about having them talk positively about the Thomas Pink brand and creating word-of-mouth generated interest in their brand and products. To get the information needed, the staff need to know the customers' stories and there needs to be a corporate sensing mechanism. That mechanism is a frontline staff focus group or retreat. Quarterly is good, monthly is better!

Someone should facilitate the meeting and, ideally, another should act as scribe, keeping track of the customers described. Use sticky notes and flip charts or white boards. Encourage a conversation, not just one person talking but an active discussion amongst the group, building upon and reinforcing stories with similar experiences as they hear them. Make the clustering a group collaborative exercise. Have some fun with naming the clusters. If your staff don't have training in facilitation or aren't comfortable showing that leadership, consider getting them suitable training or using a professional facilitator. We are leery, however, of the effect a professional facilitator can have— too much ritual and focus on the facilitation and the meeting loses its relaxed informality. It's important that staff can speak candidly, in a safe environment. They must trust that telling the truth as they see it won't be punished. You don't want a situation in which they feel they should describe what management wants to hear rather than the actual truth of their frontline experience.

The outcome of these focus groups needs to be reported to senior executives, strategic planners, and marketing executives. Perhaps the forum for this is a Strategy Review meeting or a Strategic Planning retreat. The results shouldn't be presented by some middle-ranking marketing manager reporting the focus group results. Instead, invite perhaps two of the representatives from the frontline focus group to the meeting. For them it will be both a thrill and hugely intimidating—they may be meeting senior executives for the first time—but it is hugely important that they get to tell their stories first hand. There are other valuable side effects. Connecting the boardroom with the frontline and shop floor is a means to improve social capital and trust within the firm. Having the results reported directly engages emotions. It isn't a dry report from a neutral third party, it is narrative from those who have lived it—those with skin in the game—which likely makes a far greater impact on executive decision making. Another benefit is that any results that are counter-intuitive or are at odds with existing models or belief systems can be queried and challenged directly. The frontline staff get to tell their stories and see the impact of engaging senior leaders directly.

The strategy review meeting should consider the new information with respect to existing segmentation. Have any new segments been identified? Do we wish to exploit these segments? What would be needed to do so? What do we believe are the fitness criteria for these new segments? Should any existing segments be retired? If we are retiring a segment, do we need to take any actions? Are we discontinuing a product or a service delivery offering as a result of retiring a segment? Does this mean that our marketing communications need to change? Is there any impact on our channels to market, distribution, or online web and mobile presence as a consequence of retiring a segment?

These questions are rightly the stuff of executives and the forum should be a strategy review. The focus group's purpose is to gather the raw frontline information, while a strategy review presents that information to executives for decision making.

In smaller businesses, it is possible to combine these meetings; customer narrative clustering, fitness criteria judgment, and strategic planning can all happen in the same meeting. At larger scale, it makes sense to separate them, but maintain the connection by inviting real frontline staff to make the presentation to the executives.

And finally, it is a good idea to mix it up, ask different frontline staff to focus groups from month to month. Perhaps a small overlap in attendees will provide some continuity from session to session, which may be valuable. Equally, you should change out the senior executive reporting duties. Let the boardroom see a variety of faces from the front line. Let them experience diversity in who they are hearing from quarter to quarter.

The output from these sessions—the segmentation and the insights on fitness criteria for each segment—can be used as input into existing, well-established marketing and user experience design techniques. Personas[47], described in Chapter 13, Von Moltke's Goal-Directed Balanced Scorecard, can be created for each segment to communicate the market segmentation and the archetypes for target customers to a wider audience across the company. This work would be done by an existing product management or user experience design department. Representatives from this group should be present at the customer narrative clustering focus groups so that they have firsthand knowledge of the segments and the typical customers in each.

Other Inputs for Strategy Discussions

It would be reasonable at this stage to be thinking, "Hang on, this qualitative feedback is all very well but proper strategy discussions need to include quantitative inputs as well." We agree with you! The next chapter looks at using F4P Cards to get a more data-driven approach for better decision making, while Chapter 11, Blind Spots, discusses the deficiencies or gaps in our approach. This book isn't intended as a complete treatise on how to hold the perfect strategy meeting. We are simply saying that customer narrative and observed affinity groups in the narrative should be inputs at your strategy meeting. Much of what you are already doing at strategy meetings will need to stay. On the other hand, it's a valid question to ask, "What will customer narrative clustering obviate?" Ethnographic studies for persona definitions? What else are you doing for which frontline focus groups can give you richer information faster?

Identifying Fitness Criteria for Each Segment

Without the advantage of customer-reported data, described in the next chapter, identifying fitness criteria metrics and their threshold levels is only ever going to be a question of judgment.

---

47. Cooper, Alan. *The Inmates Are Running the Asylum: Why High Tech Products Drive Us Crazy and How to Restore the Sanity.* Macmillan, 1998, Pearson/Sam's 2004.

Recall the Ferrari story from Chapter 3: Customers were unhappy because of long waiting times for delivery of their vehicles. Consequently, some customers canceled their orders and the cancellation rate rose to an unacceptable level. Ferrari discovered that the customer tolerance level was twenty-one months of lead time. Twenty-one months was the threshold for lead time as a fitness criterion. They discovered this by inadvertently driving the metric way beyond the acceptable level, causing customers to cancel orders and raising dissatisfaction with their brand and service delivery. Once recognized, they reacted by gradually increasing production, reducing delivery waiting times until the cancellation rate fell back to its historical residual level. For a business other than Ferrari, this simply isn't a safe-to-fail approach. Nor is it an approach that we can readily recommend. It is an approach used by airlines all the time, however.

Airlines are constantly looking to improve profitability by widening margins. They do this by squeezing costs and looking for ways of providing the same service level at lower costs—or so they think! For example, they reduce leg room by an inch and make seats with thinner backs and cushions so they can pack more rows of seats into the plane. Or they reduce the armrests to pack ten seats abreast instead of nine. The airplane now has 15 percent more passengers competing for the same overhead bin space and the same number of toilets. Air Canada has done all of these with their Boeing 777s, hoping you won't notice or won't mind. Who remembers when international business class flights featured three choices of red wine and three of white with meals? It wasn't so long ago. And then there were only two of each. Some airlines experimented in their business class cabins with the simpler "red or white?" choice that is associated with economy class. They repeat this process across all classes of service with all aspects of the service. They are constantly making changes to reduce costs and lower the quality of service while hoping that customers won't notice, won't mind, or even if they do, they won't switch, perhaps because they have little choice—some mature markets are so consolidated that there isn't enough competition on certain routes to adequately protect consumers and provide the best possible service levels.

For airlines, it is dangerous to practice this constant war with their customers, reducing service levels again and again, and raising customer dissatisfaction while playing this game of chicken, hoping that the customer won't blink and switch their business. It leaves them open to disruptive innovation from competitors. At the time of writing it is ten years since Virgin America began operations. Virgin America, founded by a consortium that included Richard Branson's Virgin Group, followed the tried-and-tested approach of other Virgin brands—enter a market when all the incumbent players are doing it badly.

In 2002 Virgin Mobile entered the US market for mobile phone service on a similar premise. When businesses are failing to satisfy customers and are viewed as marginally fit-for-purpose, they leave themselves vulnerable to an insurgent that understands the customer better. Virgin Mobile USA initially targeted teenagers with a prepaid service. By designing a service that offered a solution uniquely tailored to teenage kids, Virgin could take market share that incumbent mobile phone network companies were underserving or ignoring.

Similarly, Virgin America introduced several innovations aimed at superior customer service, one of which was that food is served on a tray delivered to each seat regardless of class of service. Virgin America's flight attendants never push trolleys down the aisle. Blocking the aisle with food and drink trolleys is a dissatisfier because it blocks access to the toilets for long periods of a flight. Virgin was installing superior entertainment systems in the back of each headrest, with touchscreens and credit card swiping equipment so that travelers could purchase premium entertainment. Why not simply add the menu to the entertainment system and let travelers order their food from the convenience of their seat? This is the type of genius level customer intimacy that enables Virgin Group companies to disrupt established markets again and again. Virgin America was positioning itself as a full-service airline, initially operating on the West Coast of the United States and as a feeder service for their Virgin Atlantic long-haul services to Europe. Their primary competition in the region was United Airlines, though Alaska, Hawaiian, and American all have a strong presence in California. Let's consider for a moment how Virgin America's competitors have been behaving.

At the time of writing, United Airlines has been severely degrading service over a long period of years, partly by incentivizing staff to save money at every opportunity. This can lead to catastrophic failures and a loss of consumer confidence, which can do significant damage to a brand. On April 13, 2017, Dr. David Dao was dragged off United flight 3411 to make room for a member of United's staff who was "positioning" for work the following day. It took a couple of days for video of the incident to go viral on the Internet and for the story to be widely reported. However, on the following Monday, United's stock value dropped by over eight billion US dollars. Only then did the company take action! Throughout 2017, news feeds have been filled with stories of bad customer service on United Airlines. It remains to be seen how badly their poor reputation will affect their economic performance.

For your authors, United isn't much of a problem. David lives in Seattle and mostly flies with Alaska Airlines and OneWorld partner airlines such as British Airways. David has asked his travel agent never to quote him a United fare again. For David, United Airlines no longer exists! Alexei's home airport is Toronto and he flies with Air Canada a great deal. Air Canada is part of the Star Alliance, the largest member of which is United Airlines. However, many United destinations in North America are already served by direct Air Canada flights, many of which are code shares implemented using Air Canada equipment and staff, so he uses United infrequently.

What has been driving United's behavior is a constant drive to save costs. The metrics and staff incentives they have in place are designed to minimize costs at the inconvenience of customers. On July 5, 2017, United had to apologize to Shirley Yamauchi, a teacher from Hawaii, because they had given away a seat she had purchased for her 27-month-old toddler on a flight from Hawaii to Houston, to a stand by passenger. They had sold the seat twice, assuming that the toddler could be repositioned as a lap child. Yamauchi had paid $1,000 for her toddler's seat and yet United made her carry the child on her lap for almost eight hours. Some member of staff was clearly incentivized to focus on this extra revenue from an additional passenger. It cost United yet another news cycle of bad publicity, not to mention refunding the price of the child's seat. How many other young parents empathize with Ms. Yamauchi, a schoolteacher, and will think twice about flying United when they next have to travel with their children? Throughout 2017 this steady stream of news stories has shown us that, for many customers, United Airlines really isn't fit-for-purpose! Making your service worse until customers complain or switch to alternatives isn't a recommended method for establishing fitness criteria thresholds.

So, recalling the stories of Ferrari and Tesla from Chapter 3, why can these companies get away with it when we aren't recommending it as safe for you to try?

Ferrari's brand is incredibly strong and, for true Ferrari fans, there simply is no equivalent alternative product. Also, Ferrari buyers aren't posting their dissatisfaction on social media channels such as Twitter. There is no Slack channel for disgruntled and impatient Ferrari buyers. Ferrari can lower service delivery to an unacceptable level and get away with it for a while. Tesla's brand is also very strong: their cars are incredible, and for Tesla buyers there also is no equivalent alternative product. Tesla can unveil a car, take lots of orders, build the factory while customers wait, and that is still acceptable. Almost certainly your brand isn't so strong and your product or service isn't so iconic as Ferrari's or Tesla's. For the rest of us, lowering service levels to the point where customers complain or switch simply isn't a safe strategy. It may even be a catastrophic strategy and hence we can't recommend it.

Taking Action, Observing Results

What if you believe you are overserving a market segment and you wish to reduce service levels?

Reducing Service to an Overserved Market

First, what leads you to believe that you are overserving it? Probably because you aren't hearing any complaints. If all of your customers are always happy, it is likely you are over-shooting and you could trim your product specification, service design, or service delivery levels, and thereby reduce your costs, increase your margins, and maintain your current revenues and market share. So how do you go about reducing service levels for a market segment if you believe you are overserving it?

The answer is to use judgment from the sample set of available narratives. If you believe you are overserving a market and want to reduce service levels, create a controlled experiment, perhaps in one branch or geographical market, for a fixed period. Reduce the service level or product specification and test-market your proposed change before rolling it out to an entire segment or to your global customer base.

David has used this approach when pricing his events. If some people aren't complaining, usually via social media, that an event is "too expensive" and they "won't pay," the price is probably too low. Many attendees of Lean Kanban conferences report that the events are of exceptionally high quality and that the content and access to speakers is incredibly valuable. Many happy attendees report that they believe the events are excellent value for money and probably underpriced. And yet there is residual rhetoric on the Internet about the prices being too high. If this were not present, prices would almost certainly be too low. If there are no complaints, you are overserving your market. Learn to develop a thick skin and embrace a residual level of complaining from non-customers while celebrating the positive feedback from your happy customers.

Improving Service to an Underserved Market

The other problem is harder. What if you are confident you are underserving your market—you have anecdotal reports that paying customers are unhappy or subscribers are churning off your service or going dormant. What is the right service level? What is the right threshold? How can you establish it? Does it become an internal metric, a KPI, intended to drive improvements and modify employee behavior? Or must it be implemented in your product or service design, specification, or operational capability? Can any change be easily rolled back? Or is a change that, were it not to work, were it not to satisfy customers, it will simply have increased your costs—whether variable or fixed?

It turns out that we can learn from Ferrari. The way they approached improving service delivery by increasing production to reduce the delivery wait time was iterative and incremental. With month-by-month increased production volume, the delivery waiting times fell. They monitored the cancellation rate and how long a customer had waited prior to cancellation. When the cancellation rate fell to an acceptable level, they then paced production to the new order rate to stabilize the delivery waiting time, or customer lead time, to twenty-one months. As we recall from Chapter 4, the production rate (of cars) is a general health indicator—faster is healthier—the cancellation rate is their improvement driver, and lead time is the customer fitness criteria or key performance indicator. Lead time is what the customer cares about and what determines fitness-for-purpose, while cancellation rate is what Ferrari monitored to determine the fitness criterion threshold. Notice the indirect approach: Ferrari knows there is alignment between the improvement driver—the cancellation rate—and the lead time as the fitness criterion. They know this because they've collected and analyzed reasons for cancellations. If they weren't confident of this alignment, they'd need to monitor customer satisfaction and use it as part of their feedback loop. This would cause additional delay while survey results or narrative from frontline staff was collected and analyzed.

You should improve service levels iteratively and incrementally. Establish an improvement driver metric—something you can measure, ideally quantitatively, on a regular basis. Put in place the instrumentation to get feedback on whether your changes are affecting your improvement driver. Assuming you have confidence that an improvement driver is aligned to a customer fitness criterion, you can use that to establish whether your product specification, service design, or service delivery is at an acceptable level. If you aren't confident of alignment—a direct causal relationship between your improvement driver and your fitness criteria—you will need to continue sampling customer sentiment to know whether you've improved service sufficiently.

You may also want to put in place instrumentation to assess the return on investment of improvements. Can you quantify the value of improved customer satisfaction? That's a tough one to put a monetary value on. You may, for example, be able to correlate an investment to improve fitness-for-purpose with an improved Net Promoter Score (discussed in the next few chapters), and hence, you are more likely to win referral business. Quantitative analysts or operational research analysts should be able to provide a risk-adjusted value to the likelihood of a referral. At the same time, quantifying the costs of improvements should be relatively straightforward. This will enable you to make informed decisions about improvement opportunities. Would you prefer to refresh the training to teach your flight attendants to smile more, and authorize them to serve free drinks, or would you rather reconfigure your aircraft to add a premium economy cabin with two extra inches of legroom for each row of seats? Of course, the costs here aren't always equivalents—the former is a variable cost, an operational expense, while the latter is a fixed cost, a capital expenditure. However, if you believed the impact of either change was similar, you might prefer to spend the money on training and alcoholic beverages rather than refitting the interiors of a hundred aircraft.

Once you've achieved fitness-for-purpose, stop there—at least for the time being. There is no need to overserve a market. Your focus can switch to improving margins without loss of customer satisfaction. Inevitably, competitors or market innovation will change customer expectations and the cycle will repeat; you will once again need to focus on improvements. The tighter you can make your feedback loops, the greater agility you can exhibit as a business, the faster you can sense and respond. This will minimize the negative periods of poor customer satisfaction and maximize the good times when customers love you, your brand, your products, and your services. Managing this cycle, avoiding complacency and hubris, and responding to changing externalities such as fickle shifts in customer tastes and ever rising customer expectations will be fully addressed in the second book of this trilogy, *Built to Last*.

Summary

- Use customer narratives to identify your customer segments by purpose.
- Position your business with respect to different customer segments:
  - Some segments are central to your business. Encourage and grow them.
  - Some are important but you may not be able to acknowledge their existence or advertise or sell directly to them. Apply indirect tactics.
  - Some are worth a neutral stance.
  - Some are not your target segments. Consider switching them off when they become problematic.
- Bring your frontline staff into strategy discussions.
- Identify fitness criteria and thresholds separately for each segment.
- Reducing service levels and hoping customers won't notice is dangerous unless you've got a very strong brand.
- If you're overserving your market, validate this first and then reduce the service levels.
- If you're underserving your market, increasing the service level is a more difficult problem. It will take:
  - A combination of KPI, health, and improvement indicators
  - An iterative and incremental approach
  - Determining the right threshold
  - Deciding where to focus: design, implementation, or service delivery
  - Considering the costs and the ease of rollback

9 Using Surveys and Data

There are times when you simply don't have direct customer access. In Chapter 7 we looked at businesses and business models for which direct consumer access is delegated to a channel partner such as a retailer. There are other times when you'd simply prefer to have more quantitative data or quantitative data as a "second opinion" that validates and amplifies anecdotal reports from your frontline staff. You may be supplying SaaS applications or mobile applications, or you may be in a world where competitive pressure is pushing you to eliminate your front line with automation. In any and all of these cases, you still need to sense the market, to gather information from consumers. Even in our own professional services businesses we've seen the need for quantitative data and a means to sample attitudes from a large percentage of our customers. We've developed a means to survey for that information, which we call Fitness Box Score surveys. These were inspired partly by Net Promoter Score (NPS) surveys, in terms of format, and partly by a major deficiency in NPS surveys. We explore those deficiencies and how our approach compares in Chapter 12, "It's Your Future, Be There!" For now, we'll explain how to use Fitness Box Score and gather quantitative data from your customers about their purpose and their opinion of whether your product or service is fit-for-purpose.

F4P Cards/Surveying Customer Expectations

The Fit-for-Purpose Card, or the F4P Card for short, is a simple tool we've developed for surveying customers' purposes and expectations and getting to know their stories. Figure 9.1 shows the current F4P Card design.

F4P Card

Date: Dec. 12-13   **Name:** _____

Kanban System Design (KMP I) 2-day training class

(to be filled in by the Customer)

(office use only)

Service Request Type

Question 1: Tell us *why* you chose our offering? Select **up to three** reasons or objectives you had when choosing it:

(a) KANBAN AWARENESS / BASICS
(b) PROMPT INTERNAL CONVERSATIONS
(c) REFINE CURRENT PRACTICES

Question 2: For each reason or objective in Question 1, please indicate how fit for purpose you found our service in fulfilling your expectations. Please score each reason or objective separately using the following scale:

	(a)	(b)	(c)
5. My expectations were exceeded	5	5	5
4. My expectations were fully met	4	4	4
3. My expectations were mostly met but a few minor concerns remained	3	3	3
2. Some significant needs were unaddressed	2	2	2
1. I got some value but most of my expectations were unmet	1	1	1
0. I found nothing useful. It was unfit for this purpose	0	0	0

Question 3: Tell us why you gave the score(s) in Question 2.

(a) THOROUGH TREATMENT OF THE TOPIC
(b) GOOD USE OF SUPPORTING STORIES
(c) A VIEW BEYOND THE TEAM

Figure 9.1 F4P Card design

The top section of the F4P Card identifies the customer and the service request or work item they consumed. Therefore, what the customer reports to us on this card can be traced to a specific item or instance of service delivery.

In Question 1, the customer can give us up to three statements of purpose for why they chose to bring their business to us.

Question 2 is framed to steer customers away from rating or judging our product against some abstract or unstated criteria. Instead, they connect their assessment with the specific purposes they themselves reported in Question 1.

Question 3 provides the space to capture customers' narratives and gives customers an opportunity to explain their assessment and tell us about their expectations. Such explanations are factual because they compare the customers' stated expectations against what they have already purchased and received from us.

The questions asked on the F4P Card can be customized for certain types of products and services. In the management training business, the generic, "Please tell us why you chose our product or service" may become, "What was your purpose in signing up for this training class?" or, at a conference, "What reason or objective did you have in mind when deciding to attend this event?" An enterprise service producing software features might use a question such as, "What was the original purpose of the feature?" A help desk might ask, "What was the purpose of your service request?" and so on. Question 2 can be rephrased accordingly.

The F4P Card layout is simple and compact enough to fit on a small piece of paper (5.5 by 8.5 inches or A5) handed to the customer at the delivery time. Figure 9.1 shows an F4P Card given regularly to participants of Kanban training classes.

When the delivery volume is large, F4P Cards can be implemented electronically using available forms software such as Google Docs or surveying applications. As long as the software supports simple text input fields and multiple-choice questions, it would be fit-for-[such]-purpose. The form can then fit on a web page or a mobile application screen

Even though the F4P Card design is simple, we had to make several important design choices and then test those choices one by one.

There are several reasons why the F4P Card asks certain questions and why it presents those questions to customers in a certain way and gives them certain choices of answers. There are subtleties to the simple design. Understanding such subtleties is important for practitioners to use F4P Cards effectively. It may also be important for maintaining the quality of translations of the F4P Cards, customizing them for different types of products, and for the future innovations that will be made to the F4P Card. Let's walk through them.

Question 1 limits the number of possible purposes the customers can report to three. We tried different choices here and learned that the average number of purposes per customer is usually around two. The limit of three focuses the customers on the reasons and objectives that matter the most to them. At the same time, it doesn't force them to make the difficult choice of reporting only the single most important reason or objective.

The way we present the multiple-choice Question 2 strongly links the customer's answer to their original purpose. We don't ask how likely they are to recommend our product or service to their friends or colleagues. We don't ask the customer to speculate about their future behavior; instead we ask them to report existing facts based on their experience. They can report factually how they experience our product or service. We don't ask them to speculate on how another customer might judge its appeal.

For example, participants in Alexei's quantitative project forecasting workshop—a class designed to teach mathematical methods for planning project schedules and setting expectations around delivery dates—reported that they took the workshop because they wanted pragmatic guidance on the topic and had a high comfort level with the math involved. But most of their friends and colleagues (who weren't in the workshop) didn't share this professional interest and weren't the workshop's target audience, so they said, "While I personally find this workshop very useful, I wouldn't recommend it to most of my colleagues."

These narratives highlight one of the issues with the well-established Net Promoter Score method, which we discuss in greater detail in Chapter 11, Blind Spots.

The six choices in Question 2 are intentional, too. Psychology studies[48] have shown that it's difficult for people to give meaningful answers to multiple-choice questions involving too many options. Each of the six levels is also explicitly defined, such as meeting or exceeding expectations or falling short of those expectations in some way. This makes the answer scale factual and free of calibration errors common in questions such as, "Rate this on a scale from 1 to 10": one person's 3 may be another's 5.

The free-form Question 3 is about serendipity. Customers have an opportunity to tell the stories that multiple-choice surveys cannot capture. They can tell us about the purpose they had in mind when they chose our product or aspects of their experience with our product that we didn't necessarily think about. Their answers can also help us learn about their satisfaction criteria and the threshold values of those criteria, as well as help us discover previously unimagined purposes or uses for our product or service. When customers adopt and use a product for a purpose the designer didn't intend, this is known as "exaptation."

Exaptation is a concept in evolutionary biology that refers to an aspect of the design of a creature that is adapted for a secondary use for which it wasn't originally intended. For example, feathers initially evolved to regulate temperature, then later exapted into display mechanisms for mating rituals, and eventually exapted again to become a means of providing both thrust and lift for flight. Exaptation exists for products and services, too. One famous example is how Western washing-machine manufacturers discovered that their top-loading machines were being modified in India so they could work as mixing machines for lassi yoghurt drinks in restaurants. This exaptation wasn't discovered until field service engineers—note that they are frontline, customer-facing staff—started to report this bizarre, unexpected customer behavior. It took years for the manufacturers to recognize that they'd discovered a whole new market segment—an entirely different purpose—for washing machines. Washing machines feature in another famous exaptation—the story of how modern bicycles spin on sealed bearings.

---

48. Such as Bousfield and Bousfield, 1956, in which they showed that, without mature analysis skills and a well-defined taxonomy, participants struggle to organize unstructured information into greater than six sets.

In 1992 eccentric Scottish racing cyclist Graeme Obree had designs on breaking the world record for the longest distance traveled in one hour. Obree understood that both aerodynamics and friction are the enemy of the race cyclist. While designing his own bicycle, known as "Old Faithful," he repurposed the bearing from an old washing machine for use as the bottom bracket. He was looking for minimal friction while turning the pedals. Obree broke the long-standing one-hour record held for nine years by Francisco Moser, at Hamar in Norway, on the sixteenth of July 1993, during the middle of the Tour de France. He caught a lot of attention. He went on to break the record again in 1994, and win gold in the world championships at the 4,000 meter pursuit, breaking the world record for that distance as well. While Obree had trouble with the Union Cycliste Internationale (UCI) banning his bicycles and riding positions, his bottom bracket innovation was standard on most high-quality road- and mountain-bike racing machines by 1997. In this example, bicycle manufacturers didn't need feedback from frontline staff; Obree's achievements were widely reported in the cycling press. His story was later portrayed in the movie *The Flying Scotsman*, with Jonny Lee Miller, best known today for his role as Sherlock in the TV show *Elementary*, playing Obree.

When you don't have the benefit of massive press coverage of innovation or unconventional approaches to exceptional performance, the F4P Cards should enable product designers and service providers to discover customer exaptation of their products or services so much sooner than they otherwise would. This should enable firms to respond to new market segments quickly, exploit them to the fullest, and establish a defensible position. Customers in these niches are likely to become extremely loyal. People respond emotionally to the recognition of their needs and the empathy that the producer or provider has shown for them.

What we call F4P Cards is also a choice. We've learned to avoid the words "survey" and "feedback," as they can make our customers feel they're about to fill out yet another customer satisfaction survey. The term "F4P Card" is more neutral. When presenting F4P Cards to customers, we prefer language like this: "Would you please fill out this small card? This will help us make our products better tuned to our customers' needs."

Fitness Box Score and Scoring Techniques

Fitness Box Score (sometimes called the F4P Box Score) is a compact summary of a representative sample of F4P Cards, collected from the customers of the same product or service.

We use the term "box score" to highlight the analogy with American baseball box scores—compact sets of numbers that describe a baseball game with more detail and nuance than the game's final score alone can tell.

Here is an example of a compact F4P Box Score:

74/23/3 (35) 16/20

Here is how to read the box score, starting on the right side:

20: We've delivered this product or service 20 times and asked our customers to fill out and return F4P Cards.

16: Out of the 20 customers, 16 filled out F4P Cards and returned them to us.

35: The 16 customers reported a total of 35 purposes for choosing our product (averaging 2.2 purposes per customer).

74: Of the 35 reported purposes, the customers scored 74 percent of them (26 out of 35) as 4 or 5 in Question 2—meeting or exceeding their expectations.

23: Of the same 35 reported purposes, the customers scored 23 percent of them (8 out of 35) as 3. We consider this a neutral or mediocre rating—expectations mostly met, but with some reservations.

3: Of the same 35 reported purposes, there was one case (1 of 35 is 3 percent) for which the customer gave us an unsatisfactory rating of 2, 1, or 0—significant gaps between customer expectations and what they received.

There may be a few alternative ways to calculate the F4P Box Score. For example, instead of calculating the percentages of the reported purposes (rated positive, neutral, or negative), we could have calculated the percentages of customers who rated us positive, neutral, or negative. If a customer reported multiple purposes and gave them different ratings, we'd have to decide if we should choose (a) the highest,

(b) the lowest, or (c) count the customer as partly positive, negative, or neutral. Yet another method (d) could be to assign the purposes some weight when averaging them to maintain equal weighting of customers who may be reporting different numbers of purposes.

Applying these four alternative methods to the above example, the 74/23/3 score would turn into:

94/6/0
62/31/6
78/19/3
80/18/2

As you can see, counting the highest or the lowest rating from each customer can really skew the results, while the other, more reasonable methods produce similar box score numbers. Our recommendation is not to sweat the small differences between these methods; simply pick one method you're comfortable with and stick with it. In our practice, calculating the percentages of purposes rated positive, neutral, or negative proved the simplest. The focus should be not on the math, but on understanding market segmentation by purpose, the actionable feedback, and our decisions about the strategy and positioning of the product.

If we assume that a purpose adequately fulfilled is a strong proxy for customer satisfaction, then reporting the F4P Box Score based on purposes is a more useful and actionable metric than reporting it based on just raw numbers of customers. The latter would give us a popularity rating—a vanity metric—whereas the former tells us how well our strategy is working and whether we need to do something about it.

Identifying Segments Based on Customers' Purpose

After calculating the F4P Box Score, we can do further analysis by organizing the same or similar purposes reported by different customers into clusters, give each cluster a name, and calculate the box score separately for each cluster. This tells us specifically how well we are doing in each segment.

The true value of reporting scores related to purposes is that the score directly relates to market segments that are being served well or those that are slightly or highly underserved. The box score also tells us about the size of each segment—how many customers share its purpose. Given our strategy, we can then assess how well we are doing against that strategy—are we good at what we set out to do? Are we serving customers appropriately? We can then do further analysis to identify specific segments that may need attention. We may try to improve our capability and performance in a given segment or we may decide we would rather switch it off by better communicating our intended target markets and appropriateness of our product or service. So reporting based on market segmentation—customers' purpose—seems to make the most sense to us. Weighing the value of given segments based on size or value can be evaluated separately.

The previous F4P Box Score example (74/23/3 (35) 16/20) was taken from Alexei's management training class. There were 20 people in the class; 16 of them returned their F4P Cards, reporting 35 purposes. These 35 purposes clustered neatly into 6 affinity groups, that is, many of the purposes were sufficiently similar that we need to track only 6 purposes. The actual clusters identified are as follows:

Cluster 1: Learning. F4P Box Score: 94/6/0 (18). The customers in this cluster reported their purpose for deciding to enroll in the class as "learning, understanding, or applying the management method being taught." They used words and phrases such as these: "learn it," "understand it better," "apply it," or "my project uses this method, therefore I need appropriate training." These people's choices were motivated by their desires and needs to learn a new method and show competency in their peer group. Their purpose statements show this motivation quite clearly.

Cluster 2: Professional Development. F4P Box Score: 67/33/0 (6). The customers in this cluster were looking for professional development opportunities in general—our offering was available to them, so they signed up. They described their purpose using words like "personal growth," "further training in the field" and "this training was available."

Cluster 3: Certification. F4P Box Score: 100/0/0 (1). One customer admitted her purpose for taking our training class was making progress toward a professional credential to put on her résumé (and this customer's purpose was satisfied). There is some overlap with Cluster 2. However, we offer certified training, which is a controlled market space with a high barrier to entry—trainers must be qualified and licensed to offer the certified training. Cluster 2 represents a segment for which alternative (perhaps inferior) offerings exist. This customer segment is tiny for now, but has a high value to our organization. We'd like to grow this segment because of the barrier to entry and the stickiness customers have to the brand. They cannot get certified training in this field anywhere else. Hence, there is value in identifying and tracking this segment. We can watch it over time and monitor whether it is growing. If we didn't care about the business benefit and value this segment can bring, we could simply bundle it with Cluster 2.

Cluster 4: Best Practices. F4P Box Score: 67/33/0 (3). All customers in this cluster used the words "best practice" when describing their purpose for choosing the training class. This doesn't align well with what we teach. Our training materials and instructional design aren't about best practices, they're rather about pragmatic guidance, decision framework, and comprehending that there are choices and consequences. Our customers—who manage to deliver something to their own customers in their own business—are trained to think in their own context and make their own choices. The people in this cluster are choosing our product looking for something that we don't sell. Therefore, this is quite a fragile segment. We can expect it to decline over time, or we can expect its continued existence to lead to poor reviews and bad word of mouth about our brand. We choose to track the Best Practices segment separately from other learners because it's a segment we may wish to switch off in the future.

Cluster 5: Recommendation. F4P Box Score: 50/50/0 (2). These customers reported their colleagues' recommendations, rather than their own motivation of some sort, for why they chose our product. In other words, they had time and money to spend and trusted their colleague's advice on how to do that. It may be worthwhile to track these customers as a separate cluster even though it is too small for now to draw meaningful conclusions from it. It is at least useful to know what percentage of our business results from actual recommendations from earlier customers.

Cluster 6: Dysfunction. F4P Box Score: 20/60/20 (5). These customers stated their purpose in various ways, but they were all incoherent somehow. For example, taking a foundation-level, no-prerequisites class "to increase my leadership" in the subject matter. We might view this segment as chaotic or random. It's entirely fragile and we shouldn't rely on it in our future plans, nor can we take any specific actions to reinforce this segment. We should monitor it to ensure this segment never becomes too large and so we don't become dependent on its revenues. Any action with respect to this segment is of low priority at this time.

Combining the compact F4P Box Score with the scores for each cluster gives us the full F4P Box Score, shown in Figure 9.2.

Customer segment by purpose	+	0	−	#	
1. Learning	94	6	0	18	
2. Professional Development	67	33	0	6	
3. Certification	100	0	0	1	
4. Best Practices	67	33	0	3	
5. Recommendation	50	50	0	2	
6. Dysfunction	20	60	20	5	
TOTAL	74	23	3	35	(16/20)

Figure 9.2 Full F4P Box Score

Marketing personas can be developed for the two or three most populous clusters. A diverse cluster, such as "Learners" in this example, may require more than one persona.

Now, let's consider interpreting F4P Box Scores, overall and by cluster, discovering insights and turning them into action.

Interpreting Results and Taking Action

So, we have compiled our F4P Box Scores and discovered our customer segments by clustering the purpose statements reported by our customers. Now we want to interpret this information to understand our purpose-defined market segments: what fitness criteria matter to each segment, how fit our product is with respect to these criteria, and what actions we should take with respect to the whole market or any individual segment.

Choosing our actions well requires us to clearly understand our go-to-market strategy. This includes knowing who is—and who isn't—our target customer. Suppose a particular customer segment may or may not be our target. We may also be serving this segment currently in some satisfactory or unsatisfactory ways. This can lead to several different situations, summarized in Figure 9.3.

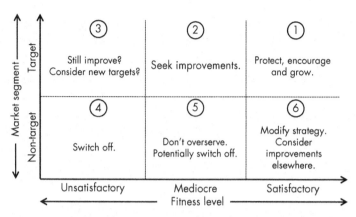

Figure 9.3 From F4P Cards to taking action

First, if the customer segment is our target and our product is fit for this segment, we want to keep it that way. Our potential actions might include monitoring our service delivery process to ensure continued satisfaction, avoiding actions that might put it at risk, helping our satisfied customers spread the word about our product and thus grow the market, creating new products to win our loyal, satisfied customers' repeat business, and so on.

Second, if the customer segment is our target but our product or service is mediocre or unsatisfactory, we need to find ways to improve the product or service to close the gap with customer expectations. Our potential actions may seek to improve our product's design, implementation, or service delivery. Customer narratives, found in their answers to Question 3, can provide clues to those expectations and how our product fell short of them.

Third, if our product is largely dissatisfactory for our target segment, we might have a significant gap between our strategy and our capability. We may need a serious conversation about whether we've even got the right strategy for our business.

Fourth and fifth, if our product is mediocre or unsatisfactory, but the market segment isn't our target, it's a very different situation. We have somehow attracted "wrong" customers to our product and they're unhappy and complaining. Our potential action might be to change our marketing to switch off the undesired customer segment. It might also be important not to cater to this segment, as such "improvement" can switch off another customer segment that is our actual target.

At the origin of the McDonald's hamburger chain, in its first location in San Bernardino, California, when the business was still owned and operated by the McDonald brothers, they made specific choices to focus on families, providing a family-oriented menu and restaurant. They specifically didn't want their restaurants to be hangouts for potentially delinquent teenagers and college kids. That second segment would have had the effect of switching off the first, so it was important to dissuade the older teens and college kids by creating a concept, a menu, and an environment that discouraged them.

David has used simple actions like these in his own business, such as increasing the price of some events so as to turn off segments (attendees) who were attracted to his conferences for the wrong reasons and then dissatisfied that they didn't get the experience they expected. He knew the strategy was working when in the following year some people from those segments complained via social media that the price of that year's conference was too high and they wouldn't be attending. It isn't always as easy as tuning prices to switch off segments, but this illustrates that often the action required can be as simple as a policy change.

Notice the contrast between these situations: Improvement actions can be diametrically opposite, such as changing prices or changing marketing communications to dissuade a segment; improving a delivery capability or changing a specification or set of product features; or changing either our delivery mechanism or our service approach. Choosing between these alternative actions is impossible without understanding our own strategy.

The sixth scenario shows that if the product is fit, but the market segment isn't our target, our set of potential options is still different. We may choose to take such customers to put the money in the bank and then switch them off in the future. We might also modify our strategy to include the newly discovered segment as a target—we might have discovered a new, unexpected purpose such as our washing machines are being used as yoghurt mixers.

Let's summarize the types of improvement actions we can potentially take:

- Improve the design, implementation, or delivery of our product or service because one of our target market segments is currently dissatisfied.

- Decrease our levels of service to the overserved segments.
- Change our go-to-market strategy to get more happy, desired, "right" customers and avoid "wrong" customers.
- Take no action because our customers are satisfied and the dissatisfied customers are not our target customers. Sometimes inaction is the most appropriate action!

Let's now consider the management training class example started earlier in this chapter and translate the information such as the F4P Box Score and segmentation data into some actions the managers might take to make the product fitter.

The first segment, Learners, is the largest, comprising slightly more than half of this training group. Being in the management training business, this is certainly our target market segment. We currently serve it well (94/6/0) and want to keep it that way. To perfect our delivery to this segment, we ought to pay attention to the narrative provided by the customer who found it mediocre. This individual came to the class for the right reasons, but expected to receive guidance on localized, team-level improvements. However, the key point of the training was about leading whole-organization, rather than local, improvement initiatives. This person couldn't reconcile, by the end of the class, the difference between what she thought the training would be and what it actually was, and she left the class somewhat dissatisfied. One of the trainers suggested sending the trainees a very condensed summary of the training material ahead of the class to help close such gaps. Notice that the improvement action for this segment is all about tweaking or improving the delivery.

Related issues seen in other surveys include requests for printed material. Part of David's firm's strategy is to create classes in which attendees are paying attention and are highly present in the moment. Providing printed materials that allow students to become distracted and browse through later sections whilst not paying attention to the current section is against company policy. It isn't the atmosphere and environment David wants to create in his training classes. We discovered that setting expectations beforehand can be enough to mitigate dissatisfaction. Again, it is a simple policy change implemented with minor tweaks to the training material—reminding trainers to set the expectation that printed materials aren't provided during class and that electronic materials are made available at the end of the class. Meanwhile, students are free to take notes by whatever means they find appropriate.

The Professional Development market segment is still served reasonably well (67/33/0), but not as well as the Learning cluster. Also, none of the Professional Development customers found that the class exceeded their expectations. This market segment is somewhat accidental for us. We may choose to take them as our customers and maintain a certain level of service so that they are not dissatisfied. We will prioritize improvements of our fitness for the Learners' segment over the needs of this Professional Development segment. We may also choose not to encourage this segment with discounts or invest in promotions. These choices, of course, rest on one important assumption: that our business's strategy includes helping people change the world of work through better management and not simply to cynically harvest a share of corporate professional development budgets. Our own sense of purpose is an important part of our strategy and a vital filter on our decision making when choosing how to make changes aimed at improving customer satisfaction.

The Certification segment—management trainees taking classes for the sake of collecting a badge of completion—isn't our target segment. This segment doesn't align with our own purpose. People collecting certifications aren't actually changing the world of work by implementing better management methods. Instead they live in the existing environment but use their badge collection as a means of boosting their self-esteem, perhaps as an antidote to survive in a dysfunctional and unfulfilling environment. This badge collecting segment is tiny right now (only one customer in 20, fully satisfied), but it bears watching. If it starts to grow, we may choose to discourage it, for example, by raising the certification bar. Or we can choose to accept it as a strong source of revenue that we put to good use elsewhere in some line of business that better aligns with our own purpose. If our brand was viewed as a "certificate factory," would that put off our most desirable customer segments, the way delinquent teenagers hanging out at McDonald's in San Bernardino in the 1950s did? If so, then we'd want to switch off the "badge collector" segment.

Among Alexei's training offerings are two kinds of two-day classes, leading to a certain professional credential for the students who complete both. Both classes are often offered in the same city during the same week. Many students like to take the first class and then take several months to apply what they learned before taking the more advanced class at the next opportunity. Some students prefer to take the classes back to back. Alexei's firm provides options to purchase registration for each class individually or both together. It sets the price of the four-day program equal to the total cost of the two classes purchased individually. This is done consciously, in order not to encourage the "badge collector" segment, which consists almost entirely of people who live and work in the city where the class is offered. Offering a bundle discount would have the effect of encouraging the less valuable Certification segment while risking turning off the more valuable Learner segment. Taking time off between the classes, which many Learners prefer, would appear to be more expensive. Some Learners would then feel pressured to sign up for the back-to-back classes even if they lacked experience and weren't ready for the more advanced class. Finally, to implement the discount practically, the prices of the individual classes would have to be raised a bit, potentially switching off some cost-conscious Learners.

The situation is different in David's training center in Seattle, where most participants fly in from across North America and the local badge collector segment just doesn't exist. A bundle discount for taking four or five days of training in the same week helps out-of-town Learners, who already are making a big investment in their professional education, including significant travel costs.

The Best Practices segment (67/33/0) is close to the Learners, but smaller and somewhat less satisfied with our product. Similar to the Learner who gave us a mediocre rating, some Best Practices customers struggle with the gap between their notion of training and what they actually get. We could take an approach like the delivery tweak we identified previously for the Learners segment and better communicate the purpose of our management training ahead of the class.

The Dysfunctional segment is the one we want to switch off. The segmented F4P Box Scores help us see a pattern: customers whose purpose is clear—such as learn, understand, or apply our management methods—tend to be more satisfied. Customers seeking best practices or the simple need to spend their professional development budgets are satisfied a bit less. Customers whose reasons or objectives aren't even coherent are the least satisfied. We can discourage the Dysfunctional segment through our marketing communication by making our product less appealing to them, or through pricing. However, the incoherent segment often do not read marketing communications with intent to understand and internalize the implications, so marketing communications often fail to switch these people off. Price can be highly effective, but there is a danger that raising or lowering prices will coincidentally switch off another segment that we wish to nurture. Because of this, price changes must be considered carefully and their impact assessed across all segments.

What we have found to work very effectively for this Dysfunctional, incoherent segment is to make a friendly contact when the client first registers for a training class. This method has been highly effective at small scale but would be problematic to replicate at large scale for consumer products. One of our marketing managers contacts our trainees before the class, sometimes only if there is reason to be suspicious based on company name, location, job title, or some other information that isn't typical of our clientele. The point of the call or email is to learn about the client's purpose in purchasing from us. And if the purpose appears incoherent or is not well matched to our target segments, we could potentially dissuade that client from taking the class, with which they most likely would be dissatisfied. When there aren't too many individual customers for each member of our frontline staff, this approach is workable and can improve satisfaction and F4P Box Score results. Otherwise, if such customers still show up in our training classes, it is important to recognize them, teach to the satisfaction of our core audience, and not let the non-target audience get in the way. As part of our train-the-trainer program, we educate our trainers to cope with potentially disruptive or incoherent attendees who have unfortunately wandered into our classroom for the wrong reasons.

Optimizing F4P Cards in Mature Markets

David's home lies just outside the Dungeness Recreation Area, also known as the Voice of America Park in Clallam County, Washington. Occupying 216 acres, the park features hiking and horse-riding trails through diverse habitats that include wetlands, forest, meadows, and marshes, as well as affording some spectacular views from the sand bluffs (cliffs) above the Straits of San Juan de Fuca at Dungeness. The park, which features a popular campground with camping sites close to the ocean, is operated by Clallam County. After about a two-mile hike from the entrance, the jurisdiction changes to the Dungeness National Wildlife Refuge, primarily a bird sanctuary operated by the US National Park Service. A trail runs for a mile down through the forest to the Dungeness Spit, a five-mile-long promontory that extends north and east into the Straits, a thin strip of land formed by the combined forces of freezing, wind, and tidal erosion pushing sand off the bluffs and down the coast. A five-mile hike along the rocky beach, scrambling over driftwood logs, brings you to the New Dungeness Lighthouse. On a clear day, the Spit area affords beautiful views: majestic Mt. Baker to the northeast, always snow-capped, even in summer; northwest across the Straits to the city of Victoria and Vancouver Island; and westward toward the town of Port Angeles with Mount Angeles and Klahane Ridge sitting 6,000 feet above it. Entrance to the Wildlife Refuge costs three dollars per household, or an annual pass can be purchased at the office for twelve dollars. Regardless of whether the visitor has an annual pass, a form must be filled out. In recent years, the entrance is patrolled by a small army of volunteers, each day three or four of them ensuring that visitors fill out the forms and pay their fees. The form is printed on an envelope, which must be filled out with a pen and then delivered through a slot in a box. It's pretty primitive technology.

The form asks for name, city/state/country of residence, type of pass or cash paid, and the number of any annual pass, if applicable. It takes only a few seconds to fill out, but how useful would it be for the Park Service if the form had just one more question, as shown in Figure 9.4.

Purpose of your visit (check all applicable)

☐ Exercise / regular walk
☐ Beach Recreation
☐ Sightseeing
☐ Photography
☐ Bird Watching / Nature
☐ Lighthouse Hike
☐ Other (please specify) —————————————

Figure 9.4 Checkboxes for Purpose

In this example, the six most popular purposes for visiting the Dungeness National Wildlife Refuge are well known. There is no new information in learning these purposes from visitors, although the numbers pursuing each purpose may assist in investment decisions and portfolio management problems. The new information is in the "Other (please specify) _____" section. This is the one to monitor for changes in usage and behavior.

For mature markets with well-understood, popular reasons for consumer selection, it makes sense to provide the respondent with an enumerated set of choices. This minimizes the need for narrative clustering and makes simple analysis easier, faster, and cheaper.

Meanwhile, the Park Service has the benefit of their small army of local volunteers who stand by the entrance each day and chat up the visitors, who need help filling out the forms and paying the fees. For the National Park Service, managing a facility like Dungeness National Wildlife Refuge, both options are available to them—the techniques from Chapters 8 and 9 will help them understand their visitors' purposes.

In this example, the Park Service isn't trying to establish fitness-for-purpose—they aren't a business—their job is to preserve habitat for wildlife and not to pander to tourists looking to enjoy the beach. However, the Park Service is funded by taxpayers, and understanding the purposes the public have when visiting will help optimize spending decisions and focus their budget where it is most needed.

Summary

- F4P Cards are a simple tool to capture customer purposes, level of fitness of the given product or service for each of those purposes, and customer narratives explaining the reported fitness levels.

- The F4P Card design shows some attention to implementation. The parts of the F4P Card layout have been thought out and tested to make the card fit-for-[its own]-purpose.

- Fitness Box Score (or F4P Box Score) is a compact summary of a representative sample of F4P Cards, showing details such as the percentage of purposes that were served in satisfactory, mediocre, and unsatisfactory fashion, the total number of customers, and the purposes reported in the sample.

- F4P assessments can be clustered by purpose to understand how fit-for-purpose the product or service was for any given customer segment.

- Depending on whether the customer segment (1) is or (2) is not our target, and whether the service is (1) satisfactory, (2) mediocre, or (3) unsatisfactory, we can take at least six different actions in response to the F4P data.

- F4P Box Score is not a single number. There is no single metric anymore, so you won't be driven to maximizing at all costs, including chasing wrong customers and overserving happy customers beyond their real fitness thresholds.

- For mature markets where common purposes are known, it makes sense to optimize the F4P Cards by including an enumerated set of options with check boxes while leaving the option for a narrative to capture "other" insufficiently common reasons for consumer selection.

10 It's Not Luck!

Exploiting Market Opportunities

"CAN WE DESIGN A SERVICE TO WIN Neeta's other pizza purchasing business?" It's a valid question! If you recall in Chapter 2 Neeta buys pizza for her office from Zak's Artisan Pie & Crust while for home delivery for her children she uses Westside Pizza. What if we were to learn that we don't have all of Neeta's pizza business, how might we design a service such that Neeta selects us every time?

Westside Gets Lucky!

In Chapter 6, Neeta participated in her local community 5K run and accidentally discovered that Westside Pizza had some more sophisticated recipes. The spicy fajita chicken and bacon with ranch sauce was such a contrast from the lukewarm cheese pizza the previous Friday evening! Back at the office on Monday, Neeta decided to check out their website. Sure enough, there it was, the new Gourmet Menu—exotic toppings, spicy sauces, and even some vegan offerings without cheese. And while they started as a suburban strip-mall chain, they now have a downtown restaurant recently opened in one of Toronto's underground shopping malls not so far from her office. "I wonder if they would be faster at delivery than Zak's?" Neeta thinks to herself, storing that away in her memory. "The monthly service delivery review meeting is coming up at the end of this week. We'll be catering that meeting and we have the new website release to celebrate. I'll mention it to Christine," the office manager, "perhaps we can give the new Westside gourmet menu a try."

From a marketing perspective, there is nothing new here. Westside broadened its offering. They promoted it at a local event. An existing customer learned about their new menu through a combination of a promotional event and later checking details via their website. In this case, the customer did the discovery. Westside had speculated that there might be a market for a gourmet menu on the basis that competitors were already doing it. It worked, at least in Neeta's case. This form of experimentation has a potentially high failure rate because Westside had no better reason to try the new menu other than "other restaurants are doing it, we should follow their lead." This is relatively low-maturity speculation. It's hit or miss. It's luck!

Now let's consider how understanding your customer's purpose might make you smarter and enable customized design of products or services with a far higher likelihood of success.

Planning for Expansion at Zak's

Zak of Zak's Artisan Pie & Crust is approached by Bill, a local Toronto financier and entrepreneur. Bill's company has been buying Zak's pizza for their office events. Some of his team are also lunchtime regulars at the restaurant. Bill's impressed with Zak's concept and he believes the Toronto economy is booming, and that, with increasing household incomes, suburban dwellers are ready for Zak's brand of premium pizza. He wants to partner with Zak and open a chain in suburban strip-mall locations, under Zak's supervision as executive chef and full partner in the expansion business.

However, the suburban strip malls are already awash with places to buy pizza. Sure, Zak's has a superior menu and a superior reputation. People make a point of visiting Zak's on the occasions they need to come into the city center. Bill and Zak agree to hold a staff retreat to talk about strategy for the expansion. Two weeks prior to the retreat, Zak briefs his frontline people. He tells them about the retreat, when and where it will happen, and its purpose—to discuss plans for a possible expansion of the franchise into the suburbs, opening several new locations. Before they do this, though, they want to understand the market better. Meanwhile, their existing customers all work in downtown, but many of them live in the suburbs. So Zak wants his team to pay attention, to chat up the clients a bit to get to know about where they go for pizza outside the city, and why they go. What are the occasions or reasons for visiting suburban pizza restaurants?

Bill arranges for a function room at the Westin Harbour Castle on Toronto's waterfront. It's an all-day meeting the following Tuesday. To ensure a prompt start he arranges that they'll cater a hot breakfast as well as lunch and a morning and afternoon break. There is nothing more powerful to get people up early for a meeting than a free cooked breakfast. Zak's staff are mostly hourly paid workers, so they are on the clock from 8:30 a.m. The cost of the meeting is easily measured, and they are hopeful that the information value produces an ample return for the time and money.

Zak facilitates a frontline staff focus group like the one described in Chapter 8.

Pete is the delivery person who regularly delivers to Neeta's WSIB office. From chatting up his customers a bit he's learned two key things. When Neeta goes out for pizza close to home, it is always a family affair, perhaps even an occasion such as a birthday party, or an end-of-season soccer team celebration with the whole team, coaches, and many parents present. There are always children involved. If she's out for a romantic evening with her husband—the kids under the supervision of a grandparent or a babysitter—or on a girls' night out with her friends, she never goes for pizza; it is always something a little more special, usually authentic ethnic food, often Asian. If she's ordering pizza for home, it is always for the children. Maybe she steals a slice with a glass of red wine—a guilty pleasure.

Currently, the Zak's concept isn't anti-children, but there is also nothing specifically pro-family about it, either. Guests aren't turned away if they have children, and the licensing for the premises allows children to sit in the restaurant while adults are served alcoholic drinks, but that is about it. There's no children's menu, for example. They don't do crayons or provide special entertainment or distractions for children. There is no play area or games room.

Pete explains that Neeta likes Westside—they have a great menu for kids, they are very close to home, she loves the convenience, and they are pretty quick to deliver.

As more of the team share their experiences and learning, it becomes clear that there is a partial identity crisis for Zak's if they are to extend to the suburbs. Aspects of the concept—in the language of this text, the "design" of the business—may need to change to be fit-for-purpose in the suburbs. It isn't just a question of whether suburban adults like exotic toppings and can afford Zak's premium prices, there needs to be a family-friendly element to it.

Bill speaks up, "We're going to need a kids' menu."

"We don't do kids' menus at Zak's," replies Zak. "We're not that kind of a pizza place," he asserts.

"It needs to sound fancier," says Bill. "We need to disguise it."

"How about 'Zak's Bistro Selection'?" he suggests.

"I like it!" says Jo, the sous chef. Jo has been invited in case the discussion has an impact on either the design of the restaurant concept or the menus, but also to assess any impact on the kitchen and the implementation of how pizzas are prepared and baked. "Maybe five pizzas, including a margarita, just plain cheese for the kids. It's a kids' menu but it isn't. Maybe we throw one recipe on there that is really just for adults? A misdirection so that it doesn't look like a kids' menu. With garlic, no cheese, no tomato sauce. Something kids would never order!"

"What if we did express delivery with a guaranteed delivery time, maybe 25 minutes, or you don't pay?" adds Pete.

"I don't like that. We'd be giving away too many free pizzas" says Zak.

"Not if we designed the service correctly," replies Bill. "And what if it was 'guaranteed 25-minute delivery, or your next one is free'? How many people would really exercise that free option? What would it take?"

Jo stroked her chin and gazed up and to the left, looking for inspiration. "We'd need to have the pizzas prepared in advance. If we could limit it to just the Bistro Selection menu, it's doable."

"We'd need guaranteed capacity in the ovens to bake the pizza as soon as we take the order," says Zak.

"And delivery riders on standby with scooters or motorbikes," adds Pete.

"What if we forgo the happy hour we offer in our current location, and instead turn it into a family focus time with express delivery only from the Bistro menu?" Jo is beginning to envision a full-service offering.

"So what time of day do these busy working parents place orders for kids' pizza?" asks Bill.

"After work!" Zak, Pete, and Jo exclaim.

"That's it," says Zak. "Zak's Express Bistro Service, weekdays from 4:30 to 7:30 p.m. Guaranteed 25-minute delivery, but to where?"

"That depends on location" says Pete. "With a motorbike, you could probably service each suburb where you open a restaurant, within that 25-minute deadline. So long as the delivery rider is standing by. We've got maybe 15 minutes, so limit the radius to, like, 8 kilometers?"

Bill summarizes, "So if we can choose a central location within each postal code or set of postal codes, we can provide this differentiating service aimed at winning the home business of our existing city-center corporate customers?"

"Yes!" they all reply.

"Everything will need to be in place," says Zak. "We'll need the right locations, a kitchen designed with sufficient reserve oven capacity, a team of delivery riders on standby at each location, a Bistro Selection menu with a stock of pre-prepared pizzas ready to bake the instant we take an order on the phone or via the website."

"We could stagger the shifts of the delivery staff," adds Pete. If you stagger the shifts, you could have double-staffing during the express service period. "It might not cost any more than it would otherwise."

"Genius!" Zak points at Pete with a broad smile. "I knew there was a reason we hired you!"

What Just Happened at Zak's?

While the story above is fictitious, it is based on composite elements of reality. David actually ran a market research experiment with an audience of professional working mothers in Stockholm, Sweden, where there was not only enthusiasm for a service similar to the one described here, there was even consensus that they'd be prepared to pay a premium of sixty Swedish crowns (SEK) for the express delivery service. Over the past decade this sum fluctuated in equivalency to between six and ten US dollars. Although Stockholm is an expensive

European city with a high cost of living, this premium is still significant. It represents an opportunity that can be exploited by a smart business with a strong market-sensing capability.

Really, What Just Happened at Zak's?

Together, as a team, Zak's identified a market opportunity and designed a service to exploit it. They identified a segment based on purpose—busy, stressed parents, who come home late and have hungry children to feed. They believe the service they envisage will be more fit-for-purpose than current alternatives. To implement it, aspects of the design, implementation, and service delivery capability at Zak's will need to change. This isn't just a new menu and a marketing promotion, they will need to change all of the following, and probably more: the way they organize and manage their kitchen; the way certain pizzas are prepared, which may have impact on the purchasing of ingredients; the working patterns and shifts for delivery riders; switching to motorbike delivery from drivers with vans; and the system for taking orders and prioritizing baking of pizzas will all need to change.

The outcome, we hope, is a service, highly tailored to a specific market segment, which is highly relevant to that segment because the design is based on an understanding of the customer's purpose. Because the service is more than just a change to the published menu and a marketing promotion, because there are infrastructure and capability changes as well as capital investment required to make it happen, the implementation of Zak's Express Bistro Selection should be difficult to copy—there is a barrier to copying the concept. This barrier will buy Zak's time to build market share and brand loyalty. Once Zak's has earned Neeta's home pizza delivery business—so long as they keep her satisfied—why would she switch away from them?

Think Like Pizza Guys

The lesson to take from this is that different market segments— customers with different purposes, different goals, and different risks to manage—need different designs, different fidelity in implementation, and different classes of service. If you have a range of functional designs, but just one level of implementation and one class of service, you may not be serving the market properly. In Chapter 7 we discussed the idea that if Silicon Valley was in the pizza business there would 1,024 designs, but little attention would be paid to suitable levels of implementation, and service delivery would be inadequate, ad hoc, or at least highly unreliable. This is because many of these businesses value ingenuity and product design above implementation capability or customer service.

The pizza business is actually highly diverse and has attracted a lot of innovation in implementation and service delivery as businesses seek to differentiate and find suitable niches. Papa Murphy's is a large chain that advertises "take 'n' bake." The concept is that they make the pizza but don't bake it. They also don't deliver. Instead, you pick it up from their store, take it home in your own vehicle, and bake it in your own oven. Papa Murphy's is tuned to a particular set of fitness criteria. Papa Murphy's customers like their pizza fresh and hot from the oven; they like fresh ingredients and don't want a frozen grocery store pizza. And they have time on their hands. They can plan and schedule the baking, and they have time to drive to the store and collect it. Papa Murphy's customers are almost exclusively domestic, using the oven in their own household kitchens because offices often have microwaves but full ovens are unusual. Hence, take and bake isn't viable for most office workers staying late and looking for hot food.

Zume is a small California operation with a limited service area whose pizza is baked in a van, allegedly by robots, while they drive to deliver it to your door. Zume's clients presumably don't have the time available to collect a pizza from Papa Murphy's, and they may not have an oven. Although Zume might have domestic clients, they are also likely to have a large corporate following.

Like Zume, the larger and better-known Domino's chain has experimented with modified versions of the Chevrolet Spark, called the Domino's DXP (for Delivery Expert Vehicles), which feature a warming oven designed to ensure the pizza is hot and tasty upon delivery.

In theory, Zume should outperform Domino's DXP on delivery time, because the pizza is baked in the vehicle, while Domino's first bakes the pizza at the store, then simply keeps it warm while delivering. Of course, the density of retail locations and the journey distance will affect lead time, too.

Square Pizza (*Pizza al Cuadrado* in Spanish) is originally based in Madrid, Spain. They have only one restaurant, but the chain has focused on opening concessions in gourmet food courts of department stores, such as *El Corte Inglais*, and high-end shopping malls. Square Pizza sells pizza by the inch (or centimeter). The pizza is baked in a long rectangular sheet. Customers don't buy a slice or a whole pie, they choose the recipe or recipes they prefer and simply ask the vendor to cut off the length they want with a large pair of scissors. Square Pizza customers want to avoid overeating; they also want gourmet flavors and premium ingredients—fresh and organic. The dough for the crust is made onsite and fermented for up to 72 hours. It tastes delicious! Square Pizza appeals to foodies and gourmet enthusiasts, many who are also people counting calories, watching their figures, on a diet, or just simply health conscious—aware that overeating is bad for your body and can cause significant health issues. Quality is core to the identity of Square Pizza, and they've carefully selected a strategy that enables them to be successful without sacrificing their values.

Figure 10.1 Square Pizza has carved out a defensible and profitable niche by understanding their market and segmenting it carefully.

Square Pizza, like any other by-the-slice vendor, is baking to forecast and speculating that there will be demand for certain recipes. The pizza is partially baked and lies cold on the counter. When selected, the slice is heated in an oven until perfectly baked. It arrives on the table fresh and sizzling. So, Square Pizza buyers trade off instant availability

—it takes maybe five minutes to finish baking—in exchange for just the right quantity and gourmet flavor toppings. By focusing on high-end department stores and shopping malls, anticipating shoppers with discerning taste, Square Pizza avoids direct price comparison with by-the-slice alternatives. In most cases, there isn't another concession selling pizza in the same location. Square Pizza may sell slices of pizza to people who might otherwise never choose pizza. There are some additional advantages of the Square Pizza model: rectangles fit into tight spaces better than circles, and hence, in tight food court concessions, more varieties of pizza can be displayed, and greater choice can be offered. While other chains such as Papizza use the same rectangular model, their mass-produced product is offered through their retail stores on the Spanish high street. By understanding their market and segmenting it carefully, through smart selection of location, Square Pizza has carved out a defensible and profitable niche.

We see lots of creative innovation in the pizza business—lots of willingness to experiment with different implementation and different service delivery approaches to best exploit different niches— niches based on managing purpose, goals, and risks.

Classes of Service Are a Powerful Tool

If your market isn't homogeneous—and it almost always isn't— offering a variety of classes of service for what is otherwise the same functional product is an incredibly powerful way to exploit and extract greater value from a market.

Innovation in service delivery, sometimes called "business model innovation" can be powerful. For product companies relying on technology innovation, the alternative of service delivery innovation can often be faster and cheaper to bring to market than a new product.

What Do We Mean By a "Class of Service"?

A class of service determines how something or someone will be treated based on their needs and, perhaps, the price they've paid. They may pay more for better service because of specific goals, risks, or purposes. Specifically, a class of service refers to things like the queuing discipline. If you buy a business class ticket for a flight, you get to queue in a different line; you may get a separate line for security. In general, you expect queuing times in the premium lines to be shorter. A higher class of service translates to faster. Customers with a greater cost of delay will be willing to pay for faster.

A business class ticket may also come with lounge access. The airline lounge may be a quieter, less crowded, and more comfortable environment than the general seating area. Some passengers may wish to pay to reduce their stress levels, relax before their flight, or get some work done. Airlines, such as the big three in the United States, that also sell memberships to their lounges should recognize that a business class lounge packed with people—nowhere to sit and nothing worth eating or drinking—is worse than the general airport concourse, not better. On several occasions, we've experienced lounges packed to capacity in Atlanta—Delta's main hub—and San Francisco—a significant United hub. David was turned away from a United lounge at SFO because it was full, even though he was holding a business class boarding pass for a long-haul flight to China. A higher class of service in name only isn't an improved class of service, it's arrogance or hubris on the part of the vendor. Classes of service must mean something tangible, not just an excuse to charge more and hope the customers feel superior and pleased with themselves. On the other hand, if the business realizes they're overserving their market, they could note the opportunity to turn the part of the service where they exceed fitness thresholds into a premium class of service, providing that they can identify a niche that isn't overserved at the current level of service. If this is the case, why not extract a premium from these customers? For services, people generally value time, space, peace and quiet, variety, choice, and fidelity of experience—we will pay to reduce stress and maximize other opportunities in our lives. When you design a class of service you should be thinking

- How can we make it faster?
- How can we provide more space?
- How can we make it more peaceful?
- How can we provide more choices?
- How can we provide better quality?

Classes of service should be designed to align with fitness criteria metrics for a given segment and their threshold values. As we saw with the Zak's expansion example, it may be necessary to develop capabilities or change an implementation method to enable a class of service. Zak's was going to have to switch to motorbike delivery to enable their Express Bistro Service.

One of David's clients is a travel industry firm in Auckland, New Zealand. Rugby Union is the national sport of this country. The capital, Wellington, is said to have more registered Rugby players than in all of Scotland. The national team is known as the "All Blacks" and is famous for their native Maori war dance, the haka, before each match. At the time of writing, the team is ranked first in the world.

It may come as no surprise, then, that during a workshop with this travel firm, one team of managers decided to design a service for laundering rugby strips (team uniforms) for local clubs.

The class of service they envisaged was that a cleaning service would contract for the whole season and guarantee delivery of clean uniforms prior to each club game—match-day delivery for home games, and night-before delivery for away games. Dirty strips would be collected after each game—same day for home games and the day after for away games. This would give them typically three to seven days to clean and return the strips before the next match fixed on the calendar.

Imagine a discussion similar to the one at Zak's offsite meeting. What would it take to create this service, and how would it affect other business?

The laundry is offering a fixed-date delivery against a known match schedule for six to nine months of the year. When they first receive the dirty strips, they can choose to wash, dry, and press them whenever they have slack capacity as demand ebbs and flows during the week. If the uniforms haven't been cleaned by the day prior to the match due to heavy demand for regular laundry, they can expedite them on that day and still meet the deadline—at the expense of slightly delaying other items by effectively giving priority and preference to the rugby team uniforms.

How did a travel company know enough about this for it to become a focus of a management training workshop? Because many of them played rugby or served on the organizing committees of local clubs. They were the customers and they knew exactly the class of service they needed for it to serve them best, for it to be the most fit-for-purpose. An Auckland-based laundry service was missing an opportunity to dominate a market niche because they didn't have the frontline market-sensing capability to detect the needs of the rugby club segment. Business opportunity comes from identifying customers' needs. When you segment a market based on purpose, these insights reveal themselves.

Service Delivery and Economics Must Be Balanced

Mayrhofen, in the Austrian state of Tyrol, lies at the southern end of the deeply glaciated valley of Zillertal before it splits into five tributary valleys that lead to the high Alps and the Austrian-Italian border some 25 kilometers to the south. A popular ski resort founded in the 1950s, the village has been a destination for summer tourists since the 1880s. The village history dates back to 1500, and some of the oldest family hotels have been open since the early 16th Century. During ski season this picturesque little village of around 1,500 residents swells to over 24,000, with tourists from the EU, UK, Russia, and Israel filling up the slopes on two mountains above the village: the Penken and the Ahorn.

The Ahornbahn cable car (Figure 10.1), with a capacity of 160 passengers, is the largest in the world. Mayrhofen has both the largest and second-largest cable cars, the other being the Tux/Pendelbahn Wanglspitz, with a capacity of 150. The Ahornbahn rises 1,300 meters to its summit above the village on the slopes of the Ahornspitze with a journey time of around seven minutes. The cable cars run every fifteen minutes from each station during the mountain's normal business hours.

The Ahorn ski area is the much smaller of the two areas accessible from the village of Mayrhofen. It offers a couple of drag tows and two chair lifts, providing access to some easy, wide, blue runs for beginners and a longer,

Figure 10.1 The Ahornbahn

slightly steeper, red run for intermediate skiers. There isn't much variety. As a result, the mountain isn't busy. It's mostly for beginners who take the cable car up in the morning and back down again late in the afternoon.

However, the Ahorn offers the knowledgeable tourist and the locals the option of a 1,300-meter vertical drop back to the

Figure 10.2 Tux/Pendelbahn Wanglspitz

base station via the exit run, or *abfahrt*. The game the locals like to play is "race the cable car." Exit at the top of the mountain, a short walk out of the station to the snow, on with your skis, and off you go. A reasonably fast run is seven minutes. Allowing for the setup time at the top, it is less than ten minutes since the cable car docked and disgorged its load of up to 160 skiers. On a good day, a little younger and in better physical shape, David has finished this run in eight minutes, usually arriving at the bottom just as the cable car returns to the station.

The other monster cable car in the Zillertal region is the Tux/Pendelbahn Wanglspitz (Figure 10.2), holding up to 150 passengers, which connects the other Mayrhofen ski area of Penken and Horberg with the Rastkogel, above the village of Lanersbach, in the Tux valley.

Most skiers in Mayrhofen access the Penken area via the Penkenbahn gondola (Figure 10.3). This is a mass-transit system constructed of gondolas hanging on wires approximately 100 meters apart, each holding up to twenty-four passengers seated and additional standing. The Penkenbahn can transport around 2,880 skiers onto the slopes in an hour. Compare that to the

Figure 10.3 Penkenbahn

Ahornbahn, running four times per hour with a total capacity of 640 skiers per hour.

Gondolas move more people per hour; they are more convenient, faster, and provide the skier a better experience than do the cable cars. A Penkenbahn gondola leaves the station every forty-five seconds if the system isn't overloaded and there is no queuing, in which case boarding is instant. This is true in summer and at off-peak times in winter. The journey time is around nine minutes including the slow period inside the station house. While the average waiting time for the Ahornbahn is seven and a half minutes. From a customer service perspective, the gondola system is more fit-for-purpose. Instant boarding and departures every 45 seconds compared to waiting five to seven minutes to board and yet more time until departure. Skiers and snowboarders prefer not to wait for a lift, so the Penkenbahn will always be more popular.

So, if gondolas are better, why did the Zillertal ski area recently build two of the largest and most sophisticated cable cars? Why connect the busy Penken and Horberg areas, with the more difficult red and black runs on the Rastkogel above Lanersbach, with a cable car? Why not a gondola? A gondola would be more convenient for skiers and would provide a smooth, ski-down, ride-immediately-back-up experience.

The explanation is simple—economics!

Gondolas provide a flow system, whereas cable cars provide a batch transfer system. The gondola's flow system reduces waiting time and maximizes skiing time. However, a gondola must be operated constantly, so it costs a lot more to run than a cable car.

The lift company estimates demand and forecasts it out over a ten- to twenty-year period in the future. They know which days and times are likely to be busier, what skill levels the skiers who are visiting the resort are, and which types of runs they prefer. They know all of this because they collect data from the RFID tag lift pass system. They have mountain usage instrumented! They can judge skill level by speed and choice of route on the mountain.

If they anticipate peak demand at, say, 600 skiers per hour connecting between Horberg and the Rastkogel, then a 150-person cable car operating once every fifteen minutes is the economically optimal way to move those skiers. The question is whether an average seven-and-a-half minute waiting time is sufficiently within skier tolerances that they will consider it fit-for-purpose.

We can understand that flow systems are more desirable. They offer the shortest lead time, which usually correlates to the highest level of customer satisfaction. However, a flow system might not always be the most economically efficient. A discrete batch transfer system might be better for our business, even if customer satisfaction is lower.

There are times when you have to treat the business owners, the shareholders, or the taxpayers as first-class stakeholders and make economic decisions accordingly. Offering a gondola on the Ahorn or connecting to the Rastkogel would no doubt meet with customer approval, but it would be overserving the market. The cable car with a fifteen-minute cadence is sufficient, even for the cable car racing locals who need time to catch their breaths, while it provides better economic results.

When designing services, it's important to know the thresholds for fitness criteria and not overserve them at the expense of running a profitable and successful business.

Natural Segmentation Based on Usage

Some markets naturally segment based on usage. For some, the functional requirements for any kind of differentiation map directly to usage, for example, bicycles. Shopping bikes, racing bikes, mountain bikes, and folding bikes are all clearly segmented by usage, so a known use leads to a functional specification and a design. Usage maps to purpose in the broadest sense. A shopping bike is for carrying home the groceries. If you limit your understanding of purpose at this level, then we've satisfied a purpose-driven market segmentation. However, if the true purpose is to have fresh, organic, locally produced food each day, while living a healthy lifestyle and exercising regularly, then a shopping bike is a means to an end. If the true purpose is to fight cancer by leading a low-stress, quiet life while eating a healthy, fresh, locally grown, in season, entirely organic diet and living a healthy lifestyle, then not only is the shopping bike a means to an end, but the groceries carried in the basket are also a means to an end.

When a bike manufacturer designs a shopping bike, they probably aren't thinking, "cancer survivor" as a market niche, and yet in the ZIP code where David lives, this niche is very tangible.

Some usage maps to the fidelity of the product—heavy usage implies a more durable design—commercial versus consumer or recreation usage affects many aspects of non-functional requirements. Bicycles are again an example. Delivery riders need a different class of frame and build. So do bike-rental and bike-transportation businesses. Professional racers need yet more fidelity to their bicycles, even more so than amateur racers.

We see the same in bicycle carrying racks. Consider the racks designed to be mounted to the front of service buses—highly durable, easy to use, fast to load and unload a bike, made of rust-free material, built to last, and can fold up in front of the bus when not in use. At the other end of the scale, we have the occasional use, recreational bike rack designed for a sedan or saloon car that straps onto the trunk or boot or through the tailgate of a hatchback. Usage and the style or type of usage affects design, and the fidelity of the design affects the price, performance, and value of the product.

There are many similar markets, such as power tools, landscaping and lawn maintenance equipment, even building materials. Generally, if you can buy it at Home Depot, it's likely that the market is segmented by usage and nature of that usage. For such markets, the Fit-for-Purpose Framework adds less value. They are already fairly good at mapping product and service designs to purpose.

True, the shopping bike designer may not understand that they are selling their product to cancer survivors, and knowing this might be useful information for targeting marketing communications, but it will affect the design very little, if at all. The real value of the Fit-for-Purpose Framework is in markets and product and service sectors where the vendor actually doesn't "know why you fly," even when they say they do!

Bloatware

"Bloatware" is a term that refers to heavy personal computing applications designed to be used for many different purposes. Perhaps the archetypal example is the Microsoft Office suite of applications.

In general, bloatware means big, heavy, and over-featured. It's easy to understand how such products evolve. The manufacturer has success in a niche—perhaps for a single purpose, or usage scenario—so then they add more features and seek to broaden the appeal. In the language of this book, they broaden the segments to which the product is designed to appeal. Gradually, the product gets heavier and heavier and contains more and more features and functions. As the market appeal of the product broadens, its design gets more and more complex, and its ease of use and appeal to its original audience is diminished. This opens up a market opportunity for a late entrant to develop a simpler, pared-down product, perhaps targeted at the original niche, segment, or market and win their business and loyalty, while the incumbent and original creator of the product category loses out.

Over the last thirty years of technology product markets, this has been seen, perhaps, as an unavoidable dilemma. The original product has a brand, a franchise, name recognition, a fan base. From a marketing perspective, it has been far too easy to simply keep adding to the existing product rather than to develop another one. There has been a massive failing in under-the-hood, technical implementation capability. Physical product designers such as in the automotive industry have become adept at designing product lines, platforms, and product architectures that facilitate reuse of components and even entire platforms. Volkswagen was one of the earliest and most adept with this engineering expertise. One platform would enable them to produce a whole family of vehicles such as the Golf, Jetta, Beetle, Seat Ibiza/Leon, Audi A3, Audi TT, and so on.

For close to two decades now, similar "platform" technology has existed in the software industry, but most programmers are not skilled in its implementation—or even aware it. Indeed, for most of the last twenty years, there has been an active movement in the software industry that favors craftsmanship—solutions hand-built from scratch every time—over reuse, software architecture, and the technology known as software product lines.

Another approach to focusing on usage, or goals, was designing different user interfaces based on usage, purpose, or user goal. If the software could understand the user's role, then the functionality could be tailored to that user. The product was delivered as bloatware—you got the lot, including the kitchen sink—but, based on an understanding of your role as a user, the product was crimped and the interface tailored to your needs. While this was a great theory, few products and firms implemented it successfully.

So, the emergence of bloatware happened because it was easier and simpler to market, and easier and simpler to engineer. Bloatware products were often described by software engineers as "monoliths"—implying that the program code was tightly coupled, with poor cohesion and impossible to divide into components or modules suitable for reuse as a platform across a product line.

Into this landscape arrived web technologies, web services, and mobile applications. So-called service-oriented architectures have increased the amount of reuse of software code. For some reason, perhaps due to the flat structure and loosely coupled nature of the web protocols for communication, a greater number of software developers appear to be capable of using web services successfully. It is now much more viable to think in terms of product lines with products tailored to market segments based on purpose. The products can potentially be delivered via mobile applications.

At the time of writing, we perceive that the skills in user experience design exist to design products based on purpose but marketing and user experience design aren't well aligned. At the same time, the engineering skills exist in sufficient numbers to build products based on web services platforms and deliver product lines as SaaS or mobile applications, but companies don't take advantage of platform engineering often enough. What is currently lacking is the alignment of marketing and strategic planning to think of the market as a set of segments based on purpose. To strengthen their fitness-for-purpose, companies need to align market segmentation with design, and at the same time take advantage of platform engineering and its flexibility to provide segment-aligned variety in their offerings. We discuss this in greater depth in Chapter 13 when we consider mapping the Fit-for-Purpose Framework with Goal-Directed Design, a twenty-year-old technique, well established in the field of user experience design.

Summary

- We've considered stories of two similar businesses making expansion plans. One firm speculated that there was a market for a somewhat different variety of their product. They took the gamble.

- Another firm identified a market opportunity as a segment based on purpose and designed a service to be more fit-for-purpose than the existing alternatives. It's not luck.

- Classes of service are a powerful tool. Class of service determines how a customer or their order will be treated based on their needs or the price they paid.

- When designing a class of service, think about how you can make something faster, with more choices, or with higher quality. Align classes of service with fitness criteria and thresholds.

- When designing a service, always consider economics and don't overserve a segment or market at the expense of profitability.

- Some markets are segmented naturally by usage. In such markets, the Fit-for-Purpose Framework adds less value. as the product and service design already map well to the purpose.

- *Bloatware* is a term to describe a problem that has challenged the high-tech industry for decades. It refers to products containing too many features trying to satisfy too many customer purposes. Web and mobile platform technologies have created an opportunity to move away from bloatware toward a family of products or services tailored to individual market segments based on purpose.

SECTION IV

Mind the Gap

Our final section continues with more pragmatic, actionable guidance. The focus, however, turns outward, to comparisons, connections, and integrations with various other existing methods and tools, and to gaps or recognized limitations in our approach. Each chapter in this closing section deals with one type of gap or another and concludes with an overview of how to extend the Fit-for-Purpose Framework to enable the long-term survivability of a business. Chapter 14 gives you a taste of the future books in this trilogy.

Chapter 11, Blind Spots, identifies gaps within the Fit-for-Purpose Framework. These "blind spots" define its limitations. They represent the situations in which you may not be able to use it effectively and will need to complement it with other methods. Chapters 12 and 13 describe connections with various other methods and tools. The gaps we discuss in Chapter 12, "It's Your Future, Be There," are wider, and we expect them to stay that way, as the Fit-for-Purpose Framework often provides deeper insights than these existing approaches. The gaps we discuss in Chapter 13, Von Moltke's Goal-Directed, Balanced Scorecard, are narrower, and we close them tighter by describing how to integrate them with the Fit-for-Purpose Framework.

Chapter 14, "Be Paranoid!" presents our conclusion, revealing several surprising gaps that we hope will inspire you to look beyond what we've written here. It closes with our final call to action.

11 Blind Spots

THIS BOOK WOULD NOT BE COMPLETE without a discussion of the weaknesses, limitations, failings, and areas where the Fit-for-Purpose Framework remains underdeveloped or is simply not applicable. In these cases, you need to resort to existing techniques to augment your understanding of the market: build a full picture of who your customers are, what motivates them to select your products or services, what their expectations are, and whether they are truly satisfied. This chapter seeks to address those gaps—to identify the blind spots and give you pointers on what to do about them.

Metrics

Chapters 4 and 5 looked at metrics and how they drive behavior. Like all business books, the metrics offered were simple, meaning one-dimensional. We used examples such as lead time as a fitness criterion, cancellation rate as an improvement driver, production rate as a general health indicator, and on-time departure percentage as a vanity metric. Business books tend to promote a world view in which simple solutions magically solve the world's management and leadership problems. Clearly this isn't true, or there wouldn't be a market for yet more and more business books as today's leaders look for new ideas to tame the challenges they see in their organizations.

This book was never intended to provide a deep treatise into metrics. We could have included a discussion on how metrics can be gamed. For example, Alaska Airlines' twenty-minute baggage handling guarantee is based on first bags onto the carousel and doesn't address the range or nature of the distribution function over time.

If first bags appeared in twenty minutes but most didn't appear for an hour, there would be plenty of customer dissatisfaction—and yet the target would have been achieved. A baggage handling firm could game their service level agreement with Alaska by increasing the multi-tasking across aircraft and extending the range of baggage delivery times.

Cynics also jump at metrics with glib assertions such as "all metrics can be gamed." This is patently untrue. You can't game your finish time at the Boston Marathon, for example. What we will offer, for good guidance on metrics, is that they tend to come in pairs. Good metrics are vectors with two dimensions. As David discussed in his first book, *Agile Management for Software Engineering*, in 2003, cycle time for a task should be paired with quality. The denominator in each dimension of the pairing should be the same, and ideally it is something of customer value, such as a feature for a software application. So, cycle time per feature should pair with escaped defects per feature. The first is a productivity measure that we seek to minimize, and the second is a quality measure that acts as a constraint, ensuring that we don't sacrifice quality in the name of speed, and again, we seek to minimize it. This concept is illustrated in figures 11.1 through 11.3.

$$Production\ Rate = \frac{1}{Cycle\ Time}$$

$$i.e.\quad Features\ per\ hour = \frac{1}{Hours\ per\ feature}$$

Figure 11.1 How Production Rate relates to Cycle Time

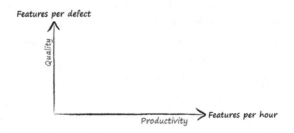

Figure 11.2 Productivity and Quality as a two-dimensional vector metric

It is generally a good idea to focus first on quality, the how something is done, before we focus on speed, how fast something is completed. Anyone who has ever learned a new skill understands this; for example, learning to swing a golf club in slow motion before you attempt to swing it at full speed and hit the ball a couple of hundred yards. Gymnasts, dancers, and martial artists all practice in slow motion first. Quality first, then speed! This concept is illustrated in Figure 11.3.

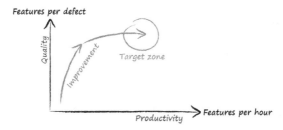

Figure 11.3 Improve Quality before Productivity

So, metrics as pairs of related system effects are common. Typically, one metric provides feedback on the other and prevents a focus on one causing a negative effect on the other. It becomes hard to game metrics when they are offered up in pairs. How would you game average productivity without sacrificing quality? It might be possible to have severe spikes in productivity where quality is sacrificed. The spike would have the effect of improving the average. This would work only if the spike in productivity produced only a minimal increase in defect rate. In reality, at least with a software industry metric like this one, even a mild increase in speed produces a dramatic and nonlinear increase in defects. Vector metrics are very hard to game. They are also, however, very hard to communicate in a marketing campaign and harder for both the consumers and the workforce to get their heads around compared to a simple, one-dimensional number, such as, "First bags on the carousel within twenty minutes of the door opening." It wouldn't be so easy to say, "First bags out within twenty minutes without any increase in lost or damaged bags." It's hard to envisage a vector metric appearing on a poster, regardless of how important it might be.

So, a simple but final word of caution on metrics, as a summary to close this topic—beware individual metrics, they may drive nasty—and at times unforeseen—side-effects. Proceed with caution.

Emotional Motivation for Selection

What if all the choices in a product category are fit-for-purpose? What breaks the tie? The answer is an emotional motivation and affinity for a brand. Brand marketing becomes most relevant in well-established and commoditized markets where everyone is making something generally fit-for-purpose. Automotive man-ufacturers, which nowadays all make cars that are beyond "good enough," have long since learned to sell to the identity of the buyer. Subaru appeals to people who like outdoor sports and an active lifestyle, while Audi's *vorsprung durch Technik* campaign was aimed at people who identified with the engineering excellence and the technological innovation both in the vehicle's features and in how the vehicle was made. People are either Coke people or Pepsi peo-ple. "The choice of a new generation" is an identity-related mes-sage. This book and the Fit-for-Purpose Framework haven't sought to address this emotional, identity-related issue in selection. David will consider this deeply in the third book in this trilogy, *First Who, Then Why*. The Fit-for-Purpose Framework is designed to deal with underdeveloped markets where there is room for innovation and the opportunity to tailor the design, the implementation, and the service delivery to specific needs related to the customer's purpose. It's for markets where logically assessed choices are still important. The Fit-for-Purpose Framework addresses logical concerns, often concerns that can be quantified, such as delivery time, or percentage on-time arrival.

Building affinity for your brand is a strong way to mitigate the effects of being only partially fit-for-purpose. If your firm isn't good at implementation or your channel is weak at service delivery, then the identity of your brand and how strongly it resonates with con-sumers is a powerful way to mitigate shortcomings in capability. The emotional content of selection overrides logic or causes a consumer to pause and delay purchase in the hope that their favorite vendor will provide a suitable solution. How many Americans who identify with the flower-power, hippie era—a dream of a lifestyle they wish they had—and love the Volkswagen brand, but could have used the utility of a SUV sooner, instead waited for years until Volkswagen launched the Touareg and later the Tiguan models?

So, while the Fit-for-Purpose Framework may be blind to emotional motivations for selection and focuses on logical and quantifiable criteria, firms that have strong brands may be blind to the fact that their products aren't fit enough and competitors are serving the market better. This is a fragile position to be in. It isn't sustainable forever. Often brand strength is based on earlier superiority in the market. If complacency or hubris has caused that to slip, the business is vulnerable. Perhaps the best targets for insurgents are incumbent firms with a dominant market share whose products or services are tired and increasingly less relevant to the consumer and their evolving purposes or motivations for selection. These firms with strong brands are unlikely to be paying attention to fitness-for-purpose or sufficiently intimate with their customers to understand them. They don't segment the market based on purpose, based on why consumers selected them. Are your competitors savvy with their front line? Can they sense the market better than you? What are you going to do about it?

Small Scale Works Better

We associate the term "economy of scale" with the 20th Century mass-production era, but we think it also applies to the emergence of broadcast media, first with radio, then television, and to direct, person-to-person communication network technology such as telephony, and later, mobile phones. In the 21st Century we now have the Internet and the platforms that run on it. We have eCommerce capabilities such as Amazon, but also Expedia and eDreams, and search engines like Google, social media such as Facebook, and messaging applications like WhatsApp. We have cloud storage and application development platforms—once again Amazon—but also Microsoft, Apple, and Dropbox. Finally, we have a reversion to broadcast-like media with streaming services such as Spotify and Netflix. So, economy of scale applies as much to the 21st Century as it did to the 20th Century. It isn't only a physical manufacturing business phenomenon.

Recall *The New Yorker* cartoon shown below, "On the Internet, nobody knows you're a dog."

"On the Internet, nobody knows you're a dog."

Figure 11.1 *New Yorker* cartoon, Peter Steiner, July 5, 1993.[49]

This cartoon was published only four years after the invention of the World Wide Web technology that would make the Internet platform accessible for a mass market. Most readers of this book would not have had Internet access at that time unless through an academic source such as a university where they were a registered student. The cartoon is, however, a prescient commentary. As we discussed in Chapter 7, today, many firms making use of contemporary Internet technologies such as mobile apps struggle to know their customers—who they are, and their purpose in selecting their product.

In the era of massive scale, we can track users with cookies; we know it is them, but we know very little about them, with the possible exception of Facebook, which has access to a lot of personal data about its users. However, see the next sections on "customers who don't buy" and "people lie" to consider just how much Facebook really knows. In 2016, pop singer Lady Gaga reflected on how people

---

49. en.wikipedia.org/wiki/On_the_Internet,_nobody_knows_you%27re_a_dog

create a fake persona online with the first single from her fifth album, *Joanne*, titled "Perfect Illusion."[50]

The mobile application Koolooks is designed for followers of fashion who want to A | B test clothing, accessories, and fashion looks with a trusted audience of friends. It's a social network application designed specifically for people who want a second opinion before they get dressed in the morning. Founder Barbara Ruzicka envisioned the application being used by fashion enthusiasts to feel confident they made the right choice before leaving home, or the right purchase before leaving the store. When your sister or best friend doesn't live with you, how else do you get advice before leaving home clad in a fashion faux pas? When you are shopping on your own, how else do you avoid that dumb purchase that seemed like a good idea at the time? Judging by its website, perhaps she also envisioned a future for the business as an eCommerce site, enabling other users to buy items they see their friends modeling. Coincidentally, the mobile application works well as a general-purpose A | B testing tool. Consequently, some users have adopted it to test pictures for their beautifully groomed Instagram pages. Rather than "Which top looks cuter on me?" they post "Which picture should I load to Instagram?" This type of exaptation, how a product gets used for a purpose that the creator didn't intend, will be fully examined in the second book in this trilogy, *Built to Last*. In this instance, this story serves to illustrate that online personas, such as Instagram profiles, present the "perfect illusion," and as marketers, we can't interpret them at face value.

At massive scale, even in the Internet era, we lack customer intimacy. We still don't know why our customers are choosing us and what their purpose is in doing so.

Most of the examples that formed the experience to enable this book were in businesses that work on a human scale, such as management training, where the trainer is the front line, interacting with the customers, and the scale of customers to staff is perhaps 20:1. In other examples we've used, such as airlines, the customer-to-staff ratio is still below 100:1. Even in the cases where we've been using surveys and data, the scale is still small. However, we know that the

---

50. en.wikipedia.org/wiki/Perfect_Illusion

Cognitive Edge company has used its Sensemaker technology to cluster customer micronarratives from Net Promoter Score surveys on a relatively large scale, so we know the F4P Card technique will work at greater scale.

An open question at the time of writing, in summer 2017, is how many customers do we really need to sample to establish that a segment exists? The answer is probably quite small. If we had three examples of a segment from 100 surveys randomly sampled from a population of 100 million customers, we've probably identified a significant and important customer purpose. More work needs to be done to develop guidance in this area. A slightly harder problem is to know the size of the segment, "the total available market" in traditional marketing terminology. This will probably need more work from the quantitative analysts in our professional community before we'll have solid guidance on the size of segments from large-scale customer sampling.

Automation or the Human Touch?

Throughout this book, we have strongly advocated for humans in the front line, sensing the complexity in the market. For some of our readers, this is going to sound terribly old-school. Some of you may be deeply involved in automating your front line, or you're in businesses such as mobile applications where there is no concept of a human front line because the entire customer interface and distribution channel is automated with technology. If you are working in these sorts of markets, then thank you for sticking with us this far into the book. We appreciate it!

There are clearly things you can do with technology to gather information about customer purpose. Most SaaS and mobile application services exit-survey people closing their accounts to ask why they are leaving. David is writing this section on the day he closed his premium subscription to LinkedIn, the professional social media network whose primary reason for existing, and original purpose, was helping match employers with suitable employees. LinkedIn duly surveyed David to ask why he was leaving. He clicked the radio button for "It's too expensive!" At $66 per month, or $800 per year, this is actually very expensive for SaaS products and, compared to most social networks, which are free to join, it is extortionate. David is, of course, the chairman of a business, and there may be some value in LinkedIn's services. However, David's real reason for leaving was that he is taking a sabbatical and doesn't need their services for at least the next 18 months. We could go further and suggest that LinkedIn's premium service is primarily aimed at recruiters, really serving only one segment, one purpose, with one class of service. LinkedIn ought to have a range of plans aimed at different segments identified by customer purpose. For example, there will likely be many independent consultants and trainers such as Alexei who wish to use LinkedIn to promote their ideas, their services, and so forth. There may be premium features they'd pay for that LinkedIn either is not offering or is currently giving away for free. At the time of writing, LinkedIn, despite its wealth of data about its user base, is actually not very smart about designing its services to be useful enough for users to pay a premium.

How might you do this better? There is clearly value in interstitial screens that solicit small, simple pieces of information. If these are used frequently and if the questions asked cover a diverse range of topics, firms could use their technology to build a richer picture of their customers' purposes, and perhaps even their fitness criteria and threshold values. Facebook is already quite good at this. Others must do better. Businesses need to get smarter at using technology to hold an unobtrusive conversation with their users, gradually building a picture of why they are selecting them and what their goals and objectives are for using the technology.

For many people, LinkedIn is just a constantly up-to-date professional Rolodex—an address book. It's a useful tool, but if we were LinkedIn, there are few features on the site that tell us much about a customer's purpose in using it. To add value people will be willing to pay for, you need to solve valuable problems. Understand purpose, goals, and desirable outcomes, then design your product or service to fulfill those. If you are flying blind or speculating about customer intent, then focus on developing better customer touch within your products—frequent, unobtrusive, interstitial screens that "chat up" your users and help you build a picture of who they are, why they come, and what they hope to achieve. That will help you tailor your product to make it fit-for-purpose in the eyes of your customers.

Existing Market Research and Quantitative Data

Throughout this book we haven't said much about existing market research. In general, we've found that fit-for-purpose surveying provided additional information about things to which we may have been blind—customer purpose, the reason behind people picking our product or service. We very much see this new technique as augmenting existing market research techniques rather than obviating them. We do believe that segmenting your market based on customer purpose is hugely important, and therefore if you must limit your research, we would argue that you should prioritize discovering "why" and sacrifice something else you are already asking.

Here is just a short list of things that our fit-for-purpose survey method doesn't tell you:

- Where your customers are from
- Who is paying for the product or service
- Age, sex, race, ethnicity, marital status, and other demographic information
- How people feel about specific features in your product or service
- How they feel about your brand
- Who they think they are, or how they identify themselves
- How they compare your product, service, or brand to competitors
- How much money they may spend with you
- How much repeat business you are likely to get
- How often they consume a product or service similar to the one you provide

You will almost certainly want to augment fit-for-purpose surveys and Fitness Box Score with other information. We are making no claims to the notion that Fitness Box Score is the only metric you will ever need. We are saying that using Fitness Box Score to quantify how fit-for-purpose your products and services are is a vital survival mechanism that will enhance your competitiveness and longevity.

Customers Who Don't Buy

Fit-for-purpose surveys and Fitness Box Score won't give you information about people who don't buy from you. With a human front line, you might be able to sense information about customer rejection. The "Did you find everything you were looking for today?" question is something you can sense with frontline staff focus groups. However, for many businesses, how would you know why you weren't selected? How does an airline know why a customer didn't fly, or bought a ticket on another airline? We aren't trying to solve the non-customer problem with the techniques in this book. In Chapter 9 we addressed the customers who only give us a portion of their business and how we might exploit information on customer purpose to find new segments, identify customers in those segments, and design products or services to meet their additional needs. If, however, we don't know these people at all because they aren't customers, then this text has nothing to offer in addition to what you might already be doing to identify new markets and new opportunities.

Promoters and Referrals

Fit-for-purpose surveys and Fitness Box Score don't give you information about likelihood to recommend, referral, or repeat business. They simply aren't a replacement for Net Promoter Score or similar market research, if this is the information you desire. In Chapter 12 we look more closely at Net Promoter Score and referral business research. We don't view Fitness Box Score as a replacement for NPS, nor think that it obviates the need for NPS. Instead, we see it as an augmentation and an approach that is more immediately actionable.

In general, we prefer facts to speculation. So, asking an existing customer, "How did you learn about us?" or using a coupon or discount code technique to track referral business is much more appealing to us. As discussed in the next chapter, NPS asks customers to speculate about their future behavior. Speculation about the future, and especially about human behavior, is a notoriously unreliable source of data for decision making.

People Lie—Hidden Purposes

Even with anonymous surveys, we've found that people fail to disclose all of their reasons for consuming one of our products or services. In some cases, the reason given is, in fact, a misdirection or credible cover story.

In 2016, two women who worked as project management contractors for a contingent staffing organization—the sort that labels its service as "consulting," but really it is only staff augmentation—attended one of David's events, the Asia-Pacific leadership retreat in Bali. They didn't fit the profile of typical attendees for the event, but when approached by organizers some time in advance, they confirmed that they had correctly registered and were confident it was the right event for them. By coincidence, David sat with them during the opening session and learned that they'd previously attended several of the mainstream conferences offered in Europe. They described the London event as "boring" and implied they didn't learn anything from attending it. Their officially stated reason for coming to Bali was to seek answers to a somewhat intractable problem with their current client, a large financial institution that had asked them to produce a detailed plan—with fixed timeline and budget—for a very loosely defined research project. Given that the scope of the project was poorly defined, they were struggling to resolve the issue. They persuaded their bosses to send them to David's event on the basis that they would "find the answer" to this knotty problem, and so their travel and registration expenses were approved.

Note that the choice of Bali as the location for the Asian-Pacific leadership retreat wasn't made to give participants a vacation-like experience. One of the requirements was visa-free access for citizens of several countries, including at least China, India, Russia, Australia, New Zealand, and the United States. This narrowed the choices considerably. Another desire was to find somewhere central, an easily accessible and neutral territory, as cultural and historical issues still deeply separate much of the Asian market. Denpasar, the capital of Bali, has Indonesia's best-connected international airport. Of all places within Bali, David picked a traditional Hindu retreat resort near Ubud—inland and as far as possible from the beaches and other distractions of the touristy locations on the island's coasts.

The two atypical visitors were given ninety minutes on the event program for a session to discuss the challenges with their client. During this session, they duly received free consulting from several very experienced, top consultants from Australia and New Zealand, each having experience with large financial industry clients, as well as input from both of us. However, despite the many suggestions made, it appeared they were not comfortable with any of them. They were, as they saw it, going home empty handed. They were the only attendees to score the event negatively on the F4P Cards, one going as far as to claim that the event was falsely advertised. A quick check on the website revealed that the first sentence of the first paragraph of copy on the home page identified who should attend, and why. In other words, these customers hadn't read past "Bali, June 2016," and had sought an excuse to have a beach vacation at their employer's expense. This was self-evident as they rushed off to Kuta as the event closed and their social media feeds lit up with posts from their holiday.

The true purpose behind their trip was "extra vacation paid for by my employer." Even on an anonymous form, they wouldn't disclose this, even as a secondary or additional reason. People lie! Doctors will tell you that, too. Doctors can't trust what people tell them on forms, even when confidentiality of medical records is guaranteed. F4P Cards are blind to hidden purposes and deliberate misdirection.

As David has owned and managed an event planning business since 2008, he's studied the market, particularly in North America. There are several categories of events, or reasons why event organizers are in business. Some events are primarily:

- Tribal in nature, and organized by social bodies such as professional societies
- Informational or educational
- Vacations paid for by employers[51]

---

51. Readers from regions of the world outside of North America may be surprised by this analysis. The reality is that in the United States, most employees receive only two weeks of vacation per year, and commonly most Americans are afraid to take all ten days in case it makes them look disloyal or insufficiently dedicated. Consequently, Americans look for opportunities to "get out," to travel and relax, while they are officially working. This market segment really doesn't exist in Europe. Often within Europe, firms organize their own retreats and take their employees on vacation, even though these same employees also receive up to six weeks of paid annual leave.

While events tend to offer features in all three areas, it is clear from the design of an event which category is its focus. Tribal events are often organized by the society or professional body, and the attendees are members of the body, such as the Bar Association of Washington State. The venue may be oriented toward a relaxed retreat location to facilitate the social nature of a tribal event. These events may happen over a weekend or at a time of year when there is minimal impact to billable work.

Informational or educational events tend to be organized by third-party providers and open to a broad audience. The venues are often chosen for convenience, and the days and price are tailored to who is paying—the attendees with their own money, or their employer.

Then there are the "b-oliday" (business holidays) events. These are held in locations such as Las Vegas, Orlando (in Florida), or New Orleans. With this latter category, some attendees literally pick up their lanyard and goodie bag at registration then head off to the casinos, the pool, or Disney World. The organizers know the business they are in, they know why they choose the venues they choose. The conference program is entirely designed as a suitable misdirection. Everyone involved has "plausible deniability" about what is truly happening.

In the example of this third category, everyone knows—the event planning company knows its market, the consumers know why they are attending, and their immediate managers signing off on the expense also secretly understand, yet no one would admit it. All will claim that people come for the program, the educational content, the personal development, and the potential application to employer's issues. However, if the organizer moved the event to Chicago the following year, attendance would drop dramatically. This market is real. The companies servicing it are successful, profitable, and long-lived. However, no formal market research method such as F4P Cards will reveal it exists—everyone involved will lie! In this example, the human approach to sensing the market is irreplaceable.

So, in summary, our fit-for-purpose approach works where a market is both functional and reasonably logical. It won't work when a market is dysfunctional or dishonest, or is driven by almost entirely emotional factors.

Dysfunctional Markets

The Fit-for-Purpose Framework will also not protect you from dysfunctional markets.

Returning to our story of London taxis from Chapter 1 and their ability to offer a robust challenge to ride-sharing application Uber: As we go to press, Uber's CEO Dara Khosrowshahi is due to visit London.[52] He intends to negotiate a renewal of Uber's license to operate a minicab business in the city, with the regulator, Transport for London (TfL). TfL and the current mayor of London, Sadiq Khan, refused to renew their license on the grounds that Uber failed to meet a number of regulatory requirements, including safety concerns and sufficient standards for background checks on its 40,000 drivers in the city. Effective from the end of September 2017, Uber is not licensed to operate in London, though they may continue to do so until the appeals process is exhausted. After the news was announced on September 22,[53] more than 680,000[54] mostly young Londoners signed a petition asking for an extension. It seems that the convenience of a rideshare minicab-hailing mobile application and saving a few Pounds, mostly for late-night rides home, outweighed their safety concerns, despite it coming to light that in 2016, there were, in London, thirty-two reported cases accusing Uber drivers of rape.[55] This data produces the shocking observation that as many as one in every 1,250 Uber drivers in London may be a rapist. This statistic is based only on alleged and reported cases in a single year.

You may recall that safety in food preparation was a core fitness criterion for Neeta ordering pizza in Chapter 3. However, she trusted that local authorities would enforce health and safety standards on her behalf and she did not feel the need to verify these herself. Regulatory authorities have a duty to protect those who aren't willing or at liberty to protect themselves. Young people tend to believe they are invincible or that it simply "won't happen to me." They tend to play the odds on "likelihood" rather than mitigating or avoiding the

---

52. www.bbc.com/news/technology-41450980

53. www.bbc.com/news/uk-england-41358640

54. www.bbc.com/news/business-41440887

55. www.independent.co.uk/news/uk/uber-drivers-accused-of-32-rapes-and-sex-attacks-on-london-passengers-a7037926.html

potential "impact" in risk assessment. In the regulator's opinion, Uber wasn't fit-for-purpose as a minicab operator in London.

This story highlights that our current Fit-for-Purpose Framework isn't good at capturing the criteria of stakeholders other than consumers. We currently don't have a strong solution for capturing regulatory requirements, for example, the non-functional quality requirement that a driver isn't a rapist, or has other criminal history that might put passenger safety at risk. This weakness in the framework needs to be addressed in a future revision.

Uber has a history of losing its license to operate as a consequence of more stringent requirements on driver background checks. The city of Austin, Texas, passed a plebiscite, known as Proposition 1, requiring that Uber fingerprint its drivers as part of a background check prior to acceptance as a driver.[56] Uber and its rival Lyft immediately pulled out of the Austin market. This immediately created an opportunity for rival applications to replace Uber's ride-sharing service within the city, most notably, the Ride Austin nonprofit app that became popular with locals.

Uber is believed to have spent $10 million lobbying against the proposition—a sum that far outweighs political spending on any local issue in the region. Uber was determined to vehemently oppose barriers to acceptance of new drivers, and any additional overhead in the recruitment process. Eventually, Uber regained its ability to operate in Austin when Texas state law overruled the Austin local law and did not require fingerprinting as part of new driver background checks. Uber's return to Austin caused one new rival, Fare, to close within a week.

While Ride Austin had gained popularity with locals, visitors to the city were once again able to use Uber. Uber has been able to use its scale, its deep pockets, and its lack of a need to operate profitably to squeeze out fitter competitors. Drivers for Ride Austin report that they may get ten requests for Uber trips to every one they receive from Ride Austin. Ultimately, they need to make their own living, and gradually the power of Uber's network is squeezing out rivals from both sides—the passenger and the driver. While the Fit-for-Purpose Framework might help an upstart such as Ride Austin create a fitter ride-sharing application, it won't protect them from a dysfunctional market or a rival with

---

56. www.bbc.com/news/technology-41450980

a strategic advantage such as a large network, or a strong cash position, and the ability to affect legislation in their favor. The Fit-for-Purpose Framework isn't protection from behavior that may attract the attention of antitrust investigators some time down the line.

Another example of a typically dysfunctional market is government contracting. In many states, provinces, and countries, civil servants are legally bound to accept the lowest bid from a set of responses to an RFP (request for proposal). This encourages dysfunctional behavior: vendors deliberately lie in their responses, quoting prices that aren't sustainable at a level of service that would be fit-for-purpose. Their intent is to claw back any deficit from the quoted price by manipulating the system for change requests in order to eventually make a profit from the contract. Once again, the Fit-for-Purpose Framework won't protect you from such dysfunctional markets. When there ought to be several fitness criteria but the selection is made purely on only one criterion—price—then the market is open to manipulation and will operate dysfunctionally. The solution is greater transparency and explicit agreement around a full set of fitness criteria for every contract. This isn't so easy to embed into law as a simple rule such as, "Accept the lowest price." Lawmakers need to do better to better serve their constituents and taxpayers. Equally, corrupt markets, where bribery and graft are core elements of selection, will not be helped by the Fit-for-Purpose Framework unless you are willing to explicitly include the need for such emoluments as fitness criteria in your assessment. This is highly unlikely, as paying such bribes is illegal in most countries, and financial auditors are often professionally and legally obliged to report such behavior if and when they find it. If you can't have clean, explicit fitness criteria, the Fit-for-Purpose Framework will be of limited use to you.

If, for example, you understand that "lowest price" is really the only fitness criterion in a public-sector bidding process, then your aim is to optimize for that. Now imagine some vendor bids one dollar for some government contract. You can say, without knowing anything about the contract, that one dollar is not enough budget to provide adequate service. Therefore, other, non-financial, fitness criteria exist and there are some minimum threshold levels of performance and capability expected—what scrupulous, professional vendors would consider the minimum acceptable levels of service. These levels may, in some cases, be greater than what the evaluation committee deems "good enough for government work." In other cases, the evaluation committee may lack qualifications to make a sound evaluation. Scrupulous, professional vendors can lose bids to cheats who lie about their capabilities or what they intend to supply as they underbid everyone else. In this latter case, the market is known in economics as "a market for lemons"[57]—the customer is unable to determine good from bad. The result is that good quality vendors drop out of the market. The Fit-for-Purpose Framework cannot protect you from a market for lemons, because selection of products or services that are unfit-for-purpose has become the standard in the market.

---

57. en.wikipedia.org/wiki/The_Market_for_Lemons

Summary

Like many business books, this text describes many simple, one-dimensional metrics. Metrics are generally better understood as probability distributions and coupled in pairs of measures, so that one measure acts as a feedback mechanism and constraint upon the other. You should generally beware of experts touting pursuit of simple numbers as the magic solution to business success.

Understanding customers intimately in large-scale markets is challenging. While technology exists to gather feedback, it is hard to properly understand customers' true purposes without direct contact at relatively human scales of one vendor staff member to less than 150 customers.

The Fit-for-Purpose Framework isn't a replacement for existing market research, although we believe it may be more actionable and more valuable for the long-term success of your business than some approaches you may be currently using. Fit-for-Purpose won't help you under the following circumstances:

- Markets in which all alternatives are good enough, and selection is emotional, e.g., Coke versus Pepsi
- Knowing where someone is from
- Understanding identity, gender, age, ethnicity, and so on
- Whether someone referred them
- Hidden purposes and misdirection in stated purpose
- Dysfunctional, corrupt, or poorly educated markets unable or unwilling to make rational decisions

12 "It's Your Future, Be There"

OUR BOOK WOULDN'T BE COMPLETE without exploring comparisons and connections of the Fit-for-Purpose Framework and its pragmatic, actionable guidance with a number of other popular approaches and concepts. In this chapter we deal with two particular cases for which we believe the Fit-for-Purpose Framework provides much deeper and more actionable insight.

Fit-for-Purpose and Jobs-to-be-Done

"Jobs to be done" is a concept created by the renowned innovation expert Clayton Christensen. In his 2012 book *How Will You Measure Your Life?*, based on the powerful speech he gave at the Harvard Business School graduation ceremony in 2010, Christensen gives a concise explanation and example of this concept. In the example, Christensen's son Michael buys assemble-it-yourself furniture from the famous Swedish furniture store chain IKEA. But he doesn't really buy furniture or choose IKEA as the place to shop. He hires IKEA to do a job for him. His job-to-be-done is to furnish his first apartment, one he just rented after getting his first job upon graduating university. The job has several requirements. The furniture must be delivered quickly. Indeed, you can choose the items you like in the IKEA showroom, pick up the boxes with the corresponding codes, take them home, and assemble them on the same day. The furniture must be easy to fit into his apartment and living situation. Indeed, IKEA provides many configurations for its furniture models. The furniture must not be difficult to move to a new apartment. The quality must be higher than the quality of used furniture he would pick at garage sales for his undergraduate residence. But it doesn't need to be as high as what he and his future spouse might buy later on—in the middle of their careers, raising children, and settling into their family house for many years to come. IKEA delivers the right level of quality at the price level he can afford. IKEA thus gets the job done that it was hired to do.

Several years later, the notion of jobs-to-be-done is popular with product designers, who trace various features of their designs to jobs their customers hire their products to do.

You might notice some similarities with examples earlier in the book and even reinterpret them using the jobs-to-be-done language. For example, you can infer that Neeta's jobs-to-be-done were to reward her colleagues for the extra work effort and to feed her hungry children.

Zocor and Dan Reeves: A Pharmaceutical Example

Dan Reeves is a famous American football player and coach. He played for the Dallas Cowboys and won the Super Bowl, the championship trophy of the National Football League. After the end of his playing career, he worked as an assistant coach for several years and soon became the youngest head coach in the league. He led two different teams four times to the big game during his 22-year career as a head coach and his 190 wins in the NFL rank in the top 10 on the all-time list.

In the 1998 season, Reeves, aged 54, led a remarkable turnaround of the team from his home state, the Atlanta Falcons. But with only two games left in the regular season, he had to be hospitalized to undergo quadruple-bypass heart surgery. He managed to return three weeks later, just in time for the playoffs, and coached his team to reach the Super Bowl. He was named the NFL coach of the year. Following this story, Dan Reeves began to appear in television commercials advertising Zocor, a drug prescribed to heart disease patients to lower their cholesterol.

The tagline of the commercial was, "It's your future, be there." Reeves was portrayed coaching his football team in an important game. The message was, take care of your health, live long enough to experience such great moments, and, if you have a heart condition, this drug could help.

Does this sound like a job-to-be-done? Yes. Reeves "hired" Zocor to take him to the great moments of his future. In another variation of the same commercial, Reeves is seen playing football with children in the backyard. That's another job-to-be-done. Live long enough to spend quality time with your grandchildren and great-grandchildren. In yet another Zocor commercial, not featuring Reeves, an aging couple appears, tells their story, and finishes it with the same tagline, "It's your future, be there." Their job-to-be-done is to enjoy their golden years together.

One can easily imagine other things people might want to do late in life that they would hire a heart disease drug for. Even curmudgeons who don't have any great moments in their future to look forward to could hire Zocor to ensure they collect more pension money from the government than the taxes they paid in during their working years to fund it.

Stories of greater quality of life are no doubt inspiring. They can motivate many workers involved in developing and delivering such life-enhancing products to their customers. To someone who came to the office or lab and faced dozens of seemingly routine tasks for the day, such stories can remind them why they chose their career and keep them going on a difficult day.

The trouble is that these jobs-to-be-done descriptions don't lead us to the fitness criteria and their thresholds, the necessary actions to change strategy, the design, implementation, or service delivery, or the company's health or improvement indicators needed to pursue such product or service changes.

Dan Reeves makes no mistake about it. He says before the tagline: "Combined with the right diet and exercise, Zocor lowered my cholesterol to 135."

Reeves has so far lived nineteen years after his life-saving heart surgery. (We wish him a continued long and healthy life.) This fact, or any of Reeves' achievements during these nineteen years, however, were not available to his doctor when he had to choose the course of treatment and select medications nineteen years ago. The selection criteria were, to start with, does he get on base this drug lower patients' cholesterol? Is it effective enough to lower the cholesterol level to the healthy range where the patient needs it to be? Further, what are this drug's side effects? What are their controllable ranges? Are they acceptable to this particular patient? How are the drug's claims of performance and side effects documented and validated? While the drug maker can motivate its lab staff with stories of people living longer and enjoying greater quality of life, the drug will be selected or not based on specific criteria related to its performance and safety and to the performance of the research development program of the pharmaceutical firm that makes it.

In the life sciences industry, like elsewhere, lead time—the time it takes to go through the full cycle of development, clinical trials, and approvals and to bring the new drug to the market—is a fitness criterion. It affects customers' selection. Even if it's years, if it's measured, understood, and managed within some range of variation, lead time of a drug, like many other products, enables its vendor to be selected a certain number of times to form a market share. Lead time, in the pharmaceutical industry, is, once again, a key performance indicator. For companies making generic drugs,[58] lead time—the duration, predictability, and timeliness of delivery, is even more important, as their window of market opportunity is generally short, immediately following the patent expiration date, and before competitors grab all the market share.

Developing and bringing to the market a complex, intellectually based product such as a drug requires contributions from many highly educated professionals in various fields. The catalog of needed skills includes many disciplines in medicine, biology, chemistry, statistics, marketing, and government regulation. It takes a large, complex organization to do it. We see many services in modern intellectual enterprises: one part of the company delivers some service, often based on their level of expertise, to several other parts of the company. The interconnected services are unified by the company's mission and can deliver to each other within the company's walls or to the company's customers outside. For example, a lab can receive samples and test them for minute quantities of various toxins. This job requires deep and narrow expertise in a particular

---

58. Merck held the patent on simvastatin (Zocor is the marketing name), expiring in 2004–2006, depending on the country. The patent expiration dates are known to any other company that wants to develop a generic equivalent and bring it to the market.

field of analytical chemistry. The lab thus delivers a shared service, and its customers are the company's various concurrent drug R&D programs. Those customers have fitness criteria, deriving from their needs to keep their R&D programs in good shape. They definitely include lead time (duration and predictability of time to receive test results) and some functional (can you detect this particular toxin?) and non-functional (can you detect one picogram of it?) quality criteria. You may recognize some of the many criteria we discussed in Chapters 5 and 6. Different programs making requests during different phases of development will have different sets of criteria—effectively customer segmentation based on their purpose. The difficult job of the lab's director is not only to advance the state-of-the-art science the lab does, but also deliver a fit-for-purpose service to its various customer segments.

You may notice that we came to revisit the fit-for-purpose guidance presented throughout the book, the fitness criteria, the different types of metrics, the customer segments, and such—and how far we've traveled from the original premise of jobs-to-be-done.

Clearer Thinking on Demand Analysis—
An Insurance Industry Example

In January 2016 Alexei conducted one of his favorite exercises, demand analysis, with one of his clients. The client was an insurance company.

The insurance industry has always depended on the information technology of the day[59] to serve their many customers—insureds—effectively. An insurance company needs many customers to effectively spread the risks. Insurance companies have been known to upgrade their operations to the next generation of technology only once it gained mainstream acceptance. In the most recent decades this included mainframe computers, client-server systems with relational databases, and, most recently, the Internet and web applications. Businesses need to make moves in response to or in anticipation of market conditions, and the competition drives a steady demand for updating and enhancing the IT systems currently in operation. Governments also introduce and update their regulations, adding to the volume of

---

59. Note: You do not need electronics, computers, or software to have information technology —even the Ancient Greeks had information technology. Mathematics and writing are the basic components needed for information technology. Insurance businesses have always employed the technology available to them to manage risk pools.

demand. If you are in the insurance business, you have to develop and sustain the organizational capability to deliver these enhancements: throughput, or the number of enhancements per year, has to match demand, while delivery has to fit within reasonable lead time and satisfy certain functional and non-functional quality criteria. For American insurance companies, the challenge is complicated further, as each state is effectively a different market and there are fifty versions of everything.

To the group of managers responsible for enhancing the IT systems powering the company's automobile insurance business, one particular source of demand provided the most insights. It was the demand for changes in the algorithms that calculate insurance rates for various cars and drivers, based on their location, car, driver's demographic attributes, driving patterns, history, and other factors. The managers saw this source of demand as one long backlog of requests to be scored, prioritized, and scheduled according to their priority order. After pondering Alexei's several questions, the managers began to see it differently. They grouped the fifty states into three categories by their regulatory regime. In the first group of states, auto insurance was most heavily regulated by their governments, and much of the demand came from the state insurance commissioner's office. The managers noted two seasonal demand spikes, at the start of the year and early in the second half of the year. The requests usually had a deadline, either the end of the year or the midpoint, giving the company six to twelve months to comply. The government regulator would not care when the company started implementing their request or how fast or predictable their lead time was. Their criterion was whether the company met the regulatory deadline. The same rules apply to all companies engaged in this business in the state, therefore there is not much room to negotiate.

The third group of states was the opposite. They were loosely regulated by their state governments, and most of the demand came from the general manager, an insurance company employee tasked with running the company's auto insurance business in this state. The general managers, while making their business moves, generated demand for enhancements in a much more even fashion, without seasonal spikes. They rarely had specific deadlines, instead having greater expectations for the duration of lead time. Trading some functional quality if it could significantly bring forward the delivery time was also an option.

And the second group of states was somewhere in between the other two.

Nearing the end of this book, you probably recognize something familiar: multiple market segments served by a business and a distinct set of fitness criteria and threshold values for each segment.

The product here is insurance, obviously. But what is the job to be done? What do people "hire" insurance for? Peace of mind? A young, first-time car buyer can "hire" insurance for only one job, to comply with the applicable law and be able to register the car (in most states, insurance is required as a condition of vehicle registration). If the buyer is taking a loan to buy the car, the bank is likely to demand proof of insurance as a condition of the loan. Then the job of insurance is to secure the bank loan. More mature drivers may see how their cars enable them to get to work reliably, to perform their job duties, and earn a living. In case of an accident, the insurance will compensate the loss and provide a temporary replacement car while the damaged car is being repaired. The driver will still be able to get to work without much disruption. The job of insurance is then to ensure the continuity of the driver's performance on the job where he or she earns a living. A small business owner or a retiree with a substantial amount of savings can buy insurance coverage beyond the minimums required by law to protect their business or life savings. We'll leave it to you to imagine other jobs you might "hire" insurance for.

These and more examples of jobs to be done, however, don't give us the hard part of what it takes to be in the insurance business. It is more difficult, but essential, to understand the demand, the customer segments, their fitness criteria, thresholds, and to develop an organizational system that can deliver well enough to all of them.

We encourage our readers who use the jobs-to-be-done concept to continue using it to source design ideas for their product features. At the same time, we urge you to apply the Fit-for-Purpose Framework to integrate the design, implementation, service delivery, and strategy to serve multiple customer segments with varying selection criteria. In large and complex enterprises, apply this guidance not only to your company's outward-facing product lines and services, but also to each connected service within the enterprise.

Fit-for-Purpose and the Net Promoter Score (NPS)

We've mentioned the Net Promoter Score (NPS) several times in previous chapters. Each mention suggested some shortcoming of the NPS or the motivation to develop a better tool. Such motivation, combined with investment of effort in experimentation and innovation, led to the guidance and tools, such as the F4P Card and Box Score, presented in Chapter 9.

For those not familiar with Net Promoter Score, you will almost certainly have seen it used in consumer surveys. There are two questions; the first asks you, "How likely are you to recommend [the product or service] to a friend or colleague, on a scale of 0 to 10?"; the second question asks you to state the reason you gave the answer to the first question. If you answer with a score of 9 or 10, you are considered a "promoter" of the product, who will generate word-of-mouth referral business. If you answer with a 7 or 8, you are considered neutral. If you answer with a 6 or lower, you are considered a "detractor." The Net Promoter Score is calculated as the percentage of promoters less the percentage of detractors. Steve Denning popularized the approach in his 2010 book, *The Leader's Guide to Radical Management* by demonstrating the correlation of high NPS scores to very high stock prices at companies such as Apple. He described NPS as "the one metric you will ever need" and encouraged firms to both instrument for it and optimize for it.

Several of Alexei's customers reported using NPS as a key performance indicator (KPI). One of them also linked NPS to employee bonuses. If you give your employees the "one metric they'll ever need," they will focus on maximizing it no matter the cost. If you give them financial incentives, they'll redouble their efforts. We began to see the emergence of NPS as a vanity metric as consultants posted NPS results from clients or public training classes to social media, and in one case, to their website, as a boast. In general, this led to behavior in which engagements were optimized for "feel good" factors and instant gratification rather than deep, lasting results.

NPS feels like it should be a fitness criterion, because it appears to affect selection, whereas in fact, as an exit survey it only reports a feel good factor, "How likely are you to recommend this [. . .] to a friend or colleague?" It asks the respondent to speculate about their own future behavior and the needs and criteria of others. It doesn't record actual behavior of respondents or the actual needs and criteria of their friends and colleagues. With professional services firms using NPS in their social media for their own vanity, or to reward employees, we have to ask, were they actually measuring referral business and correlating NPS scores from the past with referrals in the present? In two significant cases, we know that they were not. NPS was being used blindly, without feedback or verification.

As we have presented throughout this book, it is possible for businesses to make mistakes such as serving wrong customer segments, failing to identify their target segments, serving them without regard to their fitness criteria or thresholds, overserving them at great expense, or serving a non-target segment in a way that switches off a target segment. With the perfect NPS of +1.00 as their North Star, some firms' employees focused on continuous improvement of service to make the existing, current customer population feel good and instantly gratified in order to gain high NPS scores on exit surveys. This was done without regard to any mistakes such as wrongly identifying segments, overserving segments, serving non-targets, or serving target segments in a way that didn't produce long-term results. NPS appeared to encourage short-term, fragile thinking, perhaps dosed with hubris and complacency.

Compare this instant gratification with a note David received while we were writing this book, from a class participant who attended a class four months earlier:

> I just wanted to let you know that the further away I am from the Enterprise Services Planning training I had in Hamburg, the more valuable it is. I would now say without further hesitation that this was the deepest, most thought provoking and useful training I have ever attended. I uncover how it relates to our work in new and newer ways every week.
> —Tomas Kejzlar

Clearly, Tomas developed into a huge fan over time; however, we can only speculate as to whether he'd have been a "promoter" had we asked him for an NPS exit survey. We don't use NPS, and we don't optimize our products and services for instant gratification. We prefer to deal with facts rather than speculation, even when we are asking people to speculate about their own behavior. To create long-lasting, deep results, it is necessary to understand what will help the target audience, and to do so, we must understand their purpose, then communicate it clearly so that we attract the correct audience to our services.

A More Actionable Approach

In 2013 David's clients started reporting that they didn't find the NPS actionable. The score would go up and down, or hold steady, and the executive team would not know what their company did to make it so, when they did it, what they should do next, or when they can anticipate the effect of their next action. In part, the problem lay in how the answers to the second question were being analyzed. The market research company simply presented a select collection of responses as "representative" of the sample. The executive team in question didn't find this actionable.

There are better ways to deal with the information in the responses to the second question. The micronarratives can be clustered, and then for each cluster of "reasons" given, the distribution of scores given could be displayed. This would instantly improve the "actionability" of NPS. We know that the Cognitive Edge company has run some experiments clustering NPS micronarratives for some of its clients. At the time of writing we do not know the results from these experiments. However, we suspect they show a significant improvement over simply cherry-picking examples from the survey population.

Evolve Your Product or Service Design
Based on Fitness Evaluations

This book gives the fit-for-purpose guidance your business can use to evaluate the current fitness of its products and services. In the next book of the trilogy, *Built to Last*, we'll discuss how fitness tests can guide evolutionary change of products. If you can change your product and the fitness test indicates improvement, you've now got an evolutionary successor that is fitter than its predecessor. The word "evolutionary" doesn't mean slow. If you can create variations of your products fast enough and test them for fitness fast enough, your products can evolve quickly. We might call this capability "business agility."

In evolutionary biology, random genetic mutations may take thousands or millions of years to appear, and when they do, they may not produce an immediate advantage and may not get selected for breeding purposes. The mutation remains latent in the gene pool of the species, or it may die out. If conditions such as weather change later, then a specific latent mutation, such as ability to synthesize vitamin D from sunlight, may have an advantage, and it gets selected. Over time, this may become a dominant mutation so long as the poorer weather conditions persist, preventing the human population from acquiring sufficient vitamin D from their diet, and survivability is improved by the ability to synthesize vitamin D from sunlight. Nature has an amazing knack for encouraging "appropriateness," optimizing flora and fauna for current conditions, or "periods of equilibrium," as they are known in the literature. The second book in this trilogy, *Built to Last*, will look much more deeply at changing externalities, "punctuation points" where conditions change.

It takes one set of capabilities to optimize within a period of stable external conditions, "an equilibrium," and a second set of capabilities to mutate products and services across disruptive periods of discontinuous innovation, or punctuation points. The speed of evolution of a business, its products and services, is limited by the speed of the slower of the two processes—the ability to innovate, to think of new ideas, to gather actionable feedback about those products and services, and then take action based on the feedback. The Lean Startup movement has grown up to encourage this evolutionary approach for often poorly capitalized startup businesses. Lean Startup encourages product designers to "get out of the building" to get feedback about ideas and prototypes. This is entirely aligned with the sentiment in this book that you should use your frontline staff as a sensing mechanism, or instrument your market, with a survey mechanism to get quantitative data directly from consumers. Fit-for-purpose surveying and Fitness Box Score provide means to quickly assess the impact of variations to your product or service design. You may not necessarily know what your future product will look like. With an evolutionary approach, there is no "target design" for a product or service. Instead, you make informed, guided, evolutionary changes (mutations). You let the market tell you what is working best. And although you may not know what your final product will look like, you can be sure it will be fitter for its environment. It will also satisfy customers and help you keep them loyal.

Our current approach to fit-for-purpose surveying and Fitness Box Score emerged over a three-year period, with its own evolutionary process. We're confident that our current fit-for-purpose guidance and techniques such as the F4P Card and Fitness Box Score represent substantial improvements compared to the NPS because they are both the evolutionary successors of NPS and they themselves evolved and were refined over several years of experimentation, trial-and-error, and further modification. We fully expect the technique to continue evolving as we learn more. However, we feel it is both mature enough and stable enough that it is time to share it via this book.

The Evolution of Fitness Box Score

The evolutionary journey began when David's clients reported the NPS was failing their fitness tests. The executives expected some "functional quality" in the NPS reports, some answers to at least four reasonable questions, such as: what did we do to cause our NPS to change, when did we do it, what should we do next, and when can we see the effect? But they weren't getting any such answers.

Introducing a free-form question to capture the customer narrative was the first evolutionary improvement we saw in NPS. We see that this has by now been adopted by many NPS users. When booking a hotel on Expedia, eDreams, Booking.com, or Hotels.com, you may receive a survey afterwards, asking how likely you are to recommend this hotel to your friend—with the space to capture your story provided. This version of NPS was our starting point for the evolution of the F4P Card and Fitness Box Score.

The first problem with NPS was its 11-point numerical scale. How did the scale get to be 11 points in the first place? There is well-established scientific research in psychology[60] from the 1950s that established that without a defined taxonomy, humans have difficulty categorizing unclassified information into more than 6 categories. Originally, NPS had a 6-point scale, 0 through 5. This would align with the Bousfield result on categorization in a random population of data. With a 6-point scale, the top mark of 5 was classified as

---

60. Bousfield & Bousfield, 1956.

"promoter." However, in some cultures, for example, Finland, people are conditioned to never give the perfect mark. This led to countries where no one responded with the promoter score, and yet there must have been promoters in those populations. In response to this, the creators of NPS doubled the size of the scale to 11 categories, with 9 and 10 now representing promoter scores. This enabled people in cultures where top marks are never awarded to offer a 9 out of 10 and still indicate that they are promoters. However, 11 categories is too many. Any one individual would never be able to use all 11 without the guidance of a taxonomy, so some of the values will go unused for any given individual responding to such surveys, and the unused values in the set will vary from individual to individual. Thus an 11-point scale produces unreliable responses, or "noise in our signal."

The second issue is lack of calibration of the long numeric scale. People answering the survey are not told that a 9 or a 10 indicates that they will actively promote the product or service, that a 7 or 8 means they are neutral about it, or that a 6 or below means they are negative about it. Our 9 out of 10 might be only an 8 out of 10 for you and yet we all feel the same way about the product being surveyed. We have noticed several NPS surveys, especially in the travel industry, annotating the 11-point scale with suggestions like "very likely," "unlikely," and "extremely unlikely," or highlighting the scale with colors ranging from bright green through yellow and orange to dark red. Market research firms conducting these surveys must be realizing the problems with the NPS: the lack of calibration of the 11-point scale results in noise in the survey data. We agree with them and show the way forward with the F4P Card design. Humans don't do well with unclassified numeric scales. They don't use them consistently. They do better with taxonomies. Our 6-point taxonomy of customer answers using narrative emerged as a fitter solution than the 11-point numeric scale used in NPS. We accept that it needs to be translated for local languages, but narrative is better than numbers—it is unambiguous!

Next, how factual or speculative is any given customer's assessment? Raise the fitness threshold on the factual nature of survey answers, and a survey based on "How likely are you to recommend it to a friend?" doesn't meet it anymore. NPS asks consumers to speculate about their own behavior. In turn, even if they do "promote," how likely is that to turn into referral business for a supplier? While these questions can be answered with statistical analysis of actual behavior, they are likely to vary across markets, geographies, and industries. Asking customers to identify their purpose and score the product's fitness for that purpose emerged as an appeal for factual information. The respondent doesn't need to speculate. They know why they bought and they know how satisfied they are.

NPS responses can be problematic. In one specific case after a class in Stockholm, David saw a response of 0 out of 10 explained with, "I work in a two-person company and we both attended your class, and so we have no more colleagues to recommend it to." In another response, from a woman who had been a star in the class, showing leadership and ingenuity and producing superior results from the class workshops, she responded with 3 out of 10 and explained it with, "My manager sent me to this class and I didn't want to be here." This kind of confusion, especially at scale, can only create significant noise in the signal.

So, asking for facts rather than speculation: "Why did you choose our product or service?" and "How well did it meet your needs?" was our further evolution from NPS.

Next, we found that customers were filling out our forms with up to five reasons, and that at least two or three reasons was common. It's fortunate that we started on a small scale using physical paper forms. Customers would modify the forms to accommodate their complex answers to what we believed were simple questions. Customers had multidimensional reasons for attending our training classes and using our consulting services, so we modified the form to allow for three reasons, with separate scores for each reason. The choice of three was a compromise. Yes, there were some customers who'd indicated four or even five reasons in some surveys, but there were relatively few of them and the fourth and fifth reasons were often described as less important. Choosing a maximum of three kept the forms simple enough while still accommodating variety.

Even after these improvements, our survey result was a single score. It was now more appropriately named NFS (Net Fitness Score), but, like NPS before it, it was a single number ranging from −1.00 (total unfitness) to +1.00 (perfect fitness). Closer analysis of survey results showed us that net scores were problematic and hiding

```
┌─────────────────────────────────────────────┐
│            Fit  –  Neutral  –  Unfit          │
│      (a)   0   –   100   –   0   =  0.00       │
│      (b)  50   –    0    –  50   =  0.00       │
└─────────────────────────────────────────────┘
```

Figure 12.1 Alternative scores that both result in Net Fitness Score = 0.00

information. Net scores weren't actionable. Arguably, net scores were vanity metrics.

The issue is easily illustrated by using an extreme example showing two ways to obtain a net score of 0.00, seen in Figure 12.1. Scenario (a) gives us an entire market that believes we are mediocre, while scenario (b) gives us half of a market who love our product while all the rest hate it. Which scenario would you prefer? Both your authors use this example in their strategic planning classes, and an interesting split has emerged. Senior executives almost always prefer scenario (b), while more junior ranking, often younger and less experienced participants usually prefer (a). We agree with the senior executives. Let us explain why!

A result in which 50% of our customers love us tells us our product is already very good for one or more segments based on the customer's purpose. While other customers, most likely with other purposes, are finding our product deficient. This is great news. We can amplify our marketing to find more of the people who love us and consider switching off the segments that are dissatisfied. It's cheap, fast, and effective.

The reason most commonly given for preferring scenario (a) is a two parter: nobody hates us; and, if only we can identify what is deficient, we can evolve the product to solve the problem and everyone will love us. There are two huge assumptions in this thinking: first, that the market is homogeneous and there is only one set of deficiencies, which, if solved, will turn neutrals into fit-for-purpose appreciators; and second, that making the changes is easy, or at least straightforward and affordable. What if the problem with your travel website is that your search results aren't relevant enough, making it hard for users to identify what they want from a set of maybe several thousand flight options presented to them? Or what if your investment banking trading platform is taking too many milliseconds to close trades and you need faster performance? Fixing problems like these isn't easy, fast, or cheap.

So, net scores hide vital information and affect the actionability of the results. We needed to find a method to report scores that was still compact and easy to use but avoided the problem of hiding vital information. The ability to make a clear distinction between such contrasting scenarios shown in (a) and (b) was now part of the fitness criteria for fit-for-purpose surveying. The Net Fitness Score (notice the irony) wasn't passing our own test. It wasn't fit-for-purpose. Fitness Box Score, inspired by the reporting of baseball scores in newspapers, was suggested by Russell Healy, and it emerged as the answer to the problem. Fitness Box Score enables us to denote such scenarios respectively as $0/100/0$ and $50/0/50$. This was the next evolutionary step.

We didn't set out to replace NPS. Initially we were inspired by two problems: "How do you know a change is actually an improvement?" and "Can we provide actionable improvement guidance based on data, given that NPS appears deficient in this area, at least for our clients?" These two questions defined, in broad terms, what it means for a set of survey techniques to be fit-for-purpose. And we demanded such fitness from our own survey techniques. Whenever we found them not quite fit, we mutated and tested them. For example, if we weren't satisfied with the noise level of the data, we lowered our fitness threshold to less noise. As a consequence, the 11-point NPS scale dropped out and the six-level taxonomy survived. We did not know that this line of inquiry would evolve into the F4P Card and Fitness Box Score. However, now that we have these and the related guidance and techniques, we know they're fitter. They've been field tested.

Although we still feel there are deficiencies in NPS, and our clients have reported their own feelings, we do believe that there is a continued place for NPS. It simply isn't "the one metric you will ever need." As discussed in Chapter 11, the Fit-for-Purpose Framework doesn't necessarily tell you whether you'll gain repeat or referral business. Referral marketing is hugely important to all businesses. It is one of the cheapest ways to win new customers. Consequently, we accept that many firms will wish to continue using NPS. We view Fitness Box Score as a modern augmentation. It doesn't just tell you whether your clients like you or not, it gives you specific guidance on where to apply your improvement efforts and what specifically needs to be addressed to improve customer satisfaction. In this sense, Fitness Box Score serves a different purpose than Net Promoter Score. We believe that being fit-for-purpose is so important that we've written a book about it. We'll leave it for you to decide how relevant and fit-for-purpose it is for you and whether you need to augment existing market research to enable more focused improvement initiatives.

Summary

- This chapter considers comparisons of the Fit-for-Purpose Framework with the popular concept of Jobs-to-be-Done (JTBD) and the popular surveying tool Net Promoter Score (NPS).

- We've found examples where many Jobs-to-be-Done exist, but none of them leads to the actual fitness criteria used for selection by customers, the fitness thresholds, or even what it takes to be in a particular line of business.

- The "JTBD gap" is likely to be wider for complex intellectual products made by large professional service enterprises with a high degree of specialization, using not a single design-implementation-delivery process, but a network of interdependent enterprise services.

- Using Net Promoter Score (NPS) as "the only metric you'll ever need" can lead to pursuit of short-term gain, instant gratification, and complacency.

- NPS isn't fit-for-purpose if the purpose is to know whether something is an improvement or to get actionable feedback. F4P Cards and Fitness Box Score are fitter for such purposes.

- F4P Cards and Fitness Box Score evolved from NPS as the starting point via an iterative process of mutation and testing for fitness.

- The story of the evolution of F4P Cards and Fitness Box Score is how we know they're fit-for-purpose.

13 Von Moltke's Goal-Directed, Balanced Scorecard

IN THIS CHAPTER WE EXAMINE how neatly the Fit-for-Purpose Framework integrates with some existing management and product design methods: Mission Command, Balanced Scorecard, Goal-Directed Design and Personas, and Lean Startup. We know that some of our readers are already proponents of some or all of these methods, so, to make adoption easier, we describe the basic integration points with these existing approaches.

Integration with Mission Command

On June 24, 1869, the Prussian military commander Helmuth von Moltke the elder issued a document entitled *Guidance for Large Unit Commanders*. Von Moltke himself commanded the largest unit. He was at the time twelve years into his thirty-one-year-long tenure as the Chief of the Prussian General Staff—the commander of the entire Prussian military.

In this document, addressed to his generals and officers, Von Moltke presented his system of military command, which became known as *Auftragstaktik*, later translated to become known as Mission Command[61] as its elements found their way into the doctrines of the United States and NATO militaries over a century later. The system, which had already been tested on the battlefield throughout Von Moltke's career, would achieve one of its greatest triumphs in the Franco-Prussian War of 1870–1871.

---

61. Also referred to as Mission Orders or Commander's Intent in some literature

Von Moltke realized new global trends in the conduct of war that occurred during his lifetime. First, the armies were getting bigger. The bigger the army, the less practical or even possible it is for the top commander to control it in person with precise directives. Second, the range and accuracy of weapons was increasing. This necessitated battlefield formations with more separation between the units of the same army. The officers had to make more decisions independently, yet their units still had to be able to fight effectively as one army. This was especially true in an era before radio or telecommunications. In Von Moltke's time, dispatches, or orders, and field reports were hand written and dispatched on horseback. Von Moltke was seeking *Einheit*—the unity of purpose of all army units under his command. Von Moltke's famous dictum was, "No plan survives the first contact with the enemy." He knew the successful militaries of the past were not the ones in which the top commander had a great plan and controlled its execution completely from the top down, but the ones that could take advantage of decentralization and the initiative and adaptability of its officers at the unforeseeable moments in battle.

Another trend was specific to the Prussian army. Since the crushing defeats near Jena and Auerstedt at the hands of Napoleon on October 14, 1806, the Prussians had been turning around their system of education and the training of their army officers. The mission of the General War School, established in Berlin in 1810, was to produce intelligent officers, capable of thinking independently and challenging authority. Von Moltke, who spoke seven languages, was himself a product of the new system. The new generation of Prussian officers was the perfect match for the *Auftragstaktik* doctrine.

The military command problem Von Moltke dedicated his life to solving has analogies in the civilian world, particularly in business. Instead of the independent will of the army and its enemies, of course, there is the independent will of an enterprise's customers, competitors, vendors, and employees. To paraphrase Von Moltke, we might say, "No product plan survives its first contact with customers or the competitive market." Anyone who has ever tried to produce something and sell it to customers would no doubt agree. Modern enterprises produce ever more complex products requiring contributions of many workers with many different specialized skills. Markets, value chains, and supply chains are increasingly globalized. The workforce is becoming more distributed. Leaders of various levels, separated geographically and culturally, have to make more decisions independently, yet their various organizational units have to be able to act as one enterprise, pursuing its one strategy in alignment. There is a need for organizational units to act with autonomy, yet their actions need to be harmoniously aligned with those of other units. Great plans and controlled execution are not practical answers to these challenges. To move quickly and effectively at large scale, modern enterprises need *Einheit*!

British author Stephen Bungay, who is both a military historian and a management consultant, wrote *The Art of Action: How Leaders Close the Gaps Between Plans, Actions and Results*, which provides an excellent interpretation of Von Moltke's system and turns it into accessible, practical guidance for modern readers primarily concerned with civilian businesses. American author Chet Richards looks into more recent military history in his book, *Certain to Win: The Strategy of John Boyd, Applied to Business*. Richards explains the OODA loop (Observe, Orient, Decide, Act) developed by Boyd, an American Air Force pilot and military strategist and turns it into guidance for modern civilian businesses seeking to become more competitive. Like Bungay, Richards also connects with the German military concept of *Einheit* to guide modern business leaders. This is not a coincidence. Boyd's approach was inspired by Von Moltke. Boyd struggled to gain traction for his approach within the Air Force, and ironically, it was the Marine Corps that became the strongest early adopter of his and Von Moltke's doctrine. Both of us count Bungay and Richards among our influences and we've been fortunate to meet them both on various occasions at David's conferences in Europe and North America.

To give a very brief summary of Von Moltke's system—as the subtitle of Bungay's book suggests—the *Auftragstaktik*, or mission command system, recognizes three gaps. The first is between results and plans. Bungay calls it the knowledge gap—some details of how the results will eventually be achieved are unknown, or even unknowable. To close this gap, the leader should refrain from prescribing details of the action and instead focus on very clear communication of their intent: why should something be done? The next gap is between plans and actions. Are various organizational units sufficiently aligned to act independently and at the same time pursue one common strategy?

Leaders at each level should deal with this gap—the alignment gap—by allowing the next level to figure out how to achieve the intent. Bungay identifies a key activity in filling this gap: back-briefing—lower level leaders report to the higher level frequently to ensure the common understanding of the intent and its implications. The final gap is between actions and outcomes. Leaders should close the outcome gap by giving individuals freedom to adjust their actions in line with intent. And finally, the chief commander's intent-communicating orders can't be just anything they wish to accomplish. As Von Moltke saw it, strategy adapts means to ends, which is a concept more obvious to military commanders than to business leaders. In other words, military commanders only ever pursue strategy when they believe they have the capability to enable it. They do not allow themselves to be set up for heroic failure. A strategy isn't really a strategy without the capability—whether the current capability of the Prussian armies circa 1869 or the current capabilities of various services of a modern enterprise.

To our readers who are inclined to apply Von Moltke's and Bungay's ideas in their enterprise, we want to give guidance on how to integrate this approach with the Fit-for-Purpose Framework presented in this book; but first, two examples.

Commander's Intent in Insurance

A program manager at an insurance company client of Alexei's provides one example of this approach. This senior manager introduced a new policy: all updates to their IT systems that may concern personally identifiable information (PII) must pass through a specialized group with expertise in the applicable laws and regulations. If there is need to create a new form or computer screen where such information may be collected, displayed, or processed, or to update an existing form or screen, the expert group must do the design. Simply announcing a new policy like this, or worse, prescribing additional implementation details, is unlikely to be effective, and it is likely to lead to some friction. Some subordinates will see the new policy as a bureaucratic inconvenience. They may ignore it or subvert it. In recent years, management fads have focused on team composition, structure, and empowerment. Advocates of these team-centric methods might propose that we let a small team, including a business analyst, a software developer, and a tester, handle the design. The work isn't a formidable challenge after all—a generalist skill level should be enough. Keeping the work within small teams will likely eliminate handoffs and delays in the process, producing results faster. People influenced by this thinking are apt to see their boss as "not getting it" and not up to date on the modern ways of getting things done. The gaps between the plans, actions, and results will grow where commanders and subordinates do not share the same philosophy or understanding of risk.

Communicating intent and refraining from further implementation detail begins to close such gaps. The program manager noticed that although designing a form with personally identifiable customer data isn't rocket science, the functional quality wasn't consistent enough at the scale this business operates, with dozens of teams implementing hundreds of changes each year subject to fifty-one different sets of regulations. There is legal liability associated with failure or bad design, exposure to fines due to non-conformance, and hence, a substantial amount of rework could be generated, late in the process, slowing down delivery and increasing schedule risk. It also generates a certain volume of failure demand—the need to fix incorrect functionality already released to production. This demand has to be served with a high class of service, consuming the business unit's precious capacity. It turns out that having well-functioning teams of generalists is not enough for the service delivery component of this program to be fit-for-purpose. Some jobs require expert input.

We can view the failure demand of this insurance program as a non-paying customer segment. Our desired strategy includes switching off this segment. The program manager's intent is to reduce rework to the minimum. Doing so by routing some work to an expert group organized as a shared service introduces a source of delay in the delivery process. On the flip side, the new policy also removes another source of delay downstream, and a source of failure demand, thus freeing up some capacity. Communicating the program manager-commander's intent closes the knowledge gap. Understanding the intent, the subordinates can figure out the implementation details, such as scheduling policies, leveling the load on the new expert group, appropriate definitions of ready and done, service-level expectations on the new shared service, and so on. This closes the alignment gap.

Service delivery reviews for the whole program, as well as for the new service, occurring at the regular intervals close the outcome gap.

The program manager's intent includes an "anti-goal": whereas the general direction is to reduce the rework, by all means don't let the rework rise above its current levels. The current rework level is a boundary analogous to a certain river in northeastern France—a natural boundary—that Von Moltke didn't want the French army to cross in any circumstances. As Von Moltke was setting up the decisive battle of the Franco-Prussian War, he issued one of his famous orders. While giving his generals leeway in figuring out how to attack the enemy and to respond to his counterattacks, Von Moltke was very clear about his intent: keep the French on the march at the same speed and in the same direction (north). For his plan to work, the generals had to execute its crucial part: to keep the French army on the western bank on the river and prevent it from escaping to the east.

Sometimes we need to focus on the negative side of the feedback loop rather than purely on the positive. We saw this in Chapter 3 with the Oakland Athletics. They were optimized for offense—scoring runs—which was good enough to qualify for the playoffs, but in the final games of the season in October each year, they also needed to be good at defense—at preventing the other team from scoring.

Commander's Intent in Pharmaceuticals

A company from a very different industry, biotechnology, provides another example. A strategy in the drug-making business normally includes bringing to market a portfolio of products—some original, patented drugs and some generic copies of drugs for which the original patent is set to expire. The various drugs in the portfolio are designed to treat several types of diseases; some are synthesized chemically, some are genetically engineered (think coding in the genetic alphabet letters A, G, C, and T instead of zeros and ones). The strategy builds on the company's expertise and capabilities in the different fields within medicine, chemistry and biology.

Somewhere in the middle of this large, complex company there is a lab where various samples come in every day for testing and analysis. Some tests will inform an ongoing experiment—part of the process of designing a new drug formula. Other tests are needed to validate a drug's effectiveness in trials on animal subjects and human patients. Still other tests are required for a drug's approval by the government regulatory bodies. How do the lab director and staff manage their workload? Every time they start one test before another, they effectively speed up one drug development program by a small amount of time and slow down another one by the same amount. One of these programs, however, may have a cost of delay—sensitivity to schedule—of a million dollars per month, while another one has cost of delay of five million dollars per month—and it can be the other way around several months later. The cumulative economic effect of thousands of small decisions can be significant.

The company decided to color-code all vials sent to the lab. Each color communicates how the test will be treated. The color-coding scheme is reviewed by senior management monthly and updated based on the latest cost-of-delay information. The strategic intent is quite clear: avoid the type of undesirable outcome in which a drug development program suffers a "death by thousand cuts"—the cumulative delay caused by many small, seemingly inconsequential decisions. The intent still leaves a lot of implementation details to the judgment of the lab director and the directors of collaborating labs. These include specific fitness criteria connected to the purposes of the requesting labs, service level expectations, scheduling procedures, staff and equipment allocation, and so on.

Another lab decided to keep a key piece of testing equipment at a low rate of utilization to reduce wait times. (Wait times increase greatly when equipment utilization exceeds 80 percent. They vanish when utilization drops below 50 percent.) The lab director introduced a simple scheduling device and a policy: you must sign up in advance to run your test. You cannot use this particular equipment on a walk-in basis, even if you find it idle. On the surface, this may sound as if the lab director doesn't trust her staff and tries to control them. Yet another bureaucratic inconvenience! Treating adults with a Ph.D. in microbiology like naïve children! However, communicating the commander's intent makes everything clear and achieves *Einheit*: keep utilization low to avoid long wait times. Not only is incurring a long wait time bad by itself, it can cause the biological matter—the subject of the test—to expire. The researcher would then have to start over and spend weeks regrowing it in a Petri dish, causing the lead time of the drug development program (a fitness criterion—KPI for the whole company) to increase. The sign-up policy ensures the scheduling device visualizes the current actual utilization rate. Utilization is a health indicator, and high means unhealthy. The director and staff can monitor it at all times. The scheduling device serves another purpose—and this is lab director-commander's intent, too—to continuously educate the staff on what "magic trick" ensures the key piece of equipment stays almost always available, removing delays from the research process.

Our advice to readers applying the mission-command approach in a civilian enterprise is to use the categories of the Fit-for-Purpose Framework presented throughout this book when working to bridge the gaps between plans, actions, and results. When communicating the strategic intent, refer to the specific customer segments identified based on purpose. You already know, from examples throughout this book, how some segments will need to be amplified, while others will demand improvement, still others merit a neutral stance, and yet others should be switched off. When stating the goals and anti-goals, refer to the specific selection criteria (KPI) and thresholds. When figuring out how to achieve the intent, employ the same categories as well as health indicators and improvement drivers. When you see that many enterprise services connect to each other and one acts as a customer of another, translate the fitness criteria of the customer-facing service into the fitness criteria of the other service. Finally, use the observations and input of the frontline staff to inform the strategy. The Fit-for-Purpose Framework makes it easier to follow the Mission Command doctrine in commercial enterprises. Simply put, Fit-for-Purpose helps with *Einheit*!

Integration with Balanced Scorecard

Balanced Scorecard is a popular management method for alignment of strategy and tactics with improvement efforts and measuring individual employee performance. It was developed by Robert Kaplan, an academic, and David Norton, a consultant leading a subsidiary of KPMG during the early 1990s. The concept developed as the outcome of a research project with KPMG clients and the extension of a scorecard technique in use at one them, Analog Devices. The approach was popularized by a series of three articles in the *Harvard Business Review* and then the publication of the book, *The Balanced Scorecard — Translating Strategy into Action*, in 1996.

Balanced Scorecard shares some uncanny similarities with David's Kanban Method. Balanced Scorecard is both a measurement tool and a management method intended for use at large scale. A scorecard is a tool for measurement while the Balanced Scorecard is a management method that employs the scorecard together with feedback loops to tune the performance of an organization over time. The Kanban Method is also both a tool and a management method. Kanban boards are tools used to visualize invisible work and workflows in professional services, using virtual kanban tokens to limit inventory of intangible goods work, and signal "pull" to create a "just-in-time" mechanism for professional services firms similar to that pioneered by Toyota in manufacturing and tangible goods supply chains. The Kanban Method is a management method designed to enable evolutionary improvement of implementation and service delivery. It leverages both visualization of intangible, invisible work items and virtual kanban tokens to limit work-in-progress. Visualization and constraints on work-in-progress create stress, which in turn catalyzes change. Hence, both Balanced Scorecard and the Kanban Method suffer from shallow implementations focused on simple tools where the opportunity to change the system of management for the better is overlooked.

Consequently, there are many poor, low-maturity implementations of Balanced Scorecard, where the focus is on the scorecard as a measurement tool, and the implementing firm doesn't change its system of management. Kaplan and Norton lament on these shallow implementations in Chapter 12 of *The Balanced Scorecard*:[62]

> 'I tried to tell my boss that a Balanced Scorecard was about management and not measurement.
>
> He sensed that this effort was doomed to failure, because the CEO viewed the scorecard as a narrow effort to improve the organization's performance measurement system, not as a new way to manage the business.'
>
> The measurement system should only be a means to achieve an even more important goal—a strategic

---

62. This excerpt and those on the next few pages are from Kaplan & Norton, *The Balanced Scorecard*, Harvard University Press, 1996.

management system that helps executives implement and gain feedback about their strategy.

Balanced Scorecard and the Kanban Method share feedback mechanisms in common, such as monthly operations reviews and quarterly strategy reviews. The strategy review provides "double-loop learning" designed to question "Are we doing the right things?" while the simpler, lower level, single-loop learning at operations review asks, "Are we doing things right?" and "Could we be doing things better?" at a business unit or entire value stream scale.

Equally there are many poor, shallow, low-maturity implementations of Kanban where the adoption is focused on the board for visualizing invisible work, or sometimes, on the tokens, for limiting work-in-progress and relieving workers of overburdening such that they can focus on better quality of implementation. Companies adopt Kanban as a tool and fail to adopt it as a management method, with its feedback loops and metrics and the intent to improve and optimize implementation and service delivery. They merely adopt a veneer, giving the appearance of doing so. Consequently, the results have minimal impact on business performance.

The Fit-for-Purpose Framework emerged from David's work with Kanban when asking the question, "When do we know if a change is actually an improvement?" The answer, coming from evolutionary biology, is "When the mutation is fitter for its environment than its predecessor." This led to the development of the fitness criteria concept and eventually to the entire method described in this book. So, the Fit-for-Purpose Framework is designed to integrate directly with Kanban. Perhaps it shouldn't come as a surprise that it also integrates quite nicely with the Balanced Scorecard. We believe that our Fit-for-Purpose Framework enables you to be more successful with Balanced Scorecard. It makes it easier to do Balanced Scorecard well.

When something is simple, and easily understood, its implementation at scale is likely to be reliable and consistent. When something is complicated, and difficult to understand, where there is a higher bar to proficiency, then implementation at scale is likely to be unreliable, inconsistent, and at times dysfunctional. We've seen some very poor and dysfunctional implementations of Balanced Scorecard in our careers. If you work in a Balanced Scorecard company, we hope adoption of Fit-for-Purpose will make your life and work easier, and your own annual performance goals more logical and better aligned to business performance.

There are also some parallels between Balanced Scorecard and Mission Command. In Mission Command, commander's intent needs to cascade down through at least two levels of mission orders. Mission Command has three levels—strategic, operational, and tactical. Orders cascade from generals, who develop strategy in liaison with politicians, who set direction and goals, down to middle-ranking officers such as colonels and majors, who lead operations, and eventually down to company commanders and platoon lieutenants, who lead teams of individuals to perform the actual work. Note: military work does include combat, but much more often the work is logistical in nature.

Balanced Scorecards are developed for a business unit or even a whole business. At each level of organizational unit below the original starting point, the scorecards cascade down, with the intent that measures are aligned from the strategic level, through operational layers, to tactical implementation at the team and individual contributor level in a firm.

We've already seen that the Fit-for-Purpose Framework aligns and integrates with Mission Command, and for many of the same reasons it helps with Balanced Scorecard. [63]

> The objectives and measures of the scorecard are derived from an organization's vision and strategy. The objectives and measures view organizational performance from four perspectives: financial, customer, internal business process, and learning and growth.
>
> The Balanced Scorecard should translate a business unit's mission and strategy into tangible objectives and measures. [. . .] a *balance* between external measures for shareholders and customers, and internal measures of critical business processes, innovation, and learning and growth.

The Fit-for-Purpose Framework is clearly not directly focused on financial objectives, or on learning and growth of personnel. However, it will directly help with the customer focus and internal business process improvement.

---

63. Kaplan & Norton, *The Balanced Scorecard*, Harvard University Press, 1996

As we mentioned earlier, we've seen some dysfunctional implementations of Balanced Scorecard. Kaplan and Norton recognize that some firms struggle to form consensus upon understanding of their market, how to segment it, and how to identify what each segment needs.

> one financial institution thought its top 25 senior executives agreed about its strategy: to provide superior service to targeted customers. In formulating objectives for the scorecard, however, it became clear that each executive had a different definition as to what superior service represented and who were the targeted customers.

It is clear that the Fit-for-Purpose Framework will help with this. This is the key integration point with Balanced Scorecard—market segmentation based on customer purpose and development of fitness criteria metrics and thresholds for each segment.

> The Balanced Scorecard highlights those processes that are most critical for achieving breakthrough performance for customers and shareholders. Often this identification reveals entirely new internal processes that the organization must excel at for its strategy to be successful.

While we read this quote from the book, it isn't obvious how, nor is a method codified by Kaplan and Norton, to achieve this. However, recall how, in Chapter 10, Zak's holds a focus group of frontline personnel along with senior executives and investors to strategize on expansion. Zak's discovers the new internal processes at which the organization must excel in order to serve the target segments in the expansion. And this illustrates the second significant integration point with the Balanced Scorecard. This is a key way in which Fit-for-Purpose makes Balanced Scorecard better! Thinking in terms of purpose, fitness criteria, and the implementation and service delivery needed to meet them helps you discover the internal processes that must change.

Differences

There are some ways in which our approach differs from Balanced Scorecard. Perhaps this isn't a surprise, as we are arriving more than twenty years late to the Balanced Scorecard party. If we are going to be so late, we ought to bring some innovation and new insights.

Balanced Scorecard focuses on how senior executives should establish targets for scorecard measures and even suggests that these should have three- to five-year life expectancies. Our approach to metrics described in Chapter 5 is more nuanced. With the categories of fitness criteria, improvement drivers, general health indicators, and vanity metrics, we provide greater insight. Fitness criteria have thresholds. There are thresholds at which you satisfy a segment and thresholds beyond which you are overserving the segment. Improvement drivers have targets, and in this respect, you handle them as you would currently with your scorecard targets. General health indicators have operational ranges, which, when the limits are exceeded should prompt management attention and potentially intervention actions. Vanity metrics shouldn't be on your scorecard at all—unless you need them for emotional reasons and have yet to address the culture issues that are driving them. Vanity metrics shouldn't have targets, just visibility.

Balanced Scorecard talks about managers identifying "stretch targets" and in this our opinion differs greatly. If a stretch target is for a fitness criterion, it is effectively saying, "We wish to overserve the market." This is nonsensical! If the stretch target is for an improvement driver, then W. Edwards Deming, were he still alive, would be likely to reply, "By what means?" In other words, do you know how to achieve the stretch target? Do you have a means and understanding with which to improve your capability? If not, then stretch targets for improvement drivers are actually demotivational. They will have the opposite of their intended effect. Finally, stretch targets for general health indicators are also nonsensical. Imagine someone told you that they'd determined a stretch target for your heart rate? By definition, setting a target changes a measure into an improvement driver. And if your health indicator is now an improvement driver, what is it that you are trying to improve, and in what way is it related to the desired improvement outcome?

> . . . targets for customer measures should be derived from meeting or exceeding customer expectations.

Yes, indeed! We agree with this. We've given you the tools to identify fitness criteria and their thresholds. We've also given you sufficient understanding to avoid overserving those customers.

Generic Measures

Balanced Scorecard also recognizes what they call generic measures for each of the four perspectives in the scorecard: financial, customer, internal process, and learning and growth. The generic measures for the customer are satisfaction, retention, and market share. For internal processes, they are quality, response time, cost, and new product introductions.

You may recognize some similarities to the commonly recurring fitness criteria presented in Chapter 6.

Customers and Markets

Kaplan and Norton recognize many of the same common failings in marketing and strategy that we've identified in this text: treating markets as homogeneous or using old-fashioned demographic segmentation; offering products that aren't sufficiently tuned to customers' needs and goals; and leaving gaps that insurgents can exploit to steal market share.

In the Customer Perspective of the scorecard, they identify the need for product/service attributes, customer relationship attributes, and image and reputation attributes. Product and service attributes are the fitness criteria related to design and implementation and we've taught you how to discover those. Customer relationship attributes are also fitness criteria, but typically they are related to service delivery. You have the tools to identify these, too. Finally, image and reputation attributes were touched upon in Chapter 11 as one of the blind spots. This aspect will be more fully addressed in the third book in this trilogy, when we look at identity in *First Who, Then Why*.

Kaplan and Norton also identify performance drivers for customer satisfaction as time, quality, and price. Again, these are three of the commonly recurring fitness criteria we identify in Chapter 6.

Balanced Scorecard Conclusions

In some ways, the similarities with Balanced Scorecard are uncanny. Twenty years later, we feel we bring clarity and pragmatic, actionable guidance as our innovation offerings. The Fit-for-Purpose Framework will help you implement the Balanced Scorecard better, with greater alignment, and with more consistency. It should lower the entrance bar and democratize usage of the scorecard by making significant parts of it easier to implement with consistency at scale.

Integration with Personas and Goal-Directed Design

The concept of a Persona as a description of an archetypal representative of a market, audience, or product or service user segment is widely attributed to Alan Cooper as part of his product-design approach known as Goal-Directed Design.[64]

In February 2000, David interviewed Alan for his then-blog, uidesign.net. We reproduce here the relevant section of the interview where Alan discusses Personas. . . .

DJA Let's talk a little about introducing Personas and Usage Scenarios to marketing people.

I had a client recently[65] with a lot of very expensive market research information. This research defined market segments, types of people who might be prospective customers. The problem I had with this was the vagueness of the definitions.

However, the marketing people at the client really believed that their research had nailed the problem so they were very skeptical about the persona definitions and openly said it was wasting their time. What do you say to people who raise that kind of objection? How do we get buy-in for your approach?

AC   Well, yep. That is a problem.

Everyone wants better solutions and happier customers.

Industrial Design is a discipline which has been around for quite a while and was developed as a methodology to help tame the excesses of the industrial age. Well, the industrial age is over. It's now the digital age. Now we need digital methodologies. Industrial Design was a nice thing for making real nice buttons which look pushable. It's not very good at all for making buttons which allow people to understand the consequences of their pushing them. Consequences are an interaction design issue. It's a digital issue.

---

64. https://www.cooper.com/journal/2014/04/inside-goal-directed-design-a-two-part-conversation-with-alan-cooper

65. At the time, David couldn't be specific about the client. It was, in fact, Nokia Americas based in Las Colinas, Texas, and they were anxious to design some mobile data applications to run on their 2G Wireless Application Platform (WAP) technology. David was engaged as a consultant to advise them on design and specification.

The same thing is true of marketing. All those marketing people are contemporary marketeers. They were educated in the marketing techniques of today. These were matured in the '50s and '60s when radio and TV matured to their full potential. These are broadcast paradigms.

DJA So, is it the case that marketing people are not reading Regis McKenna,[66] or Geoffrey Moore,[67] and others? Or are they reading that stuff but failing to understand it? Or reading it but taking the wrong message from it?

AC All of the above. [That stuff] is not being reflected. They have an existing method of marketing that they use. The reality is that such techniques worked for broadcast media. When you are broadcasting your message, you have to think in terms of demographics and channels to market. When you're working in the digital age and dealing with all this complex functionality, you have to be thinking in terms of users and specific scenarios.

The example I use is the guy who works on the assembly line at the automotive plant in Haywood, California. He is a working-class guy, likes to watch TV and drink beer, on the weekend he gets in his pickup truck and he goes up to the Sierra Nevadas and goes out into his favorite trout fishing stream and stands there in his waders and does a little fly fishing.

Then there is the executive, who is Chairman of the Board of the automotive plant. He eats at a fancy French restaurant. He makes a lot of money. He drives a Mercedes Benz off-road vehicle. On the weekends, he too likes to get away from it all. So, he drives up to the Sierra Nevadas and wades out into the same stream in his really expensive Orbis Hip Waders and uses his 300-dollar fishing rod and he stands not 50 feet away from the other guy who works for him on the assembly line. Both trying to catch a trout.

From a demographic point of view, there is no two more different guys. Now, if you own www.flyfishing.com then these guys are your market. It's not a broadcasting world anymore. So, all those old lessons of marketing are no longer applicable.

It's a cliché to say that the world is changing because of computerization. However, people don't realize when it's pulling the rug out from under them. Marketing people call the World Wide Web, "the New Media." The problem with this is that they then think it's just like the old media. But it isn't! They thought that TV was radio with pictures but it's not. The World Wide Web is vastly different from those broadcast media.

Marketing people used to think in terms of demographics and problems like how do you sell a toothbrush. Well that is very, very different from how you sell a [cellular] telephone. How you use a toothbrush is pretty much the same because it's a mechanical device. I don't care whether you are

---

66. McKenna Regis, *Real Time: Preparing for the Age of the Never Satisfied Customer*, 1997.
67. Moore, Geoffrey A., *Crossing the Chasm: Marketing and Selling High Tech Products to Mainstream Customers*, 1995.

short or tall, or skinny or fat. How you use your toothbrush is pretty much the same as how everyone else uses it.

However, you can be demographically speaking, the same gender, the same age, the same income and the way you use your cellular phone is dramatically different from the way the guy standing next to you is using it. That's because it is really an Information Object and not a Physical Object.

All that marketing think just doesn't apply anymore.

So, all that market research data isn't a waste but you need to turn the slant on it and make people aware that it just isn't about mass marketing anymore. It's about individual marketing.

DJA   I certainly find market research useful because it guides us to choose particular personas from the broad spectrum which might be available.

AC   Absolutely. All that research is great. We are omnivorous about data. We're hungry for market research. We'll eat it all. We also like to go out into the field and do our own corroborative stuff.

We like to poke around and look for surprises because it's always the surprises which are the most valuable. If we could predict the surprises then we wouldn't be needed.[68]

To extrapolate from this interview snippet, flyfishing.com would create a persona for a trout fisherman. The persona would reflect his goal, purpose, or objective.

Two months later, David published an article about Lifestyle Snapshots, effectively narratives describing "a day in the life of" a persona based on more traditional market segmentation. This article is reproduced in its entirety as an appendix to this book. The technique was also featured in the book, *The Essential Persona Lifecycle*,[69] to which David contributed a significant sidebar. David had developed the technique while engaged with Nokia designing WAP applications for location-based services, effectively to fill a gap in applying Goal-directed Design to more traditional market segmentation. He had persuaded the marketing people at Nokia to develop persona definitions for each of their demographic market segments. These segments had names like "business professional," "soccer mom," "teenager," and "grandparent."

---

68. Originally posted February 2000, http://www.uidesign.net:80/2000/interviews/cooper2.html

69. Adlin, Tamara & John Pruitt, *The Essential Persona Lifecycle: Your Guide to Building and Using Personas*, Elsevier, 2010.

Cooper's vision was that you should design a product for just one person, and you make it so compelling for that one person that it should be highly attractive to many people who share similar goals, purposes, or objectives. So, David worked with the Nokia team to define archetypal individuals for each segment. Together they learned the name of the soccer mom; where she lived—in a suburb of Dallas, Texas; what type of minivan she drove; what she did for a living; how many kids she had, and how old; where they went to school; and so forth.

The challenge was to envisage ways that this soccer mom might engage with the new technology. What opportunities were there in her life for which WAP applications running on her Nokia device could provide some advantage or benefit? The answer was to create snapshots of her life. The team worked together to envisage narratives for different days of the week: Tuesday, Friday, and Sunday were chosen. On each of these days, she had different goals and objectives and different activities and needs to juggle in her busy life. Each of the narratives produced different opportunities for the technology and enabled the development of Usage Scenarios—sequenced descriptions of how a user interacts with a technology product to achieve a goal or a piece-part of a bigger goal.

In reality, most organizations build personas, like Nokia did in 2000; but they build them around demographic market segments. This is not how Cooper intended it. Personas should be built around goals. To integrate with this text, personas should be built around purposes. In Chapter 1, Neeta represents just one demographic, and traditional marketing would put her in one segment, and she might represent one persona. However, on different days of the week, in different contexts, when we take snapshots of Neeta's life, we discover that she has multiple purposes or goals when buying pizza for delivery. Neeta represents two goal-directed, or purpose-driven, segments. Market segmentation should be based on snapshots of customers' lives.

So, in summary, and to make a long story very short, the Fit-for-Purpose Framework and market segmentation based on customers' purpose is entirely compatible with Goal-directed Design and Personas. A "goal" and a "purpose" are effectively the same thing. The user experience design people had it right twenty years ago. Marketing needs to align its segmentation based on users' goals or purposes and, as Alan Cooper suggests, confine demographic segmentation to the industrial and broadcast era of the 20th Century.

Lean Startup

Lean Startup is a method that emerged as a movement in the early 21st Century in response to the challenge of "discovering new business models under conditions of extreme uncertainty," in the words of Eric Ries, an entrepreneur who pioneered the method and described it in his eponymous 2011 book.[70] Even though the word "startup" evokes a small, nascent business, Ries never limited his method to companies by number of employees or years since the founding. He showed that his method works for enterprises large and small, old and young, as long as they weren't satisfied with the status quo and sought to discover new products, services, and markets. The Lean Startup movement was also influenced significantly by the Silicon Valley entrepreneur and advisor Steve Blank and his insights on customer discovery and creation.[71]

Eric Ries identifies five principles of Lean Startup in his book:

1. Entrepreneurs are everywhere
2. Entrepreneurship is management
3. Validated learning
4. Innovation accounting
5. Build, measure, learn

Dot-Coms: A Different Era

Besides official definitions, it might help to describe Lean Startup intuitively, using two contrasting examples of Alexei's experiences during and after the so-called dot-com era.

Around the turn of the millennium, Alexei worked in two different software startups based near Route 128 in the suburbs of Boston. The companies developed complicated software products for the telecommunications industry. The target customers were carriers such as

---

70. Eric Ries. *The Lean Startup: How Today's Entrepreneurs Use Continuous Innovation to Create Radically Successful Businesses* (2011).

71. Steve Blank. *The Four Steps to the Epiphany: Successful Strategies for Products that Win* (first edition, 2003; second edition, 2013)

AT&T and GTE in the United States (GTE was later acquired by Bell Atlantic, now known as Verizon). In each company, about one-half of the staff focused on solving the engineering challenges of building such products, while the other half focused on marketing and sales. The startup would change its approach from time to time and rethink which product features to build or which customers to pursue. There was some chance that the startup's product would become a big hit and find lots of customer demand. Another possibility for the startup was to be acquired by a larger company with some plan for making money from the product. Yet another possibility was to make an initial public offering (IPO) of the startup's stock on a public exchange. Many of the startups of that time had the Internet domain name .com appended to their name. That's why they were collectively described and later mocked as "dot-coms." Any one of these scenarios would result in substantial financial rewards for the startup founders, investors, and early-stage employees. However, until such scenario would occur, the startups typically operated at a significant loss and depleted the capital their investors had staked in them. There was a chance, beyond 50 percent, that the startup capital would run out, but the product would not have yet found enough paying customers to sustain the business. In this case, the investors would pull the plug on the startup to limit their losses. The employees would have to find themselves new jobs. Everybody understood the fragility of their startup and accepted the risks. Investors spread their risk by investing in many startups. They made robust portfolios out of fragile investments. Employees counted on finding a job with another software company, as there were many of them in the area. In the meantime, they honed their skills and had fun working on challenging problems together with skilled professionals—their colleagues. While working for a fragile startup, the employees relied on a resilient local ecosystem of software companies.

Of the minority of the dot-coms that succeeded at earning a positive return on their initial investment, most still failed as their promise or initial successes proved unsustainable. The crashing stock prices of dot-coms triggered a broad decline of stock markets worldwide, and an economic recession in the United States, starting in 2000. The terrorist attacks of September 11, 2001, besides their immense human toll, deepened the economic crisis. In 2002 many American companies in all industries were extremely risk-averse, laying off their staff and cutting all discretionary spending.

Dot-Coms Become Extinct

In late 2002 Alexei moved to New York City and joined an Internet advertising startup. It immediately felt different from the dot-com experience. First of all, the company, still very small, already was making money. The three founders bootstrapped it with some personal savings, earned some profits, and reinvested them to generate more profits. They didn't need to pitch their ideas to venture capitalists, hoping to raise money in the fourth financing round because they've depleted the capital they raised in the first three. Even more importantly, as many employees could feel this on a regular basis, the company could put something in front of its customers almost every day, and measure the customer's reaction. Learning from such data and observations, the company could tweak the design, implementation, and delivery of its products. The company developed and constantly monitored various health indicators. For example, the daily number of clicks on all advertisements sending a web user to the advertiser's website is a health indicator, particularly when presented as a time series. The number of advertisement "impressions" or the total number of ads shown to all users is another health indicator. Divide one by the other, and that's known as the click-through rate (CTR)—not a vanity metric, either. Finally, the number of daily users, active enough to produce impressions and clicks the advertisers paid for, was yet another health indicator, establishing the heartbeat of this business. These daily numbers were even literally called heartbeats.

It became clear retrospectively, several years later, that "entrepreneurs everywhere" had decided, "Enough of the dot-com model!" A small chance of success and a 90 percent or so chance of total loss—it doesn't have to be that way. Startup entrepreneurship doesn't have to be a gamble. Lean Startups were growing everywhere on the ashes of burnt-out dot-coms. Some of their founders, such as Eric Ries, sustained their successes, reflected on their methods, systematized their learning, and wrote and spoke about it for wider audiences. We now know this as the Lean Startup method.

At one point in 2003, the advertising startup had three major US airlines as its customers: American, United, and Delta. All three ran

nationwide (US) campaigns on the startup's network, typically getting decent click-through rates in the range of 2–3 percent. One of the
sales people, a frontline staff member, reported difficulties closing a
sale to a smaller airline. The airline was Spirit Airlines,[72] at the time
flying only from its base in Chicago to several vacation destinations.
A nationwide campaign with a low click-through rate was a waste of
money to them. They wanted their ads to be shown only to Midwest-
erners looking for vacations in the Sunbelt. The location technology
was in its infancy at the time and not very accurate. Alexei devised an
algorithm to improve the correlation of advertising impressions and
locations. He then worked with campaign managers and creative staff
to test three hypotheses:

1. The new feature will not adversely affect the performance of the
   company's current advertisement portfolio (the so-called null
   hypothesis).

2. The feature will improve the click-through rate of advertisements because of more accurate geographical targeting.

3. The improved click-through rate will entice reluctant customers like Spirit Airlines to buy.

All three hypotheses were quickly tested, one by one. First, validate that there is no negative impact on the company's existing business. Hourly analytic reports gave some encouraging early indications. In twenty-four hours, users in all time zones around the world
had seen the whole ad portfolio. The proof was there. Moving on
to the click-through rate: for the ads designed to take advantage of
the new algorithm, the CTR shot up to the 5–10 percent range, quite
a significant improvement. Spirit Airlines, impressed by what the
improved product could do for them, decided to buy advertising.
Spirit used the click-through rate for selection. It was a fitness criterion for them and a KPI for the startup. Five percent was approximately the threshold of minimal performance in the geographically
targeted travel category—validated by experiments with actual

---

72. At the time of the events, or even several years later, it would not be appropriate to discuss
specific customers or metrics. However, this information is obsolete 14 years later, at the time
of writing, and we can use this 2003 story as a good Lean Startup example.

customers. Ten percent was the threshold of exceptional performance, again validated by experiment.

There was a bit more for Alexei and his colleagues to do. The design of the new feature wasn't enough. First, they had to tweak the feature implementation to make it flexible and configurable by campaign managers. Then they needed to help the senior campaign managers train the rest of their staff—that is, the service delivery component, in the language of the Fit-for-Purpose Framework. After that, several companies in the travel industry followed Spirit Airlines' footsteps as the campaign managers grew their travel market segment substantially.

Lean Startup Summary

We find many synergies between Lean Startup and the Fit-for-Purpose Framework. Throughout this book, we've shown many examples and given guidance on discovering customer stories through direct customer interaction. This is in harmony with the Lean Startup ethos of "getting out of the building"—as in Steve Blank's famous maxim, "There are no facts inside your building, get out of it."

The Lean Startup community invented the term "vanity metrics." For example, the number of website visitors, presumably mostly non-paying customers, can make someone feel good about their Internet venture, but this metric fails to get them anywhere closer to understanding their customer segments, what would make and keep them satisfied, and sustain the business. The Fit-for-Purpose Framework gives further guidance on at least three distinct types of non-vanity metrics, how to use them effectively, and avoid undesired outcomes. Startups and larger enterprises operating in the conditions of extreme uncertainty need many health indicators to warn them about changes in their environment.

The Fit-for-Purpose Framework's guidance on market segmentation can help Lean Startup entrepreneurs find and validate fitness criteria and thresholds in specific market segments. The advice of equal attention to design, implementation, and service delivery components will keep a Lean Startup organization from emphasizing one of these three components at the expense of the other two.

We also emphasize the second of Eric Ries's five principles of Lean Startup: entrepreneurship is management. It isn't gambling, betting the farm, or hoping for luck. It isn't about having a great idea. It isn't creativity or imagination. It's about the discipline of managing both the risks taken by the enterprise in its uncertain environment, and the flow of information, which arrives constantly, eliminating some risks and introducing others. We are confident that we've given you new insights and tools to manage this better.

Summary

- We presented the synergies and integrations of the Fit-for-Purpose Framework with four popular methods.

- The Fit-for-Purpose Framework makes it easier to apply the military-inspired guidance on Mission Command (*Auftrag-staktik*) and achieve unity of purpose (*Einheit*) in large civilian enterprises. F4P helps with *Einheit*!

- If your enterprise uses Balanced Scorecard, the Fit-for-Purpose Framework will help you implement it with greater depth. F4P will also ensure a better selection and more effective use of metrics appearing on your Balanced Scorecard.

- The Fit-for-Purpose framework is compatible with Goal-directed Design and Personas. The purpose and the goal are essentially the same thing. F4P will also help your organization avoid the common mistake of segmenting markets demographically when designing personas.

- If you're a Lean Startup entrepreneur, the Fit-for-Purpose Framework will help you do a better job managing the risk of your enterprise and the uncertainty of the environment in which your enterprise operates.

14 "Be Paranoid!"

CORPORATE PARANOIA—the founder of Intel, Andy Grove, wrote an entire book about it, *Only the Paranoid Survive: How to Exploit the Crisis Points That Change Every Company*.

Former Chairman and CEO of IBM Lou Gerstner said, "You can never be comfortable with your success, you've got to be paranoid you're going to lose it."

Bill Gates was famous in the 1980s and 1990s for encouraging a paranoid attitude at Microsoft, constantly reminding the workforce that disruptive innovation could threaten the survival of the company over a fifteen-year time horizon. For example, he was known to keep Microsoft humble and avoid hubris by encouraging a culture exemplified in this quote, "The outside perception and the inside perception of Microsoft are so different. The view of Microsoft [from the inside] is always kind of an underdog thing. In the early years, that underdog, almost paranoid attitude, was a matter of survival."

So, at least three of the greatest leaders of three of the greatest high technology companies all agree—their business, and their workforce, can never get complacent. Hubris and arrogance are the seeds of failure. Fit-for-purpose today, gone in fifteen years! It's possible even for some of the largest and richest companies.

You are about to complete reading the first book in our Business Survivability Trilogy. We chose that title to communicate the benefit of having products and services that are fit-for-purpose. When you are fittest among peers, your products will survive and thrive and so will your business. We hope this book has helped you to understand how your business offerings can become fit-for-purpose. The next two books will look at how to stay that way. Book II, *Built to Last*, addresses issues of changing market conditions, changing customer tastes, and rising expectations, as well as changes in expectations brought about as a consequence of your own success. Markets move, competitors and regulators change the landscape around you; being fit-for-purpose today is all very well, but long-term survival requires that you are continually vigilant. Book III, *First Who, Then Why*, addresses issues of identity and how an overly strong attachment to an existing corporate identity can become an impediment to change—it can generate inertia, which manifests as defiance and stubbornness in the face of change, and ultimately lead to the demise of your business. The modern, 21st Century leader must be a social engineer, creating a culture and an organization that exhibits resilience and robustness to survive discontinuous, disruptive innovation, changes in regulatory environments, and dramatic changes in consumer behavior as social norms evolve from generation to generation. This closing chapter is intended to give you a taste of what is to come in the next two books of the trilogy, to give you an overview of what it takes to lead for long-term survival.

Why Fitness Criteria Change

What determines whether your product or service is fit-for-purpose changes over time. Sometimes, individual customers like Neeta change their views. Perhaps Neeta becomes vegan, a choice she makes on health grounds, and now she only wants to order vegetarian pizzas without cheese. If your menu doesn't cater to vegans, you'd lose her business. Sometimes you attract new customers and they think differently from your existing customers—what once served your existing base doesn't work for the new crowd. If you want to win their business and keep it, you need to adapt. Sometimes your competitors do things to raise expectations, and once your customers see those changes, you have to respond or risk losing their business. Sometimes customers adopt your product or service but use it in ways you didn't envisage; if a competitor spots this opportunity, they might design a solution that is a better, fitter match and you'll lose that market segment. And then there are times when you see the market moving, you sense customer sentiment changing, but you simply don't want to change; you don't want to serve these new tastes, you feel these changes simply don't match with your identity, and you'd rather stick with who you are and what you know already even if it is a shrinking market. Let's spend a little time considering each of these cases.

Technology Adoption Lifecycle

Markets for technology products are known to mature through a well understood lifecycle in which different patterns of customer behavior emerge at different stages in the product's life. While this phenomenon was observed in technology product adoption, we've also seen it with services and adoption of management methods.

The first buyers in a market are known as enthusiasts. The enthusiasts aren't concerned too much about whether your product is buggy, or unreliable, or whether it breaks down often. In fact, if it is buggy, unreliable, or even poorly designed, they'd like to help you make it better. These early market buyers are tribal in nature and want to be part of your community. For your product to serve them appropriately, they want a community feedback mechanism such as a forum on your website and a Slack channel to post messages and converse with other users and the product designers. They want their enthusiasm recognized. They want to be rewarded with social status. If they suggest a bug fix, they want credit for it. If your product is software, they want that software to be open source, so they can show off their coding skills and fix the bug for you, submitting the change through a public version control system such as GitHub.

Enthusiasts are followed by a group called "early adopters." These people are looking to use your product to gain an advantage over someone else—a competitor, or a rival. This is still very much a tribal market. These people want to feel a sense of belonging to a social group. However, they need the product to work. Early adopters need strong functional quality, at least within their own, perhaps narrow, application niche—in the language of this text, their own purpose. However, they will be willing to live with, at least initially, some limited failures in non-functional quality, providing there is a workaround or mitigation. Early adopters don't mind having to reboot every so often. **What we must recognize is that they have different fitness criteria than the enthusiast crowd.**

Companies that fail to understand this change in adoption of their products, and the change in customer behavior, will continue to serve an early adopter market as if it were an enthusiast market. Consequently, they will underserve the market with a buggy, poor quality, unreliable product, which exposes the early adopter to risk of failure and the loss of any advantage they hoped to gain.

Early adopters are followed, eventually, by a mainstream market, the vanguard of which is known as the early majority. Early majority buyers are both followers and tool users. They are not tribal. They don't want to join your tribe. They aren't interested in social status among your user community. They have a problem to solve, a job to be done, a purpose, and a goal—and they want and expect your product to solve that for them. Early majority buyers are typically following a reference competitor or client who was an early adopter. Someone they know, who looks and acts like them, who has the same purpose and goals, must already be using your product and driving success with it. This gives permission to the follower to enter the market and catch up. Early majority buyers need strong functional and non-functional quality. They don't mind high prices so long as they can have fast service and there is still a viable return on investment (ROI) at the requested price point.

Much later, and often after as much as 50 percent of the total available market has been captured, the late majority buyers emerge. These are people for whom the cost of delay was low, or they perceived it that way, or they simply can't afford the prices in the early market period, or they don't value the solution enough. Late majority buyers want low prices, and in the industrial era of mass manufacturing in the 20th Century, this meant that they entered the market once the manufacturer had acquired suitable economies of scale, after R&D costs had been amortized and dropped out of unit cost calculations. What enables the late majority market is low prices.

The tail end of a market is represented by a segment known as the laggards. Laggards are people who really don't want your product at all. They don't know why they need it. They may even view forced adoption as a taxation. For example, a laggard doesn't own a flat-screen, LED digital television. A laggard owns an entirely different product— they have a set-top box sitting on top of their analog electronic tube television. This box converts the digital broadcast signal back to analog so that modern digital broadcast channels can be viewed on older, analog technology. The fact that they had to purchase this device is considered a taxation inflicted upon them by the government because they turned off the old analog radio spectrum in order that it might be reallocated for new purposes. Perhaps there should be a subset of the laggard segment known as the curmudgeons. These are people who reluctantly buy a flat-screen, digital television but love to complain about having done so, and find no solace whatsoever in the improved picture quality or screen size.

So, as a consequence of being successful, and creating a product that survives through the full product adoption lifecycle, **the fitness criteria for your market will change four times**. If you do not adequately sense these transitions, you stand to lose market share in the new segment while you continue serving the old segment, and buyers from the new segment, such as the early majority, will select one of your competitors. You may have led and pioneered a market, but failing to detect the arrival of mainstream, early majority, tool-using followers may mean that you fail to serve them appropriately. Early majority buyers want fast and efficient service. You need to be good at service delivery to serve the early majority. Meanwhile, your business will have been optimized for design during the enthusiast and early adopter stages and will have adapted and developed some implementation capability during the early adopter stage. Now you must value service delivery or you lose the large mainstream market to an insurgent, copycat with better appreciation for customer service.

The Role Played in the Market

When you first produce a new feature, ideally aimed at a purpose-based segment you've identified, and that feature is new to the market—no one has done it before— that feature is said to be "differentiating." After a while someone copies your differentiator. We've seen this described as "playing catch-up" (at Nokia), "spoiling the party" (at Sprint), and one client referred to it as "neutralizing" (a competitive advantage).

When your competitor introduces a new, differentiating feature, your customers may see it and want it, and they will gradually become unhappy if you fail to supply it. Over time, the need for the feature becomes part of the fitness criteria.

Eventually every vendor in the market is providing the feature, perhaps because the capability was commoditized by a component supplier, and integration is easy and affordable. At this point, the feature becomes table stakes for the market. Its inclusion is part of the fitness criteria for selection. If you fail to have that feature, you aren't fit for any purpose.

Cost Reducers

There is one more role, besides that of differentiator, spoiler, and table stakes, that of cost reducer. Cost reducers are features we put in a product to reduce the cost to make it, or the cost to service it in the field.[73] Cost reducers may also be elements in the implementation of a service to save cost, for example, switching from a motorbike to an e-bike for pizza delivery, or replacing a regional jet on a short regional air service with a turbo-prop aircraft—the latter is slower and noisier for passengers but can be operated at lower costs, enabling wider margins or lower ticket prices. Cost reducers are things we do to improve our economics or enable segments at appropriate price points; they are never selection criteria for our customers. A cost reducer can never be associated in a positive way with a fitness criterion.

However, David recalls sitting in a meeting at Sprint PCS in Overland Park, Kansas, when then–Chief Marketing Officer, Scott Relf, remarked, "You know there might be just five bugs in our voice mail system which, were we to fix them, would have a significant impact on customer satisfaction with that element of our service." Poor quality of service due to minor defects in the voicemail software was certainly a source of dissatisfaction for our customers, it also drove costs for our customer care call centers when people called to complain or simply out of confusion because the voicemail system had not behaved as expected. Scott continued, "but the challenge is getting them prioritized." The problem was grounded in how Sprint PCS, the cellular telephony arm of American telecommunications giant, Sprint, viewed

73. Product developers can implement a cost reducer feature not only by adding something to their product, but by omitting it or substituting some part of the product's design or implementation at a different, usually lower, non-functional quality level. In any case, they may still choose to include the cost reducer in a product specification to identify the required rework to the current design and implementation.

itself and the state of the market. At the time, Sprint PCS was around seven or eight years old. It had been born to provide 2G digital telephony service nationwide across the United States. Since its inception, it had been focused on market build-out and subscriber growth. In this mode, a firm like Sprint PCS was all about table stakes—voice calling, postpaid billing, voicemail, and sufficient network coverage— and differentiators such as innovative new designs of handsets made mostly by Korean manufacturers like LG and Samsung—as well as the occasional spoiler such as when the firm copied Nextel's differentiating push-to-talk walkie-talkie feature. Cost reducers just weren't part of the equation.

The mobile phone market in the United States had been growing rapidly throughout the late 1990s and the great telecommunications bubble years. Until, in perhaps mid–2001, everyone in the United States who wanted a mobile phone decided they already had one, and the rest of the market had concluded it didn't need one. The technology at the time was still 2G, and renewed growth would not come until 3G and smartphones began to open up new market segments; new purposes and price points for the late majority and laggard segments had reached affordable levels—in part facilitated by increased bandwidth of third-generation digital two-way radio, in comparison to its second-generation predecessor.

The stock market noticed almost immediately that market growth had ended and subscriber numbers had flattened off. To gain new subscribers, telecom firms now had to take them from other carriers. They had to find unhappy, dissatisfied customers and make them a better offer, perhaps with a service that was more fit-for-purpose? The whole market needed to switch its attention from customer acquisition, market build-out, and horizontal growth across segments, and focus on customer retention and improving customer satisfaction. In other words, by mid–2001 it was time to focus on cost-reducing features and features that fixed dissatisfaction-causing defects in the network technology.

With twelve- to eighteen-month planning cycles for network features, and much longer ones for network build-out and new technology introduction, such as 3G, firms like Sprint PCS and its competitors simply weren't nimble enough. It took one to two planning cycles to even register the change and start to think differently. Why? Well, the firm had spent eight years wiring itself for growth. It had hired and developed people who thought about growth and innovation and differentiation. There simply wasn't a mindset to think about improving non-functional quality and reducing costs incurred by poor quality.

When it's raining, and all you have to do is hold out a bucket to catch the rain, no one pays attention to customer satisfaction or tailoring products and services to intimately serve the needs of customers based on their purpose and goals. Tools like the Fit-for-Purpose Framework become vital to survival when it stops raining. When things get tough, the fittest survive. Developing capability at fit-for-purpose product and service design prepares you for the drought, for the hard times, when holding on to an existing customer is easier than finding a new one, and might just be the difference between profit or loss, and staying in business or closing up and going home.

Half-Life of a Market Role

How long before the role your feature is playing is changed by a competitive move? How long before its status as a differentiator is neutralized? How long before it decays to become mere table stakes for the market? All of that depends on the barrier to entry.

If, for example, your new feature is based upon integration of a vendor's technology, your differentiation advantage may be short. Audi was the first automobile manufacturer to implement LED headlights on their vehicles. This innovation is famously associated with the power failure during the Super Bowl—the championship game of the National Football League (NFL)—during its forty-seventh playing in 2013. Audi's social media marketing team cheekily took the opportunity to suggest that the authorities could have lit the stadium using their cars featuring LED headlights. The feature was soon copied, first by Jaguar and eventually by all manufacturers, though at differing levels of fidelity to suit different price points. The reason the decay from differentiator to table stakes was so swift is simply explained— car manufacturers do not make their own lights, they buy them from component manufacturers such as Robert Bosch, so it doesn't take long before every manufacturer has integrated the new technology into their designs.

If, on the other hand, a differentiating feature or product has significant intellectual property associated with it and can be protected by trade secret, patent, registered design, or copyright, then the decay may be slower. Amazon has successfully protected and defended their "one-click" shopping convenience feature, for example.

If you fail to spot that an innovation has become a fitness criterion for a niche, or has opened up a new niche by enabling a new purpose, you will fail to define it in your product specification and fail to "spoil the party," "catch up," or "neutralize a competitive advantage." Equally, if you fail to realize that market sentiment has changed such that a feature is now considered table stakes for your market, you may be eliminated from market selection altogether. Your product may suffer a catastrophic failure in market share as consumers rapidly switch, in large numbers, to an alternative. Nokia's failure to spot that large touchscreens had become table stakes for the smartphone market led to the eventual failure of their mobile phone division. Were it not that they managed to sell the remains of that division to Microsoft for five billion dollars, it might have led to the demise of Nokia entirely. Instead, Nokia rises again like a phoenix with its Nokia Ventures division, investing the windfall from the mobile phone business fire sale in new, innovative products and services. Nokia gets to reinvent itself yet again and lives to tell the tale of how it lost the mobile device market.

Exaptation

Exaptation was first mentioned in Chapter 9. It describes behavior by which a feature, function, or element in a design is used for a purpose for which it wasn't first intended. In evolutionary biology, natural selection then views this feature as fitter, and it gets selected. For example, if dinosaurs develop feathers for temperature regulation, and then, separately, some dinosaurs evolve to walk on two legs, freeing their front/upper limbs to develop into more dexterous arms, the feathers on the arms might grow longer as the result of a random mutation in some individuals. If the females of the species happen to find these longer arm feathers attractive, they will select such males as their breeding partners. Eventually males will recognize that they are being selected based on the length of their arm feathers and will start to advertise through displays designed to show off their feathers. These displays have come to be known as mating rituals because they are designed to attract a mate. A virtuous cycle or reinforcing loop has begun, which eventually leads to the emergence of animals like peacocks with elaborate feathers entirely designed for attracting mates and propagating the individual's genes to subsequent generations.

As mentioned in Chapter 9, one very famous exaptation of 20th Century technology was the discovery that top-loading washing machines were being used to mix large vats of lassi yoghurt drink in restaurants in India. The manufacturer who discovers this, who senses the market and listens to feedback from the field, may start to amplify the message—to market to that purpose—and perhaps even specifically adapt their product, mutating the washing machine into a custom-designed lassi mixer. They will then communicate this message to that market segment, expecting to get selected—just like a peacock strutting his feathers hoping to find a mate.

A failure to recognize exaptation and to respond to it is a failure to tap a specific market niche. It's a failure to seize an opportunity and a market that is begging for an answer to their challenge.

Identity

In Chapter 11 we briefly mentioned the fashion application Koolooks—a mobile app designed to help people get a second opinion about what they should wear today, or which item of clothing to purchase in a store. The app presents a simple A I B test choice between two options and enables the user to ask their "buddies" to vote. It's an app designed for a very specific purpose. Its market adoption is probably still in the enthusiast stage, but users we know find it fun, even essential. The problem is that the app is also being exapted for A I B testing of photographs for highly groomed social media profiles such as those on Instagram. The founder of Koolooks isn't interested in this market segment. These users represent cost—they have to be supported—but they aren't helping Koolooks pursue its own goals in the fashion market. The identity of Koolooks is that it is a fashion company, not an A I B testing market research company, or even, more specifically, a social media picture testing and profile curating business. For founder Barbara Ruzicka, identity stands in the way of embracing this market segment and its exaptation.

How you view who you are and who you want to be will affect your decision making and your choices of which markets to pursue, regardless of whether you can see the opportunity, identify it clearly, and quantify the market and its value. Pursuing exaptations is one form of what the startup community refers to as a "pivot"—a change in direction, a change in corporate strategy. There are times when you simply don't want to pivot!

Identity Revisited

Netflix is famous for disrupting the highly successful video rental business Blockbuster, and others like it, such as Hollywood Video. Netflix entered the movie-rental market relatively late. This was both an advantage and a disadvantage. The incumbents such as Blockbuster had a large bricks-and-mortar retail presence, a well-established brand, and a loyal customer base, or so they thought. However, Netflix was conceived in the era of the Internet and, as its name suggests, conceived of its identity as an online video rental business—no bricks-and-mortar stores.

Netflix innovated in its business model and in its service delivery. Their online catalog was potentially more extensive than a physical store's inventory, but browsing online versus browsing a physical store looking for that inspiration on what to watch, are different but probably comparable experiences. Netflix's genius was to conceive of holding much of its inventory with its customers. If a customer subscribes to a plan enabling them to have five DVDs on loan at the same time, then assume the customer has 5 DVDs, and let them keep them for as long as they like, watch them at their convenience as many times as they like, and with no late fees, because there is no return deadline.

Having read this far in the book, you should be envisaging how this model aligned with fitness criteria in their target markets. Essentially, this model is enabled by a change of mindset. Netflix didn't view the inventory as being a scarce resource. Scarcity encourages you to want prompt return and to impose punishment—late fees— for failure to return on time because that prevented you from renting the scarce inventory to another customer. Blockbuster's model was born in the 1980s—an era of expensive videocassettes and true scarcity of inventory—just like books in a public library. By thinking differently, Netflix enabled a new way to rent movies—a method that would work without bricks-and-mortar stores.

However, the physical stores still had one service delivery advantage. "Want to watch a movie tonight?"

"Sure! Let's drive over to Blockbuster and pick one out!"

Blockbuster still had that just-in-time, last minute, spur-of-the-moment advantage, as well as the social aspect of browsing the store and picking out a movie together as a couple, like Jack Black and Kate Winslet in *The Holiday*. Netflix solved this by allowing its subscribers to queue up movies. Every time a subscriber returned a DVD, they were sent the next one in their queue. Meanwhile, the customer had a small inventory at home to choose from, so some spontaneity was still possible.

It's quite possible that Netflix took more of a Jobs to Be Done approach and viewed itself in the movie delivery service, while Blockbuster had a self-image of "video library"—a videocassette/DVD version of a reading library with physical books. It was, therefore, a natural transition for Netflix to become a video streaming service. This wasn't an identity change for them, it was merely a change in the method of implementation, and service delivery switched to streaming rather than handling physical discs and mailing them in envelopes. The switch was facilitated by underlying improvements in telecom network infrastructure and bandwidth sufficient for streaming at prices most households could afford. For laggard telecom markets, there was still the physical system using postal delivery of DVDs.

A careful choice of identity enabled Netflix to first disrupt an incumbent and later transition the nature of their service. Meanwhile, Blockbuster's being too strongly attached to its "video library" identity —a "who we are" rather than a "what we do" frame of mind—led to its demise.

The Innovator's Dilemma

We mentioned Clayton Christensen and one of his books in Chapter 12. Christensen is, however, more famous for his 1997 book, *The Innovator's Dilemma*. The innovator's dilemma concept refers to incumbents in a broad market who struggle to introduce innovation to negate the threat of insurgents, often using disruptive technologies, and nibbling away at the fringe of their market. For example, mini-mills in the steel industry started out as regional recycling plants processing old, used steel into low-value products such as chain-link fencing. For traditional, hot-rolling steel plants smelting freshly mined iron ore and turning it into beautiful sheets of steel for pressing into flawless car body panels, the mini-mills were initially ignored—they were pursuing markets that didn't interest the big players, often markets that were low value, low margin, and already commoditized. However, over time, mini-mill technology improved. Mini-mills were smaller, regional, and much nimbler. They began to eat into the business of the large-scale steel manufacturers.

When an incumbent begins to get sufficiently annoyed by insurgents, they often start to copy them. This is problematic. For social reasons, often the best people don't want to work in the subsidiary focused on neutralizing the threat from a smaller, newer competitor. Meanwhile, the returns are often poor, and after two or three years, the senior financial people are asking, "Remind me again, why are we funding this?" Often these subsidiary business units fail and leave the original large-scale incumbent open to assault. In the case of the steel mills, the only large-scale hot rolling mills left in business are taxpayer subsidized in countries like Germany. One of the richest men in the world, Lakshmi Mittal, is chairman and CEO of the mini-mill company he founded, ArcelorMittal. He was, in 2007, ranked as the third-richest person in the world—a clear indication that traditional steel mills struggled with the innovator's dilemma and the innovator displaced them in the market with products and services that were much more fit-for-purpose.

To understand this better, let us consider the market for operating systems for personal computers around 1990. Systems such as the early Apple Macintosh and Commodore's Amiga had set market expectations for machines with WIMP (windows, icons, mouse, and pointer) GUIs (graphical user interfaces). However, in those days the Mac was primarily an enthusiast market product with strong penetration in specific niche markets where it was most fit-for-purpose, and there were applications that focused on specific jobs to be done, such as desktop publishing. The Amiga was primarily a gaming, animation, and video editing platform. PCs with the broad and generalist business market were just beginning to catch up. Most PCs at that time still ran on the command-line interface of MS-DOS or PC-DOS (depending on whether the machine was a generic clone or an original IBM[74] machine).

Microsoft produced Windows, the first few versions of which were not considered fit-for-purpose. Version 1 didn't even have overlapping windows and looked like a toy compared to the interfaces of the Mac, the Amiga, or higher-end machines running Unix with X-Windows. Microsoft Windows was not fit-for-purpose in terms of functional quality. IBM, at the same time, had its team in Boca Raton, Florida, developing OS/2 and its GUI, known as Workplace Shell. In many ways superior, it featured pre-emptive multitasking, an ability that Windows and most PCs only gained in recent years. However, OS/2 was extremely processor- and memory-intensive and ran unacceptably slowly on lower-end PCs. Unless you had a high-end machine, OS/2 wasn't fit-for-purpose in non-functional quality—it was too slow. One particular aspect of slowness was the initial boot time, which could take several minutes and was a significant source of user dissatisfaction. Nevertheless, OS/2 enabled and dominated several market niches. One of the most notable was the ATM equipment market. Almost all automated bank teller machines in the world were running on OS/2. This was an application area for which there was enough money to buy plenty of processor horsepower and plenty of RAM, and the pre-emptive multitasking of the operating system was an important feature. ATMs couldn't run on a toy like the early versions of Windows.

It really wasn't until Windows 3.1 that Microsoft finally cracked open the wider market with a product that was fit-for-purpose, and the consumer market for GUI-driven PCs exploded. As the PC market grew and grew, the consumer portion of the market came to dominate, and Microsoft and its Windows operating system dominated with it. IBM chose in the mid–1990s to withdraw from the PC operating system business and focus instead on investing in a combination of Sun's Java technology and the open-source operating system Linux. They closed their operating system development group in Boca Raton and

---

74. At the time, IBM had the largest market share of the PC business by far, and by 1995 this share was still around 15 percent globally. IBM sold vast numbers of machines to corporate and public-sector clients. It wasn't as visible as the consumer market but it was highly profitable

moved many of the people to Austin, Texas, where they were repurposed onto these two new initiatives.

So, what went wrong for IBM? There were many books and articles written on this topic at the time, and these reach into the detail in much more depth. To simplify, we can say that IBM was blind to much of the consumer market and the purposes for which those consumers were buying PCs. IBM was focused on its corporate clients such as banks, and its public-sector clients in the defense industry. IBM was prioritizing features for vertical market solutions and ignoring the broader consumer market. They failed to see the strategic importance of owning the operating system platform and owning the developer mindshare. Bill Gates and Steve Ballmer at Microsoft were much more focused. They understood how Apple had dominated niche markets through compelling applications such as Visicalc, the spreadsheet for the early Apple II, and with Pagemaker, the desktop publishing application for the Mac. If they, Microsoft, could win the hearts and minds of developers across the globe, those selfsame developers would produce the "killer apps" needed to win the market. This strategy worked, and the rest is history—Bill Gates became the richest man in the world.

So, why did Microsoft get away with it? The simple fact is that around the years from 1989 to 1991, MS-DOS and its command line were good enough for many consumers. They met expectations. They were fit-for-purpose. If you owned a PC to play games, a typical consumer purpose, all you needed the operating system for was to bootstrap your game disk until the game's own program code took over the machine and sucked you in to its virtual fantasy world. You didn't need Windows! And you most certainly didn't need the desperately slow OS/2.

If IBM had had a better concept of market segmentation based on purpose, and had they cared enough about those segments, their design choices and product management decisions would have been very different.

Staying Fit-for-Purpose

In this chapter, we've presented some of the externalities, the market dynamics that can cause a product, a service, or even a whole business to cease to be fit-for-purpose. If you want longevity, if you wish to stay fit-for-purpose, your organization needs to be cognizant of who it is and how that identity affects its decision making. It must also be aware of the state of the market for its products and services, how that market is likely to evolve in terms of phases and transitions, and you must equip your organization to watch for the signs, while continually sampling your customers to monitor how they feel about your products and services, and how well they are serving them. Are your customers' purposes remaining constant or are they changing? Are existing segments exhausted or dying? Are new segments, with new customers, with new purposes emerging? If so, do you want to serve them, or not? If yes, how? And if not, why not? When you think like this and can answer these questions, you are exhibiting the type of paranoia Bill Gates, Lou Gerstner, and Andy Grove were all looking for in the 1990s. Paranoia hasn't gone out of fashion!

Conclusion

We believe the Fit-for-Purpose Framework will make your business fitter. Building a capability at using it will improve customer satisfaction, give your employees a greater sense of achievement from their work, and improve your economic performance. But most of all, we believe being fit-for-purpose hardens your company for the difficult, uncertain times ahead. It gives you resilience, and you will show robustness to changes in market sentiment, disruptive innovation, or political or regulatory changes. You will outmaneuver your competitors and build long-term customer loyalty by showing that you understand your customers and are prepared to innovate to better meet their needs, again and again.

We encourage you to adopt market segmentation based on customer purpose, to instrument a sensing mechanism using frontline staff or new technology and survey techniques such as F4P Cards and Fitness Box Score to adopt the right fitness criteria metrics, improvement drivers, and general health indicator metrics to drive continuous improvement of your products and services. Find new customers based on their needs, purposes, and goals. Satisfy them by innovating and designing products and services that delight by being more fit-for-purpose. Keep those customers coming back by showing that you are listening to their ongoing needs, opinions, and changing purposes. Do all these things and you'll have a brand that people love. A brand that means, "It works, just the way I need it to." We wish you the very best. Thank you for investing your time in our ideas. We hope your business continues to survive and thrive for many years to come!

Appendix: Lifestyle Snapshots

Solving the context problem in design for mobile

From uidesign.net blog, April 3, 2000

Introduction

In her recent interview with uidesign.net, Laura Arlov stated that one of her biggest design problems, when considering Wireless Internet design, was the lack of Context understanding. Optimizing a design is best done when the Context of the User's interaction with the software, device, or machine is understood. Context is a description or understanding of the actual interaction event.

For example, in a banking application, the User may be a Clerk, the Context may be that the Clerk is working at the counter with a Customer on the other side of the counter who wishes to deposit money into their Savings Account. Various interactions with the bank's computer system need to occur in order to complete the transaction. However, they are all occurring within the same Context—a single Customer, at the counter, with money to deposit.

Laura Arlov was merely pointing out that with Wireless Internet Devices, it is so much more difficult to predict the Context for an interaction.

I have had some success with a technique I am calling, "Lifestyle Snapshots." A Lifestyle Snapshot is an addition to existing techniques for defining Personas (or User Roles) and Usage Scenarios. A Lifestyle Snapshot helps us to better understand the Context of a particular Usage Scenario. Lifestyle Snapshots are particularly useful when designing for Consumer Wireless Internet.

An Airport Application

Recently, John M. Thompson of IBM revealed that they had implemented a system for SwissAir which automatically checks in a passenger when he or she arrives at the airport. The system works by using their passenger's cellular phone and the local telephone carrier's transceiver or cellsite. When a phone is detected on the airport cellsite, the IBM system checks to see if the phone is owned by a person who is also registered as a passenger on SwissAir for that day. If so, then the system proceeds to check in the passenger, receiving any confirmations required over the cell phone.

This is a classic WAP application. The airline can deliver increased passenger service with faster check in. The passenger doesn't have to stand in line and can probably afford to turn up a little bit later than normal (providing the system is reliable and is working properly).

It is impossible for me to talk about any wireless Internet work I might be doing, so we will explore a design approach which includes Lifestyle Snapshots using this IBM / SwissAir example. Imagine for a moment that this system did not yet exist. An executive at SwissAir has just asked you to improve customer service by reducing check-in time for loyal, regular customers using new technology. Where do you start?

Persona Definitions

You start by trying to understand who the passengers are. These people will be the Users. The client will doubtless have market research, demographic studies, perhaps actual passenger surveys. You start with these. However, as Laura Arlov pointed out, "demographics don't buy products, people buy products." So you must invent some real people who match the demographics. Alan Cooper has called these invented people, Personas [Cooper 99]. Cooper's observation was that you should not try to design a product for all of the target audience. You should design it for just one of them (or perhaps 3 or 4 specific people). This profound, counterintuitive observation works because people are not unique. However much we pride our individuality, the truth is that there is always someone very similar not far away.

Lifestyle Snapshots

Lifestyle Snapshots work in a similar fashion to Cooper's Personas. The principle is that you should not try to design a Wireless Internet

Application for every possible situation when it might be used but instead design it well for at least one situation when it WILL be used. By making the application precisely what is needed and as easy, intuitive, and usable as it can be for just that one situation then you are designing a great product.

So for that "just one Persona," we are going to pick that "just one Lifestyle Snapshot." A Lifestyle Snapshot gives us a Context for a design. We are going to design the feature or set of features for the wireless application for that one Persona in one Context. If we get that right, then the chances are that the design will provide good to excellent operation for most of the people, most of the time.

A Lifestyle Snapshot describes a "day in the life of" a Persona, or simply a period of time. A long enough period of time to give us a Context for usage of their wireless application.

Usage Scenarios

We use Lifestyle Snapshots to determine the Usage Scenarios for an application. From the Lifestyle Snapshot ask yourself, "At what points in this scene could the main characters have benefited from use of the technology?" "Where can the technology fit into their lifestyle in order to make it better, easier, faster, simpler, more informed?"

With each Lifestyle Snapshot a number of candidate Usage Scenarios will emerge. Usage Scenarios describe precise, exact occasions where a device or application is being used. The development of Usage Scenarios is the first stage in a Usage Centered Design approach which leads to the development of Essential Use Cases.[75] Essential Use Cases can be mapped and abstracted. There is an opportunity when doing this to make a design which delivers suitable interaction for several Usage Scenarios, hence several Lifestyle Snapshots and perhaps for several Personas.

In other words, we start with very specific descriptions of the User, the Context and the Usage, and later we use our analysis phase to examine the similarities in the requirements for different Users and deliver a good, well balanced design which is suitable for a broader audience.

Let us take an imaginary exploration of the SwissAir requirements.

---

75. Constantine and Lockwood, 2000.

Example: Zurich Airport System

So, imagine for the purposes of this paper that we have been asked to design the system for SwissAir. For brevity we will consider only one Persona, and only one Lifestyle Snapshot. In a real design you would expect to develop up to five Personas and perhaps five to ten Lifestyle Snapshots for each Persona.

Persona Definition: Hans, Senior Partner of a Zurich Law Firm

Hans is 45 years of age. He is a lawyer in a major firm in Zurich providing legal services to the banking community and major industrial concerns in Switzerland and the predominantly German speaking business community. Hans studied law at college and has been with the same firm since receiving his practicing certificate around twenty years ago. He has a wife and two children, all of whom are very costly. He lives in luxury by Swiss standards, in a large house, around 20km from the city, nestled in the low mountains, with a nice view. He drives an S Class Mercedes. Hans has all the trappings of success and in order to be successful he has to be competitive.

Hans has become dependent on his cell phone and his laptop computer. He uses his laptop for email, presentations, word processing and financial calculations with spreadsheet software.

He regularly flies around central Europe negotiating Mergers and Acquisitions for his clients. It's high value business and he needs to get around Europe quickly and easily in order to be in the right meetings at the right time.

Hans relies on SwissAir to get him there. He is a frequent flyer who flies business class and gets upgraded into first class often. He expects first class service from the airline just as his clients expect first class service from him.

Now, let us consider a Lifestyle Snapshot for Hans.

Lifestyle Snapshot: Monday Morning Business in Munich

Hans is flying to Munich to close a deal. His client is buying a small Bavarian ISP as part of their expansion of Internet Services in the German speaking world.

Hans is woken at 4:30 a.m. by his alarm clock. He gets up and checks that his phone has recharged. He fires up his laptop and checks for any last minute email. While the machine is working, he darts back and forth getting ready. It's a one-day trip so he doesn't need to pack much.

By 5:30 he is dressed, has had his first coffee of the day, has his laptop packed in its leather briefcase and his phone in his pocket. He also has a Psion Organizer with his diary for the day and week ahead. His colleagues have been tempting him with gentle nudges to buy a Palm Pilot but so far he has stuck with the Psion.

All the technology was pre-loaded with the information he was going to need, the previous Friday afternoon by Hans' private secretary.

He gets into his car, the ever reliable Mercedes and sets off for the airport.

It becomes apparent that the weather has turned poor overnight and there has been a late spring snow fall. The roads are difficult but not impossible. His journey, nevertheless, is slower than it might be and he gets stuck behind some snowploughs on the Autobahn.

He parks in the one day parking at the airport and walks to the terminal, quickly. Although, not too late, he is close to the closing time for the flight. The airport is still quiet at this time. Luckily as a business class passenger he doesn't have to wait in line. There is only one passenger ahead of him. However, he finds that there are no window seats left and he will need to take an aisle seat. He checks to see if his frequent flyer miles have been credited to his account. Seemingly not. Some mistake. A few more minutes are wasted as the check-in clerk checks his details and amends the error. Just a little bit of stress that he might have done without.

He proceeds to the business lounge which he knows well and enjoys another coffee. Breakfast will be served on the plane.

The flight leaves a few minutes later than expected with no real danger to Hans' schedule for the day. He eats breakfast, rereads his client notes on his laptop and sleeps a little. The flight arrives in Munich.

As he proceeds off the airliner, Hans realizes that he is short of Euro currency and will need to change some money. He has pre-booked a rental car and will afterward make his way to the underground garage to collect his car. The car rental company is affiliated with the airline and he wants to ensure that his airmiles are credited to his frequent flyer account. He discovers when he reaches the desk that the company is making a special offer today. He can drive a Mercedes for a small upgrade fee and earn double airmiles on his account. Slightly more time is wasted while he takes advantage of this offer. Accumulating maximum airmiles is important for family vacations. . . .

We could continue to explore the rest of Hans' day. For example, the weather at Munich could worsen and the airport might be closed in the late afternoon. Hans would then need to book into a hotel and would need to acquire some toiletries and essential clothes for the following day.

We might choose to call the whole day a single Lifestyle Snapshot or we may choose to break the day into three distinct sections. The first would be the journey from home to the prospective acquisition in Bavaria. The second would be the session at the prospect site including all the negotiations. The third would be the return journey with its subsequent overnight stay due to bad weather.

There are lots of opportunities for Usage Scenarios from this Lifestyle Snapshot. Let's look at just a small number.

Usage Scenario: Auto Check-in for Flight

On arrival at the airport, the SwissAir system is alerted that a mobile phone belonging to Hans is now transceiving with a local cell site. The system pushes a welcome message (probably via SMS) asking if he would like to check in by WAP Internet Service.

At this point Hans has probably not yet left his car or he may be already walking with his luggage towards the check-in area.

Hans accesses the SwissAir site through a bookmark and is given an easy to find navigation link to the "check-in" service. The system already knows why he is logging in. This is a key point for improved usability—we have a Context for the Interaction. He is asked to confirm his flight number and is prompted for his seat preference. Perhaps the system already knows that he prefers window seats rather than aisles.

Usage Scenario: Boarding Notification

Hans has already checked in. He is now waiting in the business lounge but the phone system does not necessarily know this. He could be shopping in the airport, drinking in the bar. It sends him alerts (probably by SMS) that the flight will begin boarding in 10 minutes, then later that boarding has commenced.

Usage Scenario: Rental Car "Push" Advertising

As the system already knows that Hans has checked in and will be flying to Munich, it should also know that he has a rental car booked and with which company. There is an opportunity to advise Hans that there is a special offer available today and perhaps allow him to confirm that he wants the upgrade and it should be billed to his credit card. Assuming that the system knows his credit card details.

Summary

Lifestyle Snapshots provide a Context for an Interaction. They help us to understand a Persona and they give us a tangible situation into which we can apply a design. They act as a "halfway house" between Personas and Usage Scenarios.

Lifestyle Snapshots have proven particularly useful when designing for wireless devices because they allow us to understand the Context of Use for a product which is ultimately aimed at a broad mass market and can conceivably be used in almost any location at any time. Lifestyle Snapshots help us to guess the most likely locations and the most likely times for a particular feature or set of features to be used.

A Lifestyle Snapshot gives us clues as to which features will be needed at or around the same time, which features are needed to work together and should be tightly integrated.

For example, in our airline example, we can see that check-in and frequent flyer miles inquiries need to happen together. Rental Car and related information would be useful. There are advertising opportunities too based on what we know about the Persona's life. It might also have been useful to offer weather and driving conditions.

The better we can understand the User and how that User lives, the more likely we are to design an information age appliance which provides what he needs when he needs it. Personas and Lifestyle Snapshots help us to do that. They are tools which help to produce great, compelling design.

Index

A

Agile Management for Software Engineering, 187
Ahornbahn cable car, 176
Air Berlin, 63
Air Canada, 102–103, 138
   packing more seats on planes, 136
Air Canada Rouge, 102–103
airline industry
   automating customer interface, 112–113
   classes of service, 174
   competition from low-cost airlines, 101
   constant war with customers, 136–137
   design, 118–119
   early boarding, 64
   eliminating human staff, 112
   fit-for-purpose, 118–119
   fitness criteria, 62
   flight cancellations, 63–64
   human staff to handle exceptions, 112
   implementation, 119
   improving profitability by widening margins, 136–139
   key performance indicators (KPI), 62
   knowing why passengers fly, 102
   market where players are doing badly, 137
   on-time arrival, 62–64
   on-time departure percentage, 62–63, 64
   outsourcing away-station gate agents, 111–112
   providing service level at lower costs, 136
   punctuality, 63–64
   service delivery, 119
   squeezing costs, 136
   time spent waiting at airport, 62–63
   undesirable behavior, 64
   why you fly, 101–121
airport application
   automatically checking in passengers, 270
   Lifestyle Snapshots, 270–271
   persona definitions, 270
Alaska Airlines, 64, 137–138
   baggage handling, 66–67, 187–188
   fitness criteria, 66
   leader in North American aviation, 66
   point-to-point service, 67
   reducing passenger stress, 66
alignment gap, 228
Alta Velocidad Española (AVE) network, 67–68
Amazon, 191, 259
American Airlines, 37, 137, 245
   advertising, 101
   annual membership, 102
   business class passengers, 102
   competition from low-cost airlines, 101
   designing products and services around higher value customers, 101–102
   hub-and-spoke model, 66–67
   OneWorld alliance partners, 102
   purpose-based segments, 102
   "We know why you fly," 101–121
Amiga, 263
Analog Devices, 232
Apple, 191, 263
   dominating niche markets, 265
ArcelorMittal, 263
argon, 20, 21
Arlov, Laura, 269, 270
arrogance, 251

CPSIA information can be obtained
at www.ICGtesting.com
Printed in the USA
BVOW03*0949271217

503133BV00018B/21/P